They Called Him Cas

The Len Casanova

Jack,
Always great talking w/ you. Enjoy this read about Cas & Oregon football & his men.
George Dames

George Dames

©Copyright 2016 George Dames All Rights Reserved

Publisher: George Dames
Year of Publication: 2016

Dedication

I would like to dedicate this book to the Casanova family and to the University of Oregon where Cas spent over 50 years of his life coaching or working for the Athletic Department.

Acknowledgments

Les Joslen and Dan Johnson in them helping me with the writing and editing on this book. Also in Dan Johnson's advising on several issues along the way to get this book finished.
The University of Oregon their help with various archives on Len Casanova.

Bethany Perry with technology issues and Margot Wells, Cas's oldest daughter, for information and several pictures.

Forward

I remember the night I met Len Casanova as if it were yesterday. I was a fourth grader attending the Medford High School football team awards banquet. Casanova's team, the University of Oregon Ducks, had just narrowly lost to the Ohio State University Buckeyes in the 1958 Rose Bowl. Flanked by Norm Chapman and Jack Morris, both Medford graduates and Ducks players, the legendary coach took the stage. Little did I know then that our lives would intersect again and his influence would shape the rest of my life.

I had followed the Ducks closely that year; as closely as a fourth grader in Medford, Oregon, could. I watched several games on television and listened to others on the radio. I followed with excitement as the Ducks won game after game and qualified to play in the Rose Bowl. I knew Coach Casanova as a visibly striking character—silver-gray hair, snappy suit, and all—on the sidelines. I knew Morris and Chapman as football heroes. Starting fullback Morris was the older of the two by four years. Between Medford High and the University of Oregon he had served in the Korean War. A talented center, Chapman had played for Fred Spiegelberg at Medford High.

That night coach Casanova talked about the game, about life, and then introduced his captains. After the program, I met all three men. That did it. From that night on it became my dream to play football for Len Casanova. Nine years later that dream came true. Not only did I get to play for Coach Casanova, I played for Norm Chapman who had become an assistant coach at Oregon, and Jack Morris and I became friends as well.

I knew Len Casanova as a coach, but also as an individual. He was a great coach, but also a good man. Every coach and player who knew him realized he was special; the hero we all wanted to emulate. He was my hero, and I want to honor him. I have written this account of his life to do just that. I hope readers enjoy some of the funny stories and accounts of memorable games and players. But most importantly, I hope the readers come to know why Len Casanova meant so much to all of us who knew him, and why his legacy matters today.

Contents

Chapter 1 Ferndale, College Football, WWII and more (1905-1950)   1

Chapter 2 University of Oregon Head Football Coach (1951-1954)   27

Chapter 3 (1955-1957 Seasons at Oregon)   63

Chapter 4 (Rose Bowl, 1958)   85

Chapter 5 1958   103

Chapter 6 Oregon Football (1961-1964)   127

Chapter 7 (1965 and Beyond)   193

My Life Timeline   225

Chapter 1
Ferndale, College Football, WWII and more
(1905-1950)

John Sebastion Casanova arrived in San Francisco on Christmas Eve, 1886. He was from a small, Romansh-speaking village in Switzerland. He spoke Romansh, German, Italian, French, and some Spanish. But his inability to speak English was a big handicap when finding work. So he gladly took any available job. He found employment in the Ferndale area of coastal Humboldt County, California, 260 miles north of San Francisco, where he worked in forestry and on farms.

While working one job, John ran into an old friend from the same town in Switzerland. John learned from him about a young woman named Marie Ursula. Marie was also from John's home village in Switzerland. Having immigrated to the United States also, she now lived in South Dakota. She had been the "girl next door" to the Casanova family, and was only 14 years old when John left for the United States. A courtship by correspondence ensued, and Marie Ursula eventually arrived in Ferndale. The relationship continued to grow and she and John were married in the Church of the Assumption Catholic Church in Ferndale in 1900.

They called Him Cas

Cas and Johnny

    In short order, a family sprung up with six children: Three boys and three girls. Leonard Joseph, the second youngest, was born on June 12, 1905, on a ranch in the Grizzly Bluffs area just outside Ferndale. At some point, Leonard became "Len" and, in time, "Cas." As the Casanova family grew, John worked for the Pacific Lumber Company as a timber faller. As World War I began in Europe in 1914, economic impacts were felt around the world. Pacific Lumber fell on hard times and John was among many who lost their jobs. His search for work in San Francisco being unfruitful so he returned to Ferndale where he found work on the Russ family ranches. Marie Ursula worked hard too. She was a midwife. She baked bread and cleaned doctors' offices and homes. She worked constantly while bringing up six children. To make ends meet, the Casanova children worked at every job they could find.

His daughter, Margo, recounted, "When Cas was a preteen, the kids would go out and stay with different ranchers around the valley," where they worked in the fields, cleaned houses, and did everything they could to earn money. She said, "They slept out under the stars on those ranches." At the end of the month, parents and children put their wages into the family pot so they could pay their bills. Margo also recalled: "Len also had two paper routes, and delivered papers in the morning and evening. One day, as he delivered papers, his bike broke. Somehow he carried it back to town, got it fixed, and still delivered the day's papers. He also worked at a meat market in town when he was older."

As poor as they were, the Casanovas couldn't afford to own a house. They were finally able to purchase one that wouldn't sell, apparently because a number of children had died from tuberculosis there. The house was purchased with $390 the family cobbled together. The ignorance and fear of others had made home ownership possible.

Marie cleaned that house thoroughly, and the Casanova family never experienced a health problem from living there. As poor as they were, they opened their humble but happy home to needy families passing through Ferndale during those hard times. Faith was important to the Casanova family and they regularly attended mass at the Catholic Church in which John and Marie were married. A daily family prayer stipulated that, "Every step I take is to the honor and glory of God."

Down the road from the Casanova home was a community gathering center called Roberts Hall. Casper, Cas's older brother, worked the door admitting ticketholders to events. Most involved song, dance, and drinking. Cas worked regularly as a hatcheck boy, and after each event he collected beer cans and bottles discarded by the partygoers. Then he redeemed them for cash. He banked the money in a savings account, and bought his first suit.

As Cas was becoming a teenager, his family lived so close to Roberts Hall they would frequently run into other Swiss families who had just stepped off the boat in San Francisco. These families often had neither job nor home and the clothes they had were the ones they were wearing. Cas would go out Saturday night not knowing who was going to be in his bed when he came home. It was not

They called Him Cas

unusual to see three or four kids in his double bed sleeping head to toe. The Casanovas were generous people, especially when it came to other Swiss families just arriving on American shores.

Ferndale was a small town of about 900. In some ways, it was an idyllic community in which to grow up. A mild climate lent itself to a Tom Sawyer existence for young boys with free time. The Casanova's house was on a freshwater creek handy for skinny dipping and fishing. As he got older, Cas and his friends went camping and biking miles from town on dirt roads, spending nights around campfires and under the stars.

But work and school were ever present. Hard times demanded hard work, and better times required a good education. Work—from the paper route to the meat market—continued through Cas's years at Ferndale High School. There he was a popular classmate, good student, and star football, basketball, and baseball player.

Football was his favorite sport and he played fullback, punter and kicker. In his first years, his mother sewed padding into his sweatshirt because the school didn't have real uniforms. Football pants were similarly improvised. Though Ferndale was a small town without proper equipment, the town was serious about sports, especially football. Storeowners closed their shops on game day so they could watch the game.

Cas was captain of the Ferndale High School football team in 1922. In his first game, as a left-footed kicker, he dropkicked a 45-yard field goal to give Ferndale a win over the Arcata Tigers. As teammate, Clark Bugbee, later recalled: "Cas wanted to be good. The coach gave him a football to take home and practice with. He practiced winter and summer and turned out to be quite a punter in college."

With seven wins in eight games that season, Ferndale was co-champion with Eureka High School. Cas graduated from Ferndale High School in 1923 as student body president. In the school yearbook, he listed his future career as football coach. But his prospects were dim. Neither he nor his parents had money for him to attend college, and as a small town kid—even though a well-rounded student and reasonably good athlete—he seemed destined for the blue collar workforce.

Chapter 1

The challenge of paying for college confronted all six Casanova children. Yet all of them attended, helping each other financially as they could. Cas and his three sisters graduated. When Casper, Cas's older brother, went to the University of California at Berkeley, he stayed in San Francisco with a cousin and commuted across San Francisco Bay to the campus by ferry. But when his sister, Dora, had to have an appendicitis operation, he quit school to help pay for it, and didn't return. Instead, he went to work testing dairy cows for butterfat in the Salinas area. Johnny, two and a half years younger than Cas, managed to go to Santa Clara University where he played baseball and football. At 20, he was signed to play for the Detroit Tigers. Sadly, his life and career were cut short in 1928 when he was killed in an accident in Eureka around Christmas time.

Cas's three older sisters went to San Jose State College and became teachers. The oldest married a sheep rancher and lived a relatively isolated existence. His middle sister, Dora, married a fellow student from Ferndale. They lived in Stockton where she taught until he died. Then she returned to Ferndale. His third sister was also a teacher. She attended Columbia University, earning both bachelor's and master's degrees. She taught in New Mexico and Ferndale, then at Western Washington State College in Bellingham, before retiring.

Cas had a friend who knew the President of the University of Santa Clara. He wrote him a letter and the president requested more information. As Cas recalled, "They asked me to send clippings and information. They didn't know who I was because I came from such a small town. So I sent the clippings and my grades to Santa Clara and they offered me a partial scholarship of $300. Thanks to a lot of beer bottles, newspapers, and sausage deliveries, I had $313.19 in my savings account. At that time, in 1923, board, room, tuition fees, laundry and books were $600 a year. So I ended up with $13.19 in my savings account and went down there."

That was only the second time in his life Cas had been outside Humboldt County. The first was in his senior year of high school when Ferndale played Ukiah in neighboring Mendocino County. That was the first time he had ridden a train—as far south as San Francisco—and a streetcar that took him on to Santa Clara. He would leave California for the first time during his freshman year at college when Santa Clara played Arizona.

5

They called Him Cas

University of Santa Clara Football and High School Coaching
(1923-1935)

Len Casanova arrived on the historic University of Santa Clara campus south of San Francisco in fall of 1923. He did not know then he would spend most of the next quarter century—indeed, all but about three World War II years of it—in the South Bay and Peninsula areas along San Francisco Bay. His immediate objective was to study and play ball, and from 1923 to 1927 he majored in philosophy, minored in history, and played football and baseball.

Football was at the top of Cas's list and Santa Clara had quite a football heritage. The small college's first gridiron contest was played in San Francisco on Thanksgiving Day, 1896, against Saint Mary's College, another Catholic school in Moraga, California. Santa Clara clobbered the smaller, outmanned Saint Mary's 46-4, and in an 1898 rematch, reprised their victory with a 56-0 win. There's no record of Santa Clara playing football again until 1902. As at most West Coast colleges in those years, Santa Clara football was primarily a student-run club sport. Games were played against almost anyone who would play—athletic clubs, local high schools, and local Army and Navy teams. But two decades of evolution changed all that. During this time many teams turned to rugby while new rules to make football less dangerous were instituted. The nation's colleges returned to American football at the end of World War I.

By the time Cas arrived at Santa Clara, the University of California and Stanford University dominated Bay Area football, and the Saint Mary's team Santa Clara had embarrassed way back when, had become a third area football powerhouse. Santa Clara returned to the field in 1919. During the 1919 through 1922 seasons, coaches Robert Harmon (two seasons) and then H.G. Buckingham (two more) began building a winning varsity eleven. A loss to Saint Mary's in the 1922 "Little Big Game"—the rival Jesuit and Christian Brothers schools' version of the annual "Big Game" between California and Stanford—proved a setback. Coach Buckingham was gone.

During the first two seasons, 1923 and 1924, Eddie Kienholz coached the team. His patient attempt at rebuilding the Broncos lead

Chapter 1

to two losing seasons that included a humiliating Little Big Game loss in 1924 that cost him his job. Team losses notwithstanding, the freshman season gave Cas an opportunity to shine. Nowhere was this more evident than in an otherwise disastrous 6-55 loss to Stanford. On one play he picked up a fumble and returned it 86 yards for a touchdown and those six points saved Santa Clara from another embarrassing shutout.

As a junior and senior at Santa Clara, Cas was mentored by a young head coach, Adam Walsh. An outstanding athlete himself from Hollywood High School in Los Angeles, Walsh had just graduated from Notre Dame where he played for the immortal Knute Rockne. An All-American center and captain of the undefeated 1924 team that beat Stanford in the Rose Bowl, he anchored the Fighting Irish offensive line, dubbed the "Seven Mules," who blocked for the famed "Four Horsemen" backfield. Adam Walsh was also known for playing every minute of the game against Army in 1924 with two broken hands. Never missing a snap of the ball, he was involved in seventy-five percent of the tackles on defense and intercepted a pass in the final minutes of the game to preserve the Notre Dame victory.

They called Him Cas

He also earned varsity letters in basketball and track. Santa Clara was looking for a head coach, and Rockne recommended Walsh even though he had just graduated, had no coaching experience, and was younger than some of the seniors on the 1924 team.

Walsh had other things going for him. He was a natural born leader known for his character, fighting spirit, and dogged determination. He openly idolized and imitated his former mentor in style, dress, and demeanor. He immediately installed the Notre Dame system of football that consisted of the famous backfield shift and alternating teams or shock troops. His pregame talks to the team were inspiring and full of fight. Santa Clara's red and white jerseys gave way to green and gold during Walsh's tenure and the team was labeled the "Green Wave." He hadn't planned on being a coach, but after rubbing elbows with famous coaches Pop Warner of Stanford and Howard Jones of the University of Southern California, he was hooked. After four years as head coach and athletic director at Santa Clara, he continued a successful collegiate and professional football coaching career. Despite his inspirational leadership and solid knowledge of the game, Walsh's teams, which often lacked reserves, could do no better than five wins and four losses in each of his four seasons.

As a senior, Cas had gone off campus on an errand. When he came back past the athletic department he saw Knute Rockne talking to Walsh. Knute was saying goodbye to Adam after a visit. Cas walked up to them as other players had too. Cas was arms-length away from the famous coach. Nothing was said and no introduction was made, but he got that close to the Legend of Notre Dame. Many of the new and innovative offenses and defenses that showed up later in Cas' career can be traced back to Adam Walsh.

Those four years at Santa Clara were good seasons for Cas. An anxious small-town boy, away from home for the first time with little money, he gained confidence as he played successful football and made the grade academically. By his junior year he was living at Santa Clara, going to school full-time, and playing varsity football under an innovative style of coaching Knute Rockne bequeathed to his protégé Walsh. It was the beginning of a love affair with football that led Cas to success in college football, semi-pro football, business, and eventually teaching and coaching.

Chapter 1

By his senior year in 1924, Cas was playing halfback, punting and serving as captain of the Santa Clara Broncos. During that year's Little Big Game with Saint Mary's—by then played annually at Kezar Stadium in San Francisco before crowds of up to sixty thousand—Cas pulled off his most memorable punt. With the ball resting on the Santa Clara two-yard line, he was called on to punt from his own end zone. The punt flew 97 yards to the Saint Mary's one-yard line. And if pre-1937 statistics were included in the NCAA record book, the punt still ranks as the second longest in college football history. That kick was the legacy of the Ferndale coach who years before gave Cas a football to take home to practice punting.

They called Him Cas

    Cas graduated from the University of Santa Clara in 1927 with a bachelor's degree in philosophy and a minor in history. He attended summer school, and in 1932 earned a teaching credential. But at home in Ferndale in the months after graduation, he wasn't sure what to do next. Someone suggested he play football for the San Francisco Olympic Club that in those years played against California, Stanford, University of San Francisco, Army, and even his own Santa Clara. A team sponsor in San Francisco got Cas a job selling office supplies. He played one season helping beat Coach Walsh's Broncos, 6-0, before deciding he didn't like living in San Francisco or selling office supplies.

    After the 1927 football season, Cas heard about a coaching job south of San Francisco in Belmont, and in early 1928 began his teaching and coaching career at St. Joseph Military Academy.

    In fall of 1928, Cas began teaching physical education and coaching football and baseball at Sequoia High School in Redwood City, California, also south of San Francisco. He recalled years later, "They hired me as a part-time coach. That's all the room they had, plus I did not yet have a teacher's credential. They got me a job in the tax collector's office in the morning, and I was at the school in the afternoon. I wasn't a head coach that first year. But I thought I was pretty good for the simple reason that the year before they hadn't won a game. In that year I was the assistant coach we tied for the championship. That head coach then went into basketball, and I took over as head football coach and also head baseball coach. At that time, you could teach physical education if you had played on a varsity football team. I had, of course." He eventually had a full-time job and taught physical education and coaching football and baseball for five years. He said, "That next year we won all the games and the Peninsula Athletic League championship."

    Tragedy struck the Casanova family on Christmas Eve in 1928. That evening a group of guys, including Cas and his younger brother Johnny, were traveling from Arcata north to Ferndale. The Casanova brothers, each in his own way, were excited about life and what each other's future might bring because of sports. They both were eager to come home and share this with other members of their family. Cas, in the front seat, had graduated from college and had full-time work he loved. Johnny, in the rumble seat, was an outstanding

Chapter 1

baseball player and had recently signed with the Detroit Tigers. The driver took his eyes off the road, and a sudden crash resulted. Johnny wound up in the hospital with a lacerated liver. He died five days later.

    Johnny's death was the first, but certainly not the last, that would touch his older brother. The loss deeply affected Cas. As a result, he frequently visited a Catholic seminary in Belmont to talk with the priests. Was this accident and his brother's death a sign God wanted him to enter the priesthood? He prayed earnestly, and the priests encouraged him to stick with coaching. They argued that he could do young men more good as a coach and as an example than as a priest. His life proved them right.

They called Him Cas

Cas and Johnny together at Santa Cara

Those who lose a loved one live with an emptiness in their hearts. They can be paralyzed by the lingering pain or channel that emptiness into something positive. Cas reacted in a positive way to

Chapter 1

the death of his younger brother in a way that defined who he was as a person and coach. He often went out of his way for players making many of them feel special, important, and loved. But this love was tempered with toughness and respect.

In 1930, Cas met Dixie Simmers of Santa Cruz. They met on a blind date arranged by mutual friends. Dixie had attended San Jose State College and was a kindergarten teacher. A relationship flourished and the couple married on June 12, 1931, in Redwood City. Never afraid of hard work, Cas taught and coached during the school year and took a dangerous job in the summertime helping build the Martinas Bridge. Putting the income together, the way his family had done years earlier, gave him enough to pay for Dixie's ring and their wedding ceremony.

Eventually, they had their first of two daughters, Margot. When Dixie was in the hospital, the football team showed up one night to serenade her with songs. They brought Margot home to share their small two-bedroom apartment.

In 1930, Cas had become head football coach at Sequoia High School. One of his students, Jack Roche, was a great athlete. His parents raced dogs. This required them to move around the country constantly. To give Jack stability, Cas invited him to live with them. Since the Casanovas only had a two-bedroom apartment, they had a folding bed in the closet Jack would take out at night and sleep on in the living room. In summertime he would move it to the garage. Jack was the third boy that they brought into their family over this period. Here we see shades of Ferndale in the opening of their home to immigrants.

Cas coached the Sequoia High School football team through several more successful seasons, and in 1935 his team again won the Peninsula Athletic League championship.

They called Him Cas

Santa Clara University Assistant Football Coach
(1936-1942)

In 1936, Cas was invited to return to his alma mater, the University of Santa Clara. He would serve under head coach Lawrence, "Buck," Shaw who had been an assistant under winning coach Maurice, "Clipper," Smith. In that position, Cas helped coach winning teams until the football program was suspended by World War II for the 1943, 1944, and 1945 seasons. Coincidentally, his Sequoia High School protégé, Jack Roche, got a Santa Clara football scholarship and became one of his many great players. Cas would jokingly say they offered him a job to ensure Jack would follow.

Cas also served as Santa Clara's head baseball coach from 1939 to 1942. He remembered coaching baseball against UCLA at UCLA. One player got to bat and walked to first, stole second, stole third, then stole home. Then he went over to the adjoining track field and entered the long jump. He won the meet with his baseball suit on. That player was Jackie Robinson.

Santa Clara won all eight of its 1936 season games and was invited to play Louisiana State University in the Sugar Bowl on January 1, 1937. Buck Shaw's Broncos upset the nationally-ranked Tigers, 21-14. Sportswriter Harry Borba of the *San Francisco Examiner* reported the post-game scene: "Those boys from the West have just torn down the north goalposts and, quite appropriately, too. Now the south goalposts are falling prey to small, joy-crazed bands of Santa Clara rooters all the way from Northern California. Their Bronco heroes have just beaten Louisiana State, 21-14, in the major upset of the post-season."

In the 1937 season, Santa Clara again went undefeated and shared the Associated Press number nine ranking with Notre Dame. The Broncos were invited back to the Sugar Bowl where they once again stunned eighth-ranked Louisiana State in a 6-0 shutout. Head Coach, Buck Shaw, and his assistant coaches continued to surprise the collegiate football world. He led the Broncos through five more winning seasons, and established Santa Clara, a small school with a student body of less than five hundred, as the "Notre Dame of the

West" and a perennial contender for national honors. After this, intercollegiate athletics were suspended as World War II broke out.

It is easy to visualize Cas in the latter 1930's recruiting, coaching, and disciplining football players with a tough love that transcended age and generations. Here was a man who learned there were no easy ways, no shortcuts; a man who believed if you really wanted to go to college, you could. Here was a man who believed if you really wanted to excel at football, you could; that if you really wanted to do something you have always dreamed about, you could. It is no wonder he was able to develop successful teams so quickly in his early years at Sequoia High School and win the Peninsula Athletic League football championship twice. Or that Buck Shaw invited him back to Santa Clara in 1936 as an assistant coach. Cas genuinely knew men and they loved him and wanted to play for him. They gave it their all because he demanded their best and because he had total confidence in them. He succeeded and they succeeded because he was a true grit guy and they knew it.

Among the great players who benefitted from an association with Cas in those Buck Shaw years at Santa Clara were: Tom Fears, Eddie Forrest, Les Palm, Jesse Freitas, Herm Meister and, of course, Jack Roche. Some of these player's sons—Les Palm Jr., Ed Forrest Jr., Herm Meister Jr. and John Roche among them—later played for Cas at the University of Oregon. And Jack Roche was his assistant coach there. But that is getting ahead of the story.

World War II

College football changed drastically when the United States entered World War II. College men entering the armed forces in droves put a crimp in player recruitment and team rosters. Team travel was limited, intersectional contests were curtailed and on the West Coast, especially, large crowds were discouraged. At Santa Clara University, the entire campus mobilized for the war effort. Every physically qualified student enrolled in ROTC or some other form of military training.

Assistant Coach Casanova was essentially without a team at the end of the 1942 season. With football suspended and his coaching career on hold for the duration of the war, Cas accepted another challenge to apply his coaching skills to the war effort. In June 1942, Cas—quickly indoctrinated in a one-month, direct-commission, naval officer course at the U.S. Naval Academy—became Lieutenant Leonard J. Casanova, U.S. Naval Reserve. He went on active duty immediately after the 1942 football season in the Navy's new V-5 aviation cadet program as a physical training officer.

To meet the need for naval aviators occasioned by the war, the U.S. Navy rapidly ramped up its pilot training program. Those who would be naval aviators were assigned to the rigorous V-5 flight training program, which had evolved from the Naval Aviation Cadet program authorized by the Naval Aviation Reserve Act of 1939. The revised V-5 program called for 12 weeks of pre-flight training before successful cadets went on to primary, basic, and advanced flight training and— for fighter, torpedo, and dive-bomber pilots— training to launch from and recover aboard aircraft carriers.

The rigors of naval aviation called for cadets who were mentally sharp and in top physical condition. Physical training was, therefore, a key component of naval aviator training. The V-5 pre-flight program, developed shortly before Japan's attack on Pearl Harbor, had four general objectives. Later listed by former physical training officer Bruce Bennett, Emeritus Professor of Physical Education, Ohio State University, as "proper physical conditioning and strength, knowledge of general naval lore, knowledge of military drill and seamanship, and elementary training in communication specialties."

Captain Arthur W. Radford, Director of Aviation Training, appointed Lieutenant Commander Thomas J. Hamilton to head the Physical Training Section of the Aviation Training Division of the Bureau of Aeronautics. Captain Radford told Hamilton to "use competitive athletics and training in athletic skills to increase the abilities of combat pilots for the Navy ... ." Captain Radford picked the right man for the job, and Lieutenant Commander Hamilton would pick the right men to help him. The Bureau of Aeronautics decided those men should be commissioned officers, not enlisted men, because they would be training prospective officers; hence Lieutenant Casanova.

Tom Hamilton packed gear for the job. A 1927 graduate of the U.S. Naval Academy, where he was an outstanding football player, he served the required time in surface ships before applying for flight

Chapter 1

training. He earned his Navy wings of gold at Pensacola and had logged two tours of sea duty as a naval aviator. He was head football coach at the Naval Academy from 1934 to 1936. According to Bennett, "He was a natural leader who could convey his enthusiasm to others. He had the broad view of the program overall but also had the patience and tolerance for the details to make it work. Hamilton was at ease with admirals and ensigns, chiefs and seamen, and led by example." He was, in a sense, another Cas.

Cas's assignments as a physical training instructor took him in rapid succession to duty at U.S. Naval Air Station, Corpus Christi, Texas, and Puget Sound Naval Shipyard, Bremerton, Washington, where he was promoted to the rank of lieutenant commander. He quipped, "My sea duty was cruising up and down Puget Sound." From there it was off to U.S. Naval Air Station in Livermore, California. There he supervised the physical training of the latter classes of more than 4,000 cadets who took primary flight training. As the war wound down and Livermore was closed, Cas was transferred to an administrative assignment at U.S. Naval Air Station, North Island, near San Diego, where he completed naval service at the rank of commander. This V-5 program trained Naval personnel how to stay in shape at sea. Knowing how and what to exercise was invaluable to these young seamen who were captive on a ship for months. Very little is ever told or known about this program.

As the war ended and release from active duty neared, Commander Len Casanova looked toward returning to Santa Clara as head coach. Among other collegiate coaches granted commissions as Navy physical training officers were Paul, "Bear," Bryant, Harold, "Tex," Oliver, and Bud Wilkinson, Bryant's senior officer. Several coaches were in this program and occasionally found time to talk offense and defense.

Cas always was on the cutting edge of new and dynamic offenses. He had survived at a small college with fewer athletes. During his four years in the Navy, he was not only an officer, but a commander. As a result, he was constantly required to make decisions and lead other men. He got things done by delegating authority and teaching other men to get the job done. His naval experience paid off when he returned to coaching. As head coach he often delegated authority to his assistant coaches and relied on them

They called Him Cas

to come through; a style and approach to leadership that paid lasting dividends on and off the field.

When the war ended, his naval mentor, Captain Tom Hamilton, returned to Annapolis to coach the U.S. Naval Academy football teams of 1946 and 1947. He then served as the Academy's athletic director for two years before retiring at the rank of rear admiral. He accepted the position of athletic director at the University of Pittsburgh where he and Cas would meet again. Cas returned to Santa Clara in time to serve as head coach for the 1946 football season.

Head Coach - Santa Clara University (1946-1949)

"The war is over! Let's play ball!"

Commander Leonard J. Casanova, U.S. Naval Reserve, like many of his commissioned coach colleagues, was ready to return to Santa Clara University and college football. Buck Shaw, with whom Cas had served as assistant coach at Santa Clara, was hired to be the first head coach of the San Francisco 49ers. The team was founded in 1946 as a charter member of the All-America Football Conference (AAFC). The team, along with the Cleveland Browns and Baltimore Colts, joined the National Football League (NFL) in 1950.

Cas accepted the appointment as head football coach at Santa Clara following Lawrence A., "Moon," Mullins, who left after a five-month search for housing in the midst of the post-war shortage. Joe Cooper Herrick had also turned the job down. So Cas came back still willing to coach football as an assistant at Santa Clara. After several others turned the job down they finally gave the head job to Cas. Nothing came easy for Cas. During the next four years his Broncos went 20 and 13, with three ties, as they faced off against many of the strongest teams in the US. In 1949, they won a major bowl game.

Shaw went on to coach and rebuild the last-place Philadelphia Eagles in 1958-1960. With quarterback Norm Van Brocklin, Shaw led the Eagles to the NFL Championship and won it in 1960. Then he retired. Mullins, who played fullback under Knute Rockne at Notre

Dame, had been head coach at St. Benedict's College from 1932 to 1936, and at Loyola University of New Orleans from 1937 to 1939. He served in the Navy during World War II in the same capacity as Cas. He ended his coaching career at St. Ambrose University and went on to become athletic director at Kansas State University and Marquette University.

Cas began by building a team from scratch, a team that had been disbanded after the 1942 season. But there was good news. As explained by Herman Meister, one of his assistant coaches: "Santa Clara offered an ideal coaching situation. It was an all-men's school with about 800 students at the time. The academic standards were solid, the students lived in dormitories and were subject to relatively rigid rules of discipline. Weeknights, students had to be in their rooms by certain times. They could not leave campus except on weekends. The Jesuit priests took care to see that the rules were maintained. The activity on the football field was really an outlet for the guys. Also, because they lived together and worked together, they developed an esprit de corps and pride that is often very difficult to get in other schools and universities."

There was more good news. Cas had picked his assistant coaches well. In addition to Meister, a Ferndale boy and coach Cas had known most of his life, he had hired his Sequoia High School protégé John J., "Jack," Roche, Santa Clara class of 1940, and Edwin, "Eddie," Forrest, class of 1943. Unlike before the war, freshmen were permitted to compete. Many were World War II veterans.

Meister recalled, "The first two years were not very productive from a games won and games lost standpoint. But a good foundation was built in 1946 and 1947 that set the scene for a couple pretty good years." During the 1946 season, Cas' Broncos won two, lost five, and tied one. They improved during the 1947 season with four wins and four losses.

Casanova's 1948 and 1949 teams fared much better. His 1948 team won seven, lost two, and tied one. They defeated Stanford and Michigan State and posted a 20-17 upset over Oklahoma in Kezar Stadium in San Francisco. Playing for Oklahoma were Jim Owens, a lineman who would later coach at Washington, and Darrell Royal, a quarterback, who would coach at Washington and then Texas. Cas would deal with both coaches later at Oregon. They also played SMU in Dallas, Texas and got killed 33-0. Meister shared a funny summary of the game: "I remember Jack Roche calling down from the press box just before the kick off saying, 'Boy if nothing else, we really looked great in those uniforms.' It was the only thing that did look great. Every time SMU would score, their mascot, a pony, would run up and down in front of our bench. Our bench was in front of the SMU routing section. As I remember it, almost every time a touchdown was scored, the little pony pranced before our bench, she relieved herself.

"At halftime, Buster Rathe, a country boy from Chico, California, nothing bothered Buster. The team baggage was strewn all over the dressing room and Cas had to kick things out of the way to get to the blackboard. He went on for about five minutes attempting to rally the team and Buster had not removed his helmet. He was sitting on a baggage trunk kicking his legs forward and lightly tapping the side of the trunk with heels. Cas looked at him and said, 'Buster pay attention.' Buster kind of shook his head and he let out the most rousing fart that one could ever hear. With his butt firmly entrenched against the hard surfaced empty trunk, the conditions for resonance were perfect. It brought down the house and relieved the tension, but the second half was no better."

In 1949 the Broncos opened with a disappointing defeat at the hands of the University of California Golden Bears.

The Cal Bear games were very emotionally charged as were the Stanford games also. Both were cross town and cross bay rivalries. One Cal Bear game in Berkeley, Dixie was in the stands behind the Santa Clara bench as usual, Cas was coaching. For some reason Cas stepped out on the field, perhaps to get the referees attention regarding a call, and a fan in front of Dixie yelled at Cas letting him know that he was breaking the rules by stepping on the field. With that, Dixie leaned down closer to the fan and started beating him over the head with her rolled up program. There were other times when Dixie and Jane Meister would connect with sports writers after the games and reason with them saying they didn't get this or that right. It was always done as good sportsmanship. It's an indication of how well versed and how into it these gals were.

Chapter 1

"After that, Santa Clara went undefeated over the next eight games, a success marred only by a 7-7 tie with Stanford. About mid season, Santa Clara was playing Portland University. They had not won a game yet that year and were large underdogs. We were so flat that the fullback of theirs, named Sans Regret, who weighed about 250 pounds and rumbled like a freight car, was running our ends and making yards. It was disgusting and Cas was fit to be tied. We went into the dressing room at halftime and Salty had the oranges and lemons cut up and in a bucket. Cas had gotten into the dressing room just about the time the players had, and Jack and myself had followed suit. As I mentioned, profanity was not one of Cas' long suits. As one of the players went for the bucket to get an orange, Cas kicked it and oranges and lemons flew all over the place. He said to the center that had reached for the oranges, 'Don't you touch that. You're not worth a bucket of shit!' It came explosively, and sort of stunned the players. Jack and I almost burst out laughing. We had to get out of the dressing room, and away from the building. We were tied at 0-0 and about to lose an easy ballgame, but we doubled up with laughter and laughed so hard it hurt. Jack and I didn't go back into the dressing room at all. After halftime, the rest of the kids came charging out of the door almost running over each other, and Cas followed almost pounding a hole in the ground with every step. His tirade had had an impact. Actions on his part like that were extremely rare, so it didn't have the same effect as a barking dog." Santa Clara won 26-13.

After nearly upsetting Oklahoma in Norman in his final game, the Broncos were invited to play in the Orange Bowl in Miami, Florida. Their opponent was the University of Kentucky Wildcats, then ranked 11th by the Associated Press. They were coached by Paul, "Bear," Bryant who had served under Cas in the Navy and later became the "All-Time Winningest Coach" in college football history after moving to Texas A&M and Alabama. Kentucky was the overwhelming favorite, Santa Clara, the 19-point underdogs.

Santa Clara traveled to Miami in a 19-car train called the "Orange Bowl Special." It stopped in Yuma, Arizona, and Del Rio, Texas, to allow the team to hold short practices. Herman Meister remembered the game well and Coach Bryant better. He characterized Bryant as "a rather formidable individual with an

They called Him Cas

engaging southern accent" who was of "rather aloof manner at times" and "most gracious to the ladies." He was also "extremely confident" and "in the men's john we found out how completely overconfident he was. Jack Roche and I were facing the wall when Bear Bryant came in. Another man came in who evidently was a southerner and a Kentucky rooter. He asked the Bear if he thought Kentucky was going to win, and Bear Bryant drawled 'Man, there's no question about that. It's just a question of how big the score is going to be.' I'm sure had Bear known who we were, his approach would have been different. People, particularly coaches, just don't say things like that. Naturally, we passed this on to members of our team. It was good ammunition because the players were looking for anything to help them get psyched up even more than they were."

Meister continued, "Jack Roche and Eddie Forrest were on the phones, and Casanova worked the bench. We wound up beating Kentucky 21 to 13. Bryant remarked after the game, 'I had better men at my disposal than Casanova had. He got more out of his men than I did.' The celebration in the Broncos' locker room after the game was a long one. Players smoked cigars and slapped each other on the back."

Meister continued, "The coaches made speeches at a gathering after the game for both teams. Cas was gracious. Bear Bryant, however, was still burning from the game. He berated his senior players, accusing them of letting down and not being good leaders. He admonished juniors and sophomores to take heed and never put on an exhibition of leadership as the seniors had in this game. It was an unforgettable experience, that New Year's night."

Meister had fond memories of Len Casanova during those postwar Santa Clara University years. He said, "One of my more pleasant experiences in coaching was the two years I spent at Santa Clara with Cas, Jack Roche, and Eddie Forrest. I had known Cas practically all my life. He was raised in Ferndale, and I had also been raised there up through my grammar school days. Cas and his wife Dixie, Jack and his wife Rennie, and Eddie and his wife, Muffy Jane, had been friends, and during those years our friendship became even closer as we suffered the trials and tribulations of defeat and the moments of victory. We were blessed with a great number of

Chapter 1

excellent athletes. We had about 44 players, most of whom had served in the armed forces at the tail end of World War II.

"Santa Clara had a succession of football coaches who seemed to fit the same mold. They were Clipper Smith, Buck Shaw, and then Cas. All were respected individuals, medium in stature with graying hair. None was a dynamic speaker, but they were sincere about the job.

Cas fit the school and the school fit Cas. As head coach, Cas praised his assistants for what went right and took the blame for what went wrong. A situation like that is ideal for an assistant coach, particularly if you are winning most of the time. Cas was deeply concerned about the personal lives as well as the athletic lives of his players. He could get close to the players without losing their respect. He worked hard, and would go anyplace anytime to represent his team. He handled the pressures of being a head coach well."

University of Pittsburgh Head Football Coach (1950)

Santa Clara University was riding high after its tremendous 1949 football season and its Orange Bowl victory over Kentucky. Head Coach Len Casanova and his assistant coach, Herman Meister, had gone to New York for the annual college coaches association meeting. The meeting seems to have been an eye opener, and Cas decided that he and his assistants should receive pay increases. He had been head coach at Santa Clara for four years at a relatively low salary, and his assistant coaches received only $4,400 to $5,000 a year.

Back in Santa Clara, Cas asked for a raise for himself and his assistants. Meister mused decades later, "I forget what he asked for, but it seem reasonable that his assistants should get a $500 raise. Larger schools were paying better money." Cas tried for other concessions, too.

Instead of offering Cas and his assistants raises, Santa Clara announced that, as a cost-cutting measure, it would drop college football in the not too distant future. Cas and his assistants—including Meister, who initially thought it might be advantageous to

They called Him Cas

his career to fill the head coach job behind Cas until the end came—decided to stick together as a staff and take the best job that might be offered. Cas let word out that he and his crew were looking, and word traveled east.

Admiral Tom Hamilton, with whom Cas had served in the Navy V-5 physical training program during World War II, and by then had retired from the Navy, heard the word. As new athletic director at the University of Pittsburgh, he was anxious to grow its football program and return Pittsburgh to a position of an athletic power. He needed a new head coach for his Panthers and made Cas an offer. Cas accepted the job for himself and his assistant coaches.

The University of Pittsburgh is located in the Oakland district of the City of Pittsburgh, then a steel-making city. It was located at the confluence of the Allegheny and Monongahela rivers where they form the Ohio River and Pennsylvania's second largest city. The University's main building is an awe-inspiring 46-story spire. According to Meister: "Called the cathedral of learning by some and the synagogue of learning by others, it had an outstanding reputation in the liberal arts and in the medical and dental fields. A downtown or commuter school, it had its own stadium and all-purpose field house.

But it was far from ideal. Living conditions for athletes were limited. They were quartered in houses, in annexes of old school buildings, in nurse's quarters, and in the stadium. It was a different situation than Cas and his assistants were accustomed to. The practice area on a hill overlooking the stadium was about three-quarters the size of a football field. Adjacent to it were the athletic offices. On one side was a cemetery, on the other side a group of medical buildings. The city was dirty; its air was polluted."

Meister remembered, "The people we met and grew to know were the nicest, warmhearted folks but the facilities were something else. Across the street from the open end of the stadium was an infirmary, the upper floor of which housed women with venereal disease. Practically every day, as we came down the street from our office to the stadium where we dressed for practice, the prostitutes hung out the windows and gave us this big hello. It was really quite an education."

"Our doctor was an exceptional orthopedic surgeon. After spring practice, he performed an operation on Joe Schmidt, who would

Chapter 1

make All American at Pittsburgh and gain fame as a Detroit Lions linebacker and coach. Doc operated on Joe's knee in June and never put a cast on the leg. This was pretty much unheard of at the time. Joe worked out and followed the therapy outline by the doctor, was ready to play in September, and played the whole season without injury.

Cas expected to have an experienced Pittsburgh team to play a tough schedule against Notre Dame, Michigan State, and Ohio State. But in June, 1950, the Korean War began and most of his football players were called into the armed forces.

And so, after spring practice, Cas and his coaches traveled the state widely to recruit players for his diminished ranks. He almost recruited a youngster from the Pittsburgh area named Johnny Unitas. Cas referred to him as a "skinny little guy." His high school coach said, "I know he's not very big, but he can sure throw the ball." Unitas could, indeed, throw the ball. Cas offered him a partial scholarship, which he didn't accept; the University of Louisville came along and offered him a full ride. Unitas later wound up playing for the Baltimore Colts with George Shaw who quarterbacked for Cas at the University of Oregon in the early 1950s. Shaw was Baltimore's starting quarterback until he was sidelined by a broken leg. Unitas took over and the rest is football history.

Things might have gone differently for Cas at Pittsburgh had he landed Unitas. His starting backfield was especially hard hit; those backfield boys were in the U.S. Marine Corps Reserve and among the players called to duty. With the season about to begin, Cas and company had to start again from scratch. As quickly as he could, Jack Roche developed a quarterback by the name of Best who had been a third-string defensive back. Jack did an excellent job with him, and he responded to Jack's good coaching. By the end of the season, Best had broken several University of Pittsburgh passing records. But that was about the only good news.

Otherwise, the highlight of that season seems to have been going to South Bend, Indiana, to play Notre Dame. "It was like going to Mecca," Meister recalled. "The facilities, the spirit, the people were fantastic. Everything was steeped in tradition— the Golden Dome, the Knute Rockne Memorial." And the game got off to a good start, too. We led Notre Dame seven to zero for a good part of the game.

They called Him Cas

Eventually, they rebounded, and we lost the game, 14-7. It would have been heaven on earth, as far as we were concerned, had we been able to defeat Notre Dame." But when a loss is a highlight—Pittsburgh won one game and lost eight during that disastrous 1950 campaign—matters can only improve. In an effort to improve his Pittsburgh team, Athletic Director Hamilton himself took the helm on an interim basis for the 1951 season.

Things could only improve for Cas and his staff of West Coast coaches by getting back to the West Coast. Cas was offered the head coach job at the University of Oregon, a dismal football backwater at the time. Assistant coaches Jack Roche and Vern Sterling went with him from Pitt to help rebuild a languishing Webfoot football team.

Meister was offered an assistant coach job at the University of California under legendary head coach Lynn Osbert, "Pappy," Waldorf who had just led the Golden Bears to three straight Rose Bowls. When he got the news, he and his wife Jane and their young son drove over to Jack and Rennie Roche's house. Jack was happy for Herm. Meister recalled, "I took on quite a few belts, but was still able to drive home. I turned the corner near our house and couldn't contain myself any longer. There was a big snowbank. I spun the wheel, gunned the motor, and slammed into the soft pile of snow. I yelled with delight."

"Cas was a very popular coach at Pittsburgh with the student body. Red Dawson took over for Cas for one year. He had a good year up to a point, but became ill before it was over and Tom Hamilton took charge. Pittsburgh went to a Bowl that year and to a Bowl the next year, so everyone at least for a time lived happily ever after."

Happiness for Cas and his crew seemed to be seeing Pittsburgh, Pennsylvania, in their rear view mirrors.

Chapter 2
University of Oregon Head Football Coach
(1951-1954)

At the end of the 1950 season, the University of Oregon football team was considered one of the worst in the country. But within three years, coach Casanova had reinvented the team. He did so by overcoming both the program's loser reputation and the Korean War's drain on its players with his own brand of leadership. That style, as University of Oregon football history shows, focused on selecting and developing his coaching staff and recruiting and training good players. This included four great quarterbacks during the sixteen seasons he was head coach at Oregon.

Cas and his assistant coaches hit the deck running. He and his staff had missed spring practice with the team. They arrived during the summer and the 1951 football season was just weeks away. It would take time for Cas to turn the Ducks' program around, but it took far less time than many thought to reverse Oregon's recently dismal football fortunes. After two lean seasons and a mediocre third, Cas led the team through four winning years and to a dream that requires an entire chapter to celebrate.

The Casanova family was visiting his family in Ferndale when the search for a new University of Oregon head coach began. Leo Harris, appointed the University of Oregon's first athletic director in 1947, approached him with the offer to replace the flagging Jim Aiken. Harris was from Cas's part of the country. Born in Santa Cruz, California, in 1904, he played fullback and guard at Santa Cruz High School before attending Stanford. He had played tackle for legendary coach Glenn Scobey, "Pop," Warner in 1925 and 1926. He coached Fresno State College football from 1933 to 1935, and won the Far West Conference Championships the last two years. He also coached Fresno State's basketball team.

His first challenge at the University of Oregon was getting its athletic program out of serious financial trouble. During his first year, a handshake deal with Walt Disney permitted the university to use

They called Him Cas

the likeness of Donald Duck as the basis for its mascot, the Oregon Duck. Thus the "Webfeet" eventually evolved into the "Ducks." After progress on the fiscal front, Harris took on the playing challenge. That meant recruiting a football coach who could get the football team out of serious trouble.

Cas came to Harris' attention when a member of the Portland Duck Club, who as a high school student had played for Cas, campaigned for his coach who had later led small Santa Clara to an unlikely Orange Bowl. This was Don Kennedy who at that time worked for Jantzen Sportswear and later became CEO of White Stag in Portland. Harris flew Cas to Eugene to check out the situation. He showed Cas the game films from the previous 1-9 season. It was not a promising program. But Cas didn't like Pittsburgh and longed to return to the West Coast. Cas said he would have to consult with Dixie, so Harris flew her to Eugene. She agreed it would be a good move, so Cas signed on.

Cas brought assistant coaches Jack Roche and Vern Sterling with him from the University of Pittsburgh. Also on his staff was Johnny McKay, a holdover from Aiken's staff, and track coach Bill Bowerman who signed on for double duty as freshman football coach. Roche would stay with Cas for all 16 years until Cas retired as head coach in 1966. McKay would stay for eight years before going on to coach at the University of Southern California in 1959. Because of the Korean War, the Pacific Coast Conference (PCC) allowed freshman players to play on the varsity team, and a junior varsity team was established that Bowerman coached until the track team, growing in size and success, required all his time.

Knowing talent when he saw it, Cas kept John McKay as an assistant coach. He had played with the Ducks from 1947-1950, playing brilliantly during the Ducks' disastrous 1950 season. Born in West Virginia where he graduated from high school in 1941, McKay was enrolling at Wake Forest College on a football scholarship when his widowed mother became ill. He returned home to work in a coal mine for a year then enlisted in the U.S. Army Air Force as a tail gunner in B-29s in the Pacific.

After the war, he went to Purdue University on a football scholarship in 1946, then transferred to the University of Oregon in 1947 where he played for and coached with Aiken. He played with

Chapter 2

Van Brocklin on the Cotton Bowl team in 1948, then he coached for Aiken, and then for eight years with Cas.

McKay always had fond memories of Oregon and the ATO house or "Animal House." I had the pleasure of being a graduate assistant during the 1971 season at USC. After training table, we would walk back to the coach's office and watch film each night during the week. McKay saw me walking behind and he waited for me. He asked, "George, do they still have the ATO house up at Oregon?" I said, "They sure do coach." Then he asked, "Do they still have the Fur Trappers Ball?" I said, "Coach, they still do." Then he asked, "Do they still have the slide? Man, do I remember that." I knew that they did, and said, "Yes, coach, they still have the slide." I can remember, we would tell people to sit down together and off they went down the back stairs. They slid on a bunch of cardboard which made up the slide down into the basement where the floor was filled with mattresses galore. He just had a kick remembering old memories of that. His face lit up and he grinned as he said he helped his fellow fraternity brothers slide down the stairs on cardboard with their girlfriend close beside them.

Of course, John Belushi made Animal House famous. That was the ATO house, and was filmed on the Oregon campus. Part of that movie is always played in the second half every University of Oregon home game.

John McKay also had fond memories of the Cotton Bowl year, but there were some issues there that would come up again in his coaching tenure at USC and we will talk about them later.

The improving Ducks tied for the PCC title in 1957 and played in the 1958 Rose Bowl. After the 1958 season, McKay moved south as an assistant coach. Then he became head coach for the University of Southern California Trojans. He led them to four national championships in 1962, 1967, 1972, and 1974, as well as the 1963 Rose Bowl victory over the University of Wisconsin. After turning down several NFL offers, he became the Tampa Bay Buccaneers' first head coach in 1976. After an occasionally controversial career in professional football, he retired in 1984 and died in 2001.

In the wake of two seasons in which Oregon football barely won a game, expectations for the 1951 football season were low. After the two winning seasons of 1947 and 1948, which Aiken owed primarily

They called Him Cas

to the presence of quarterback Norm Van Brocklin and halfback Johnny McKay, the team had fallen on hard times. When Van Brocklin graduated and moved on to the NFL in 1949, McKay took over the Duck offense and called the signals from his position as running back. Without Van Brocklin during the 1949 season, the Ducks slipped to four wins and six losses (two and five in the PCC), and lost the last five games in a row. Then, without McKay on the field in 1950—he'd graduated and become one of Aiken's assistant coaches—Oregon won one and lost nine and was winless in conference games. When seven sportswriters listed possible 1951 PCC champions, the University of Oregon and the University of Idaho definitely were not among them. The Eugene Register-Guard put it this way: "Casanova, a sincere gentleman who doesn't beat around the bush, is Oregon's 24th football coach and it's about time we have a coach who doesn't quit under pressure. Wouldn't it be refreshing to have an Oregon coach whose record is so good that we can afford to keep him? At least it would be something different and kill the longtime belief that Oregon is a coach's graveyard. Maybe Oregon will lose all of its ten games this season. So what? There is little difference in a 1-9 record. ...Casanova, very popular at Pittsburgh despite a 1-8 record, is more optimistic than that. In any case, we urge wholehearted cooperation of the fans in boosting Casanova, Jack Roche, Vern Sterling, Johnny McKay and the athletic department."

Given these dire circumstances and prospects, some found it amazing Cas and his staff turned the Oregon football program around in three years. The first year they won two and lost eight. The second year they improved slightly by winning two, losing seven, and playing one to a draw. The third year they won four, lost five, and tied one. And in 1954, the seniors from his first freshman class enjoyed a winning season of six wins and four losses.

This remarkable achievement—starting at a low point and turning a losing franchise into a winning one in such a short time—proves what remarkable people combinations Coach Casanova and his assistant coaches put together. History would demonstrate during his 16-year tenure as head football coach at Oregon what can be accomplished professionally and personally by a coach who cares

Chapter 2

enough about his players to take a "total person" approach to developing not only their athletic abilities but also their lives.

This happened before modern "big time" college football. This was when head coaches and assistant coaches were paid modest salaries; when college football offered only seven major bowl games to its most successful teams. This was when Oregon played at Multnomah Coliseum in Portland, which had a capacity of 30,000, and Hayward Field in Eugene, which accommodated 22,000. Frequently, there were 20,000 fans at Portland games and 10,000 to 15,000 fans at Eugene games.

In August 1951, Cas and his assistants watched the spring practice films and saw their first major challenge. Many of the players they watched on those films had been drafted into the armed forces and were not available to play in the coming season. More players were needed.

To recruit them, Cas and Leo Harris flew a small airplane from Eugene's old airport—just down the hill from campus—to strategic locations. Harris had been named the University of Oregon's first athletic director in 1947. Together they set off to meet alumni and potential players in Portland and Salem as well as Medford, Coos Bay, and Grants Pass in western Oregon, and to Pendleton, Ontario, and Baker City in eastern Oregon.

Just fielding a team was a major challenge. Cas and Harris met the challenge of selling the idea of playing football for the Pacific Coast Conference's second smallest school—the University of Idaho was the only smaller one—in the short three weeks they had before the season began. Cas baited his Oregon grid men with 30 minutes remaining in a lengthy September 1951, practice: "Would you like to have some raw meat?" They roared in unison, "Yes!"

One hundred players showed up for the 1951 season, and by September 16th there were 70 including both varsity and junior varsity squads. Cas experimented with different players at different positions. He changed fullbacks to guards, tackles to centers, linebackers to defensive linemen and back again. After only three weeks of practice, the Ducks began a football season in which they would win twice as many games—two—as they had won the year before.

They called Him Cas

    Cas would also inherit the staff trainer and doctor. The trainer's real name was Bob Officer but he went by "Two Gun." The team doctor's name was Dr. George Guldager. They were quite a pair. They were the physical training team for many years at Oregon before Cas came, and during the 16 years he was there.

    Dr. Guldager methods were equally unconventional. He grew up in eastern Washington and had an accident while baling hay. It resulted in him losing parts of his fingers and the thumb on his left hand. He shared one account with me on a bus ride to one of the games. He had to pass all of the operations including learning to stitch wounds with no special advantages because of his handicap. There were a few times when Novocain was accidently shot into mid air instead of the arm, forehead or leg.

    Cas's offense put a lot of pressure on the quarterback. He had to be a team leader, had to run, pass, and hand off effectively. Four players did this: George Shaw, Jack Crabtree, Dave Grosz, and Bob Berry. Shaw could do all of that and more. He also played defensive back. He was All-Coast his freshman year as a defensive back with 13 pass interceptions. It came natural to him because he was also an All-American baseball player and outfielder who would go to the college world series. A player had to run with the ball in a wide-open attack and master the handoff. Shaw was the experienced veteran in which all the qualities came together. That key player skill set the stage for the winning team that found its way to a bowl game.

    Ironically, the player that did not make it to a bowl game was George Shaw. When he came to Oregon, the program was on the bottom, and when he left the team had a winning record. Shaw was the number one pick of the 1954 NFL draft. With a smaller school with a limited numbers of players, this is what had to happen. Cas learned this at Santa Clara, when he played for one of Knute Rockne's players. When he would interact with Bud Wilkinson, or Bear Bryant or Pappy Waldorf while in the Navy. Cas knew football. He loved the creativity that fools opponents. When you don't have enough talent, you need smart multifunctional players. George Shaw was perhaps the most physically talented of all.

Chapter 2

1951 Season
Wins 8 Losses

Date	Home team	Score	Visit Team	Location
Sat. 9/22/51	Oregon	20-27 (L)	Stanford	Portland, OR
Sat. 9/29/51	Oregon	39-21 (W)	Arizona	Eugene, OR
Sat. 10/06/51	Pacific	34-6 (L)	Oregon	Stockton, Ca.
Sat. 10/13/51	Oregon	6-63 (L)	Washington	Portland, OR
Sat. 10/20/51	UCLA	41-0 (L)	Oregon	Los Angeles, Ca.
Sat. 10/27/51	Wash. State	41-6 (L)	Oregon	Pullman, WA.
Sat. 11/03/51	Idaho	14-13 (W)	Idaho	Eugene, OR
Sat. 11/10/51	Boston Univ.	35-6 (L)	Oregon	Boston, Ma.
Sat. 11/17/51	California	28-26 (L)	Oregon	Berkeley
Sat. 11/24/51	Oregon St.	7-14 (L)	Oregon St.	Eugene, OR

Season Recap

Loss to Stanford, 20-27

Oregon was expected to lose its September 22nd season opener against the Stanford Indians by 21 points as a crowd of 25,000 watched. Forty-eight players suited down 13 freshmen and six sophomores. Cas had been practicing with the squad for less than 21 days. Oregon had only an outside chance of winning. Shutting down Bill McColl, their All-American tight end, seemed like an insurmountable task. Bill McColl was 6'3" and 230 pounds and played defensive end. The consensus All-American went on to play nine years with the Chicago Bears while going to medical school at the University of Chicago. He later became a medical missionary to Korea from 1962-1964.

They called Him Cas

McKay, Roche, Sterling, Cas

Cas and his assistant coaches, Jack Roche and Vern Sterling, had played for and coached at Santa Clara. Stanford was one of their big bay area rivals. They shared strong feelings about Stanford, and did not want to be embarrassed. Cas was not afraid of defeat as much as he was about his squad losing its spirit in a terrible loss. Stanford won, 27-20, but the surprisingly close game was no embarrassment. Indeed, it was more than the crowd of Duck supporters at Multnomah Stadium could have hoped for, and it was an indication of good things to come with Len Casanova at the helm. Cas would play Hal Dunham as quarterback. The rookie George Shaw did not start but did get playing time. These decisions evolved over time and with experience. He immediately played on the defense, and was very effective.

Win over Arizona, 39-21

The victory over Arizona broke an eight-game losing streak. There was a crowd of 12,550 at Hayward Field in Eugene. This was the first victory after eight straight losses, including the prior 2 season's 1-14 record. This win was considered a miracle. Monty Breathauer had an outstanding game. Reserved seats went for $3.00.

Chapter 2

Loss to Pacific, 34-6

The Duck's first away game was a trouncing in reverse that cost them four injuries. The team traveled by Southern Pacific Railroad to Stockton where they endured a 34-6 defeat by the College of the Pacific Tigers at Pacific Memorial Stadium. They returned by train to Eugene the next night. The Eugene newspaper reported, "Passengers on the SP daylight that pulled into Eugene on Sunday night must have thought Oregon's Webfoots had registered a stunning upset football victory, instead of the 34-6 defeat suffered at the hands of COP at Stockton on Saturday night. Several thousand fans, mostly students, were on hand to welcome the Oregon team." Cas and his team were sustained by this support. With four players down, however, they would be even more challenged as they faced the University of Washington the next Saturday at Multnomah Stadium.

Loss to Washington, 63-6

The injuries in Stockton brought five junior varsity players up to the Ducks' varsity team for the October 13 game at which the Huskies handed Oregon a 63-6 defeat, and the worst loss ever in PCC history. All-American Hugh McElhaney, a future All-Pro halfback for the San Francisco 49ers, had a field day against the injury-ridden Ducks.

Loss to UCLA, 41-0

The next Saturday, October 20, the Ducks set another embarrassing record as the smallest crowd ever showed up to watch Oregon lose to the University of California at Los Angeles (UCLA) at Los Angeles Coliseum. The Bruins shut them out, 41-0. Injuries required four more junior varsity players move up to Oregon's varsity team.

They called Him Cas

Loss to Washington State, 41-6

The Ducks' trip to Pullman, Washington, to face the Washington State College Cougars on October 27th, turned out a bit better. At 41-6, their loss was not a shutout. Oregon fielded a 37-man squad for that game. Lineman Jack Patera wore a "bird cage" (a facemask was a gridiron rarity in those days) because he had loose teeth. Linemen Dick Stout and guard Howard Allman had broken noses. The entire University of Idaho Vandals' team watched this game from the grandstands as Moscow is less than ten miles from Pullman.

WSC coach, Forest Evashevski (1950-51), would go on to coach at Iowa from1952-1960 and be the athletic director from 1960-1970. His overall record as a coach was 68-35-6.

Win Over Idaho, 14-13

If the Idaho eleven were emboldened by what they witnessed in Pullman, they didn't show it the following Saturday at Hayward Field in Eugene. The Ducks ended their losing streak by beating the Vandals, 14-13, in the last few minutes of the game. With the sudden win—their first PCC win in two years—the whole team hoisted Cas onto their shoulders and carried him across the field to shake the hand of the Idaho coach. A month and a half after they first met Cas, these players spontaneously carried him on a victory ride as they scored their second win of the season. Cas had already made an impact on these guys' lives without much success in the win column. Still, with the win over Idaho, the Ducks had won twice as many games as they had the year before.

Loss to Boston College, 35-6

The Ducks' next game was neither a PCC game nor a victory. Boston College won, 35-6, at Braves Field in Boston, on November 10th. But there was more to that trip than the game. Cas said to Barney Holland, a Marshfield High graduate from Coos Bay who was on the traveling team, "This is a little different from going to California." He replied, "It sure is, Cas. On the trip to Boston we went

Chapter 2

back about three days early." After practice, Cas took his team on a tour of the city's historical sites. Holland said, "That was really neat. Cas was always big on education first."

Barney Holland was a reserve quarterback who was used successfully as the passing quarterback in certain times when George Shaw would move to wide receiver to improve the passing game. Barney also played basketball and then coached high school basketball for 32 years, mostly at North Eugene and Aloha. He would coach three state championship teams. He was good friends with Jack Roche's son, John. Barney would mentor John and mostly coached 18 years at Churchill where he had two state championship teams. John played football and basketball at Oregon from 1965-1968. His son is now successfully coaching high school basketball in Wilsonville and John is helping out. John's grandson is on the team.

Loss to Cal, 28-26

Back on the West Coast, the Ducks met the University of California Golden Bears at Berkeley's beautiful Memorial Stadium on November 17th. Thirty-seven men made the trip to the Bay Area for the game. Oregon was not supposed to give Cal a workout, but Jack Roche had designed a special defense to stop Cal's quick-charging line. The Duck's surprisingly close score showed the extent to which the brilliant defense succeeded. Close games such as this, with Cal and Stanford, continued throughout Cas and Jack's sixteen-year careers at Oregon and reflected their alma mater's old rivalry with the two larger universities. They could not get that rivalry out of their blood, and were most respected for their successful performances against these two major football teams.

Loss to OSC, 14-7

Oregon's last game of the 1951 season was a close one against in-state rival Oregon State College, at Parker Stadium in Corvallis. In the first of these annual "Civil War" games Cas coached, the rival Oregon State Beavers won, 14-7, by a touchdown.

At the end of his first year as head coach at the University of Oregon, Len Casanova had reason to be pleased. With a new coaching staff, the loss of players to Korean War service and many injuries, he, his staff and team had gone down to Berkeley and almost beat the Golden Bears on their own turf. He had beat Arizona and Idaho. Statistics never tell the whole story, but his Ducks' two wins and eight losses represented the start of something big. Cas could feel it, and so could others.

Cas was particularly pleased with the fighting spirit of his squad. Some teams fold when they suffer bad beatings week after week, but not Cas's Ducks. It was amazing to see a team finish strong even when riddled with injuries and routed on the field. Cas somehow avoided getting down in spirit, and that reflected in the team's morale throughout the season. Not only in their two victories but also in their surprisingly good showings against the University of California and Oregon State College.

In addition to the Oregon athletes who did not play because they were drafted into the armed forces, and those whose play was limited by injuries during this season, there were many athletes who learned to play college football for the first time and went on to do well. George Shaw was one of these.

The year-end football banquet at the downtown Eugene Hotel marked the end of the beginning of the end of Oregon's football doldrums. Well attended by fans, it featured a good program and a well-known speaker. A highlight was the award of the Hoffman Trophy to the team's most valuable player. Dick Patrick received the honor after being selected by his teammates.

George Shaw was All-PCC at defensive back for 1951, having intercepted 13 passes.

Cas recommended that Oregon backs play handball, turn out for track, and even engage in folk dancing. He said, "We lack agility." He warned fans not to become over enthusiastic about the next season because of the showing the Webfoots made against Cal and OSC because, "They were up for California, and OSC was a natural rival." He admitted team spirit made up for some lack of talent, but inspired play cannot be counted on week after week.

A sampling of comments from the Register Guard at the end of Len Casanova's first of 16 years of coaching reveal how admiration for him grew early at the University of Oregon:

Chapter 2

"Bill Tubman, our editor, has always had hopes that Oregon will some day find a coach who will grow old with Oregon, and it looks like Casanova will be a solid favorite toward that goal. ...

"How many student bodies can be found which will present the coach an achievement plaque the first season that included only two victories?"

Whether it was being athletic director or helping Oregon with the development fund, he would be with Oregon from 1951 to 2002; the rest of his life. How lucky we were to have Cas come to Oregon when he did.

Cas was on the way to developing the Oregon football program just as he had done at the Santa Clara. After starting with almost nothing, his Santa Clara teams got better every year. By the fourth and fifth years, the team played in two major bowl games. In that fifth year bowl game, the Broncos had taken the Orange Bowl from Bear Bryant's favored Kentucky team. This was at a small school of about 500 students. All of the students were male, but that meant about ten percent of the student body was on the football team.

Cas had a blueprint for making Oregon football better every year: Get new athletes and develop existing athletes, have good coaches, love coaching and love the players. Cas got new players every year, but from the beginning he developed three guys from Portland — George Shaw, Jack Patera, and Ron Pheister. His predecessor, Al Akins, who had resigned in June, 1951, had recruited them. Under Cas these players got better and better, becoming the leaders of the team. Each played a significant role as Oregon continued to improve and continued to win more games each year.

Ron Pheister

A native Oregonian, George Shaw had quarterbacked Grant High School in Portland, Oregon, to two state football championships.

They called Him Cas

Then he enrolled at the University of Oregon where he became a first-team All-American in both football and baseball. After his Oregon years with Cas, the Baltimore Colts selected Shaw as first player in the 1955 NFL Draft.

Jack Patera

Jack Patera was a graduate of Washington High School in Portland, Oregon. He enrolled at the University of Oregon where he played for Cas from 1951 through 1954 and earned All-Pacific Coast Conference honors as a tackle in his senior year. He was also selected to play in the 1955 East-West Shrine Game. Drafted by the Colts in 1955, he played three years for Baltimore as a linebacker and two years with the Chicago Cardinals before joining the Dallas Cowboys. His playing career ended when he suffered a knee injury in the fourth game of the 1960 season.

Turning his attention to coaching, Patera was a defensive line coach for the Los Angeles Rams from 1963 to 1967. During this time, he developed the famous "Fearsome Foursome." He was an assistant coach for the New York Giants in 1968, and a defensive line coach for the Minnesota Vikings from 1969 through 1975. During this stint, Jack developed this defensive line into the "Purple People Eaters." He then became the first head coach of the new Seattle Seahawks expansion team in 1976. His success with that team culminated in an impressive 9-7 record that earned him the NFL Coach of the Year title in 1978. After another 9-7 year in 1979, followed by losing seasons and deteriorating relations with owners and management, he was fired in 1982 and his coaching career ended.

Another Grant High School graduate, Ron Pheister, was star center of Cas's Ducks for four years and captain of the team his senior year. After graduating from the University of Oregon, Pheisterpassed on a professional football career to coach high

Chapter 2

school teams; first at Tigard High School near Portland, returning to Grant High School as assistant football and track coach, and, in 1958, becoming head football coach at Benson High School in Portland. Eventually, he became Athletic Director of the PIL.

Jack Patera remembered being recruited by Coach Aiken on a trip from Portland to Eugene with Shaw and Pheister: "Aiken came up to us, put his arm around me, and said in his gravelly voice, 'Welcome to the University of Oregon. I'm really glad you're here, and we can give you a job and buy your books and pay your tuition.' Then he shook my hand and he grabbed George Shaw and Ron Pheister around the shoulders, and walked off down the hall. My interview wasn't a priority, I don't think." Patera would learn that every player was a priority for Len Casanova.

He later recalled: "I can remember this guy from OIT in Klamath Falls came and recruited me and I said, 'No, I want to go to a regular college.' He said ,'Well, you know you could be a butcher, a baker, or candlestick maker.' In all this stuff I said, 'No, I want to go to Oregon.' He said, 'Well, you can't go to Oregon. You don't have good enough grades.' I said, 'Well, I've got four A's and a B right now, which I ended up with. I don't know why I can't qualify. 'Well, the coaches told him that I should be a baker like my dad. So that was a recommendation I got from my high school coach. He didn't think a whole lot of me. In fact, I was one of the team Capt. and he appointed a co-captain.

"Cas was disciplined. Cas was like 46. He was young, but he had so many wrinkles. I said, 'Cas, you got to be 80 years old,' when I got to know him a little bit better. He just laughed. When I met him, I thought he was 65. I was 17 years old. He had a real wrinkled face. His strong suit was interacting with people.

"I was screwing around doing something I wasn't supposed to be doing in practice. I can't remember. Cas told me to stop, and I didn't, so he said, 'Hey, you start running until I tell you to stop. Get out of here and start running.' Then practice ended and it started getting dark. You know how Eugene is. Everybody goes in. I'm running around that area next to the field with the hedges that we would practice on. Jack Roche comes out after about 25 minutes and says, 'Cas says you can stop now.' I said, 'He told me to run until he would tell me to stop running, so I'm going to keep running until he tells

They called Him Cas

to stop. 'About five minutes later, here comes Cas out. He said, 'All right,' and mumbled, 'You can stop now.'

"I think my experience with Cas was entirely different because we were rookies together. I was raw and stupid and dumb at that point. I was completely different. Had I been a little bit more sophisticated and not had a chip on my shoulder, I don't know what the hell was going on. It was the first time in my family that anyone had gone to college, so I never had anybody explain anything to me. It was like being adopted into a fine family. I came from a good family but they were a working-class family."

1952

"In the clearing stands a boxer, and a fighter by his trade. And he carries the reminders of every glove that laid him down and cut him in the face till he cried out in his anger and his shame, 'I am leaving, I am leaving, but the fighter still remains.'" Paul Simon, "The Boxer"

Forty-two men—one of the smaller squads in recent years—showed up for the twice-daily practices in September, 1952. Returning players of note were halfbacks George Shaw and Tom Elliott, and linemen Jack Patera, Ron Pheister, Hal Reeve, and Monte Breathauer

Hal Reeve was a good-sized lineman who was brought up in North Bend, Oregon. He did a good job for Cas's early teams. His younger brother played for Oregon and was on the Rose Bowl team.

Monte Brethauer was a perfect size split end at 6' 1," 180 pounds. He was fast. His senior year he received the Hoffman award. Baltimore drafted him in 1953, he was rookie of the year in 1954, and he was drafted into the Army and played for the Colts in 1955.

With talent such as this, Cas prepared for a better 1952 season. During preseason training the players were housed at the Theta Chi fraternity house within a few blocks of the athletic facilities. The preseason polls predicted an even worse season than the previous one, but the scores of most of the Ducks' games proved closer in 1952 than in 1951, and a keen eye could see Oregon becoming a better football team.

Chapter 2

1952 Season
2 Wins 7 Losses, 1 Tie

Date	Home Team	Score	Visit Team	Location
Sat 9/20/52	UCLA	13-0 (L)	Oregon	Los Angles, Ca
Sat. 9/27/52	Nebraska	13-28 (L)	Nebraska	Portland, OR
Sat. 10/4/52	Idaho	14-20 (W)	Oregon	Moscow, Id.
Sat. 10/11/52	Oregon	7-41 (L)	California	Portland, OR
Sat. 9/18/52	Washington	49-0 (L)	Oregon	Seattle, WA.
Sat. 9/25/52	Oregon	14-14 (T)	Montana	Eugene, OR
Sat. 11/1/52	Oregon	6-14 (L)	Pacific	Eugene, OR
Sat. 11/8/52	Oregon	6-19 (L)	Washington St.	Eugene, OR
Sat. 11/15/52	Stanford	20-21 (W)	Oregon	Palo Alto, Ca.
Sato 11/22/52	Oregon St.	22-19 (L)	Oregon	Corvallis

Season Recap
Loss to UCLA, 13-0

Midweek during the season, the Oregon club met at the Eugene Hotel for lunch and for an assessment of the coming opponent. A member of the coaching staff usually talked. But before the first game of the 1952 season against the UCLA Bruins, movie star and comedian Joe E. Brown entertained as guest speaker. Brown was a great fan of the Bruins. A few days later, in the September 20th season opener in Los Angeles, the Bruins beat the Ducks, 13-6. That was a great improvement over 1951 season's 41-0 shutout visited on the Ducks by the Bruins. Cas's kids played a good game, but ran out of gas.

They called Him Cas

Emery Barnes Speaker of the Assembly

Loss to Nebraska, 13-28

On the weekend of the Saturday, September 27th game with the University of Nebraska, players participating in defensive end Emery Barnes' wedding—linebacker Emmett Williams as best man and guard Ben Johnson as an usher—were excused from Friday's practice. Both the game and wedding were in Portland. Barnes, a black man, was to marry LaVerne Partin, a white woman. Cas had no problem with this. He didn't care what color a person was or who they married. He just wanted good athletes who were good students. Both bride and groom filled this bill. Others saw it differently.

At some point before the wedding, Partin was kicked out of her sorority house. Mixed marriages were unusual in 1952, and Emery and LaVerne confronted and overcame many racial issues during their married life. Emery was not shy about using his physical and intellectual gifts to overcome economic and racial barriers while emerging as a role model. The 1952 All-Pacific Coast Conference defensive end and 1953 Ducks team captain also stood out on the track as a two-time conference high jump champion. In 1952, he tied for first NCAA high jump Champ at 6' 8" and AAU Champ at 6' 9 ¾," as U.S. Olympic Team high jump alternate.

Drafted by the Green Bay Packers, the 1954 history graduate opted for an eight-year professional career in the Canadian Football

Chapter 2

League, while embarking on a career as a social worker and advocate of human rights and equal opportunity in Canada. He served almost 25 years in the British Columbia Legislative Assembly and was elected the first minority parliamentary speaker of the Assembly in 1994. Inducted into the University of Oregon Sports Hall of Fame in 1986, he was presented the University of Oregon's Pioneer Award in 1998. Cas was very proud of Emery and visited the Barnes family in Canada from time to time. Emery and LaVerne Barnes were winners in life, but the Ducks lost their wedding weekend's game against Nebraska, 28-13.

Win over Idaho, 14-20

The next weekend, October 4th, the Oregon team defeated Idaho, 28-14. Thirty-seven players went by train to Moscow. The Barber twins were two of those players. Excellent athletes and students, they also competed in track. Bill Bowerman, track coach and freshman football coach, was always up for a good prank. One day, at Hayward field, he took advantage of having twin runners. He started one of the Barber twins in a race and had the other hidden across the track behind the stadium. He got the first twin to stop running in a blind spot and the other to jump in fresh to finish the race. Those watching the race thought a world record had been broken until the first twin popped up to confess it was all a joke. Monte Brethauer noticed the twins wore the same pajamas and joked, "I suppose you have the same dreams, too!" Brethauer was right. Both Barber twins went to medical school and became doctors in the San Diego area.

Loss to California, 41-0

The point spread at the October 11th game against the University of California Golden Bears was a bit larger when Cal defeated Oregon, 41-7, at Multnomah Stadium.

Loss to Washington, 49-0

They called Him Cas

It got worse on October 18th in Seattle when the University of Washington Huskies shut the Ducks out 49-0.

Dunham, Barnes, Brethauer, Shaw &Cas in Seattle night beforethe game.

Tie with Montana, 14-14

On October 25th, the Ducks played the University of Montana Grizzlies to a 14-14 tie in Eugene.

Loss to College of the Pacific, 6-14

Also in Eugene, Oregon lost to College of the Pacific, 6-14.

Loss to Washington State College, 6-19

Oregon loses to WSC, 19-6, in yet another loss in Eugene, Oregon,

Chapter 2

Loss to Stanford, 21-20

On November 15th, Oregon defeated the Stanford Indians, 21-20, in Palo Alto, to tally their second and final win of the 1952 season.

Loss to OSC, 22-19

With a close 22-19 Civil War game loss to Oregon State in Corvallis on November 22nd, Cas's 1952 team had compiled a 2-7-1 season. But the wins and losses column didn't tell the whole story. Except for the California and Washington games, the Ducks' losses were close. There was reason for hope for Oregon's 1953 football season.

Part of the reason for hope was the team's greater emphasis on recruiting. 40 of the 50 players on Oregon's 1952 team were from Oregon, and 26 of the 30 freshmen. This mix began to change as Cas took advantage of his California contacts—including former Santa Clara players who became high school football coaches—and recruited more and more California players.

At the annual football banquet at Eugene Hotel, Monte Brethauer received the 1952 Hoffman Award. The November 30, 1952 Register Guard reported, "Len Casanova is happy as University of Oregon football coach. Len says that several alumni from Santa Clara approached him on the possibility of coming back to Santa Clara when the head job was available, but he told them he was happy here 'as long as the Oregon people will have me.' Despite a record of seven losses, two wins and one tie, plus losing the 'big one' 22-19 to OSC, this writer is convinced that Oregon can do no better and that Len and his staff, if given the necessary fan, alumni, and financial support, Cas will provide Oregon with representative teams we can all be proud of."

They called Him Cas

1953 Season
4 Wins, 5 Losses, 1 Tie

Date	Home Team	Score	Visit Team	Location
Sat. 9/19/53	Nebraska	12-20 (W)	Oregon	Lincoln, Nebraska
Sat. 9/26/53	Stanford	7-0 (L)	Oregon	Palo Alto, Ca.
Sat. 10/3/53	Oregon	0-12 (L)	UCLA	Eugene, OR
Sat. 10/10/53	Washington St.	7-0 (L)	Oregon	Pullman, WA.
Sat. 10/17/53	Oregon	6-14 (L)	Washington	Portland, OR
Sat. 10/24/53	Oregon	26-13 (W)	San Jose St.	Eugene, OR
Sat. 10/31/53	Oregon	13-7 (W)	USC	Portland, OR
Sat. 11/7/53	Oregon	26-6 (W)	Idaho	Eugene, OR
Sat. 11/14/53	California	0-0 (T)	Oregon	Berkeley, Ca.
Sat. 11/21/53	Oregon	0-7 (L)	Oregon St.	Eugene, OR

1953 proved the turn-around year for Head Coach Len Casanova's Oregon Ducks. Cas continued to develop his coaching staff and his players.

Cas added Willard, "Bill," Hammer to his coaching staff. Hammer took over the duties of freshman football coach from track coach Bill Bowerman even as he served as varsity wrestling coach. For five seasons he alternated roles as freshman team coach and varsity interior line coach. Cas also made two strategic additions to the squad in Lon Steiner and Dick James.

Dick James

Chapter 2

Dick James, 1953-1955

Dick James came from Grants Pass Oregon and made an immediate impact on an improving Oregon football team. He wasn't tall, but he played effectively at both offense and defense. He led the Ducks in rushing in 1953, receiving in 1954, and scoring in 1953 and 1954. He was also among the all-time leaders in interceptions. He rushed for 1,434 yards in his Oregon career.

With James' quickness and speed, agility and coordination, he immediately made a positive impact at Oregon both on offense and defense. He was always a scoring threat on offense and a potential interceptor of passes on defense. As a result, he became instrumental in allowing the Ducks to win more games with him playing key roles in several games that they won.

James' athleticism was evident. He played football, basketball, baseball and track and field (high jump and gymnastics). He would often walk on his hands down flights of stairs before games.

He was a Hoffman award winner and University of Oregon Hall of Fame inductee. James played professional football for the Washington Redskins from 1956 to 1963. He was the last player to play both offense and defense in the same game throughout his career at Washington. James scored four touchdowns in one game for the Redskins as they beat the Dallas Cowboys, 34-24, in 1961. He was one of the smallest players in the NFL at 5'9" and 175 pounds.

He played for the New York Giants in 1964 and the Minnesota Vikings in 1965. Here again we have the Oregon connection with norm Van Brocklin getting an Oregon guy. He was in the 1961 Pro Bowl and was included in the seventy greatest Redskins and Oregon Sports Hall of Fame. James was born in Grants Pass, Oregon and died there on June 28, 2000.

Lon Steiner, 1953-1955

Lon was brought up in Corvallis, Oregon. His dad, Lon SteinerSr., had been head coach of Oregon State University for 15 years; the longest tenure of any coach at Oregon State. In 1951, Lon SteinerSr. was fired as head coach at Oregon State. Lon Jr. went to

They called Him Cas

Grant High School for two years and played football there as a sophomore and junior. LonSr. got a job for Heinz lumber in West Fir and the family moved there. Lon played his senior year at Oak Ridge. Lon was a good-sized lineman at 6'1" and 213 pounds. Several schools were interested in him. His mother would not allow him to go to Oregon State. He had seen how hurt his father was and the way they treated him. He never forgot that even though he was brought up and had a good life in the town of Corvallis.

Cas asked George Shaw and Ron Pheister to go visit him in West Fir. They knew of him from Grant High School in Portland. The last person to visit him was Len Casanova in West Fir. While there, Cas discovered his bag was packed, his dorm room number was assigned and he was ready to go to Stanford University. I do not know what was said, but it is one of many examples of Cas reasoning with a young player and convincing him to stay in the State of Oregon. So Lon stayed and played for the University of Oregon where he became captain of the team his senior year. He went on and played in the East-West Shrine Game and thought he wanted to play professional football. He talked to Cas who counseled him against playing. He said, in effect, "You're not big enough. Go to law school instead." And Lon did just that. He went to law school and became a prominent attorney in Portland.

Win over Nebraska, 12-20

The turn-around year began with Oregon's first football season-opener win since 1949. Thirty-six players made the trip to Lincoln, Nebraska, for the September 19th game in which the Ducks upset the University of Nebraska's powerful Cornhuskers, 20-12, in the first-ever nationally televised Game of the Week on NBC. Captain Emery Barnes led a strong starting lineup that included Cas's versatile quarterback, George Shaw.

That this game was the first ever nationally televised Game of the Week on NBC created a new dynamic. The score was close during the third quarter when, suddenly, the referee ran up, blew his whistle, and called time out. Cas, on the sideline, went crazy. "Why a time out now? We didn't call a time out! Why is there a time out?" The referee informed him, "It's a commercial time out." Frustrated,

Chapter 2

Len asked, "What's a commercial time out?" And so it was that Cas learned something new about what was becoming "big-time football."

Reality set in after that opening game win over Nebraska as Oregon went scoreless the next three games, and lost four games in a row.

Loss to Stanford, 7-0

The Ducks left Eugene by train Thursday night and arrived in San Francisco Friday morning. They had a practice at Kezar Stadium Friday afternoon. After playing the game Saturday, they returned on Sunday morning. It was a jaunt that made for a long weekend considering how many hours one was on a train verses a two-hour flight.

There were 18,000 fans watching the game in Palo Alto. Oregon came twice to the 5-yard line and could not get a touchdown. George Shaw was superb in engineering the offense. But Cece Hodges and Emery Barnes were both injured and had to sit out the game. Impressive running by James and Farrell Albright and Van Leuven could not make enough of a difference to win the game.

Loss to UCLA, 0-12

A crowd of 19,500 showed up for the game at Hayward Field. Patera and James were virtual Iron Men for Oregon and the low scoring game was close. George Shaw threw the ball very well. Cas mentioned it was the best team the Ducks had met that season. John Reed, Ron Feaster, Ken Sweitzer and George Shaw played a terrific game.

Loss to Washington State, 7-0

In Pullman on October 10th, the record was getting closer to 15 scoreless periods and a fifth straight loss. It was the first time George Shaw played wide receiver and Barney Holland played quarterback.

They called Him Cas

Loss to University of Washington, 6-14

At Multnomah Field in Portland on October 17th, the University of Washington beat Oregon 14-6. But the scores were getting closer and change was in the air.

Thirty-seven men suited down for the Washington game in front of 21,677 at Multnomah Stadium. The Ducks then spent the night in Salem. The score was getting closer with the Huskies

This was the sixth game of the season to date and there had been very little offense, especially passing offense. There were no receivers, so it was Jack Roche's idea to put George Shaw at wide receiver and have Barney Holland throw the ball as quarterback. The hearts of the fans went out to the kids who had been knocking at those touchdown portals all season without much success. That fourth quarter, Saturday, proved the scoring punch was there. Cas was particularly happy with the confidence his kids had in the fourth quarter comeback. Shaw caught three passes for 81 yards. Cas was pleased with Patera, James, Hal Reeve, and Charlie Kaaihue.

Win against San Jose St., 26-13

At Hayward Field in Eugene on, October 24th, George Shaw caught three Barney Holland passes for 81 yards, and one touchdown as Oregon defeated San Jose State, 26-13.

Win against USC, 13-7

The next Saturday, October 31st, Cas's kids came of age on a cloudy Halloween afternoon in front of 17,772 fans at Multnomah Stadium. That is the day a fourth-quarter pass from Barney Holland to George Shaw put the Ducks ahead to defeat USC, 13-7.

Dick James' parents were watching him for the first time in person.

The four-sport letterman and freshman also intercepted a pass in the fourth quarter as a key play. Cas was willing to try anything that might work on offense. Any new, creative play used Barney Holland at quarterback and George Shaw at wide receiver. Shaw's speed and

Chapter 2

athleticism at that position seemed vital and effective. Emery Barnes played his best game of the season.

Apparently, some of the alumni in Portland thought playing George Shaw as receiver was not a good idea, and Cas came under pressure for doing this. The big victory over USC quieted alumni concerns.

Everyone was happy after the game. The team was in Portland, and on top of this, it was Halloween. It was a time to say, "Hey, let's do something crazy, we beat USC and it's Halloween." Somehow, fullback Dean Van Luven and tight end Jerry Nelson had the harebrained idea of flying to Coos Bay after the game. Dean's uncle had a 2-seater in Scappoose, Oregon. So they found their way out there and began their journey. Dean was a pilot.

Their plan was to fly down the Columbia River Westward until they got to the ocean. There they would turn left and fly south to Coos Bay, spend the night, and come back the next day. The rain was coming down hard and the wind was howling. They made it as far as Three Tree Point, Washington where they hit some trees on an island on the Columbia River, because they were flying so low. Somehow, the plane stuck in a tree with no major damage to either player. They spent several hours until someone discovered them. Somehow they made it back to Eugene in time for Monday's practice. Van Leuven went on to become an engineer and Nelson, Executive of Washington-Morrison Knudsen, before passing away in 2012. Ironically, he died on Halloween at age 83. Both were great Ducks and great supporters. Cas would get all kinds of calls through the years regarding player mishaps on a Saturday night, but can you imagine this one. "Cas two of your players have crash landed an airplane on the Columbia River and they are still alive." I think this takes the cake.

Win over Idaho, 26-6

On November 7th in Eugene, Dick James scored three touchdowns as Oregon beat Idaho, 26-6, and won its third game in a row. Shaw and Holland were 10-10. Shaw was 6 for 6, and 164 yards. Holland was 4 for 4 and 29 yards. It was time to get ready for anything. If it works, do it. Offense was needed.

Tied with California, 0-0

Saturday, November 14th, was a rainy day in Berkeley. Cas's 13-point favorite Ducks quarterbacked, by George Shaw, tied the Golden Bears, 0-0. It was a match that ended Oregon's winning streak, but didn't involve a loss. Oregon got down to the Cal 10-yard line three times, but was unable to score. Ron Pheister and Jack Patera both played 60 minutes.

Loss to OSC, 7-0

At mid week, Kip Taylor, the OSC coach, was interviewed. OSC had won four straight coming into the game, and was 8-2 over the last 10 years. Kip predicted an OSC win. Cas was going all out. This was his third Civil War and he hadn't won one yet.

It was Homecoming and he invited all the dads of the players to a father-son brunch before the game. He also invited the dads to sit on the sidelines with their sons. Here is a great picture of who Cas was, how he thought, and acted. He also decided to make all the seniors co-captains for the game. There were about ten. It is an emotional picture of how Cas created a moment all the young men and their fathers would carry with them the rest of their lives. He was pulling out all the stops.

It was a cold, wet day with a very hard fought defensive type battle and it all came down to one sad interception. Oregon State beat Oregon, 7-0, on an intercepted pass in the annual Civil War Game. The interception happened when quarterback Barney Holland threw a pass to George Shaw. The pass bounced off Shaw's shoulder pad, and was intercepted by Tommy Little who galloped 20 yards for the only touchdown of the game.

Dick James did not play because of injuries, and that made the difference in the game. Thus ended the third season Cas was head coach at Oregon. His team had improved noticeably with four wins, five losses, and a tie, and they were knocking on the door of a winning season. They were now a team to be reckoned with. Not to be taken lightly, they were respected. They could have been 500 or better with a few small plays going the other way this year. It clearly was the turning point.

Chapter 2

Ken Sweitzer won the Hoffman Award at the annual football banquet on Monday following the last game.

Cas was so hungry for a winning season he said, "I think that we have the makings of a team that won't be beaten next year." He had a great ability to envision things and believed the team could win every game the next year with the talent they had. It proved to be a prophetic statement. Oregon finally had respectability. They would go 6-4 but would pass through Hell to get there. After only his 4th season at the helm, the first winning season was accomplished. In spite of occasionally difficult circumstances, the tide had turned.

At the banquet, Cas was awarded a pipe with tobacco so he could spend a restful time now that the season was over.

The Duck Club of Eugene was always giving Cas something to make him feel special, appreciated, and wanted. The gifts were small by today's standards, but Cas appreciated it and took it to heart because that was who he was.

1954

6 Wins, 4 Losses

Date	Home Team	Score	Visit Team	Location
Sat. 9/18/54	Idaho	0-44 (W)	Oregon	Moscow, Id.
Sat. 9/25/54	Oregon	13-18 (L)	Stanford	Portland, OR
Sat. 10/2/54	Oregon	6-7 (L)	Utah	Eugene, OR
Sat. 10/9/54	California	27-33 (W)	Oregon	Berkeley, Ca.
Sat. 10/16/54	USC	14-24 (L)	Oregon	Los Angeles, Ca.
Sat. 10/23/54	Oregon	26-7 (W)	San Jose St.	Eugene, OR
Sat. 10/30/54	Washington	7-26 (W)	Oregon	Seattle, WA.
Sat. 11/6/54	UCLA	41-0 (L)	Oregon	Portland, OR
Sat. 11'13/54	Oregon	26-14 (W)	Washington St.	Eugene, OR
Sat. 11/20/54	Oregon St.	14-33 (W)	Oregon	Corvallis, OR

They called Him Cas

That winning season door opened in 1954. The Ducks would go 6-4, and it would be the first winning season of Cas's tenure at Oregon. All of a sudden—or so it seemed—some of America's greatest athletes were Oregon Duck football players. George Shaw was a nationally renowned quarterback and defensive back. Jack Patera, Ron Pheister, and Dick James were considered pre-season All-American choices. Along with Cas, this was the fourth Ducks season for seniors Shaw, Patera, and Pheister. It proved to be those players' first winning season even as it proved their team's first winning season since 1948. These three seniors also enjoyed some post-season play and were drafted by NFL teams.

In fall of 1954, there were four freshmen that came to the Oregon campus to play football. Jim Shanley from Coos Bay, Norm Chapman from Medford, John Robinson, and John Madden, both from Daly City, California. They all turned out for football. They hit it off, hung out together and kept their close friendships for life. John Madden left after a few months to play football at Cal Poly. He would reconnect with other Oregon Ducks in pro ball with the Philadelphia Eagles for a few seasons; guys like John Wilcox, Darrell Aschbacher, and Norm Van Brocklin. And the head coach was Buck Shaw who Cas served under for several years at Santa Clara. Madden would be the roommate of Darrell Aschbacher on road trips. Madden attributes days in the film room with Van Brocklin for inspiring him to go into coaching. Ironically, all four of these players, besides playing college ball and some playing pro ball, also coached college and pro ball.

This was the core of the squad that determined the future at Oregon. The momentum was impossible to stop.

Win over Idaho, 44-0

The September 18th opening game with Idaho's Vandals in Moscow got the Ducks off to a good start with a 41-0 shutout.

Chapter 2

Loss to Stanford, 13-18

Going into the Stanford game on September 25th, Oregon was ranked 16th in the country. This was new territory for the team. It had been eight years since Oregon had been in the top 20.

John Brodie was 8-16, for 151 yards. He would go on to play 18 years as quarterback for the San Francisco 49ers. He would also become one of the greatest pro quarterbacks in NFL history and play several years on the same teams with Dave Wilcox of Oregon.

Loss to Utah, 6-7

George Shaw was All-American candidate leading the country in total offense and third in passing. But his team lost a close one to Utah. Looking at how much happened in this season and how close some of the games were, Oregon simply failed to pull off the win.

Win over California 27-23
Loss to USC, 14-24

Cas and the Ducks bounced back in Berkeley on October 9th, defeating the California Golden Bears, 33-27. Guard Jack Patera later remembered Cas took him out of that game, "Because we were beating Cal badly." I asked Cas why, he said, 'We're beating them and I want to give a little playing time to this other guy.' That irritated me because it was the only minute of playing I missed all that year. So I put myself back in and Cas never said anything. I wanted to play every minute that year which I did except for that one minute."

Tragedy struck Cas and his team just days after this victory. Patera and his best friend and fellow guard Ken Sweitzer—to whom the team had voted the Hoffman Award as a junior at the end of the previous season—went deer hunting north of Coburg, not far outside Eugene. Jack and Ken became separated, and Jack mistook Ken for a deer. The gunshot wound killed Ken almost instantly. Patera was devastated and Cas and his wife Dixie spent much of the next few days with him, talking with him, trying to console the inconsolable. When the team was going to practice, he would pick Jack up and

They called Him Cas

drop him off with Dixie and they would talk. Dixie was quite a woman; ready for anything, strong and loving. On Friday the team bussed up to Portland for an afternoon practice before their October 16th game against the USC Trojans. Instead of practicing, Jack went to his home in Portland and hung out with his parents.

Cas said at game time, "Jack is going to play, and that's that." Cas had monitored the situation and concluded Patera was better off playing than not. Cas, of course, wanted him to play—needed him to play. Both of his guards were gone if Patera didn't play. Patera played, and despite the team's sadness and loss, Oregon played a good game under the circumstances; the Trojans won, 24-14. It was a loss that did not cost Oregon and Cas a winning season. The Ducks remained a "together" team, anticipating a winning season. What a tough thing in life to go through, especially for Jack Patera.

Win over San Jose State, 26-7

That season continued with a 26-7 victory over San Jose State at Hayward Field in Eugene, on October 23rd.

Win over University of Washington, 7-26

Someone predicted of the upcoming Seattle game: "Fierce determination on the part of the players will bring back a Husky pelt." Oregon had lost five straight to Washington, including 63-6 and 49-0 drubbings. This time was different. The Ducks came away victorious. Beating the Huskies for the first time on their home ground was quite a win as well as a rare one. The University of Washington proved to be one of Cas's nemesis; his Ducks beat the Huskies only three times during his 16 years as Oregon's head coach.

Loss to UCLA Bruins, 41-0

Red Sanders almost never lost to Cas. Oregon would lose to UCLA, 41-0, on November 6th. The game was played in Los Angeles. The train ride last week, now the trip to L.A. to play another first class team was asking too much with injuries this late in the season.

Chapter 2

Win over Washington State, 26-14

Oregon would be at home and finally beat Washington State, 26-14. The team was ending strong again, 5-4, with one game to go.

Win over Oregon State, 14-33

Lon Bryant, a student and member of the Delta house in 1954, was going over early Saturday morning and serving breakfast to Cas the day of the game. Cas's older daughter, Margo, was dating another member of the Delta house. They had it all planned that three of the fraternity brothers were to serve Cas breakfast before he left for the game in Corvallis. So they came over early and served him a breakfast of ham, eggs and pancakes. Then he left and caught the player bus to Corvallis. They won the game so Cas wanted to do the same routine each year thereafter. It went on for three years.

Lon, who became a well-known attorney in Portland, said: "I just loved ol' Cas." Cas was able to involve non players in his doings quite easily.

OSU would be Cas's other nemesis. He would have a 4-10-2 record against the Beavers. Oregon would travel up to Corvallis and play the Beavers there. They beat the Beavers for the first time in 5 years, 33-14, and ended up with a winning season of 6-4. It was the first winning season since 1948. Kip Taylor, head coach of Oregon State, was let go after the game. Tommy Prothro became new head coach in the ensuing months. Cas's record against Oregon State was 4-10-2 for the 16 years he was head coach.

Dick James scored three of the touchdowns that helped defeat the Beavers that day. Then he enjoyed one of the long showers for which he was well known. This one was a bit too long. When he got out, he found he had been left in Corvallis without a ride to Eugene. He caught a ride with a young woman named Sonia Taylor. As they drove south, they heard on the radio that Kip Taylor, head coach at Oregon State, had been fired after the game. Sonia was Kip Taylor's daughter.

Pheister, Shaw, and Patera went 6-4 their senior year. Each had started for four years. Then all three were invited to play in the East-West Shrine Game at Kezar Stadium in San Francisco. Cas was

They called Him Cas

asked to tag along and be an assistant coach for Pappy Waldorf from Cal Berkeley. Patera also played in the Hula Bowl and the College All-Star Game.

Ron Pheister would be drafted by the San Francisco 49ers, but would not go on to play pro ball. He wanted to get into teaching and coaching on the high school level in the Oregon area and he also had an injured shoulder. Ron would coach and teach at several different high schools around the Portland area and around the state including coaching at OIT in Klamath Falls. He came back to Portland and became the Director of Athletics for the PIL schools in the greater Portland area for several years. In that position he became a very positive influence on high school athletics, especially in the Portland area.

George Shaw would become bonus pick or first pick overall in the NFL draft for 1954, being drafted by the Baltimore Colts. Alan Ameche was the number one pick for Baltimore, and Heisman Trophy winner that year. LG Dupree, a running back from Baylor, was second pick for Baltimore. Third pick was Dick Szymanski, a center from Notre Dame, and fourth pick was Jack Patera, by Baltimore.

There were quite a few Ducks that had suddenly become Baltimore Colts. While George Shaw was sitting with friends in the ATO house watching TV, the phone rang and it was for George. George hung up said he had just been the bonus pick for the 1954 NFL draft. He was drafted by the Baltimore Colts and was offered $15,000. Later, an Oregon alum counseled him and asked what Alan Ameche got? Alan was the first round pick after the bonus pick. It was discovered he got $17,500. So Shaw said he would sign for what Alan Ameche got and the Colts said okay.

George not only played football, he also played baseball. He was All-American as a quarterback in football and he was All-American in baseball as an outfielder for the University of Oregon. The Ducks also played in the college World Series. George was a phenomenal athlete who could either be considered a quality quarterback or a quality defensive back; one of the great sports specimens to come out of the University of Oregon, and a multi-sport All-American. George also could have considered professional baseball.

Chapter 2

George Shaw played for the Baltimore Colts from 1955 to 1958. In 1956 he became starting quarterback early in the season but broke his leg, and Johnny Unitastook over as quarterback. You might say the rest is history. In 1958 the Colts won the NFL championship game against the New York Giants in overtime, 23-17. This would be known as the greatest game ever played. George was there with the Colts. The Colts would trade him to the New York Giants where he would play the next two years—1959 and 1960.

In 1960, George replaced Charlie Connerly as starting quarterback. During that year, Frank Gifford received a vicious hit by Chuck Bednarik during a game against the Philadelphia Eagles. Gifford missed the rest of the season and the following season as a result. The Giants picked up YA Tittle from the San Francisco 49ers and in the expansion draft Van Brocklinchose George Shaw for the Minnesota Vikings—their brand new expansion team—as their new quarterback. This happened several times where Van Brocklin would pick up ex- Oregon players. George Shaw started the first game in franchise history, but was replaced in the first half by a rookie, Fran Tarkenton, who took over the starting job.

In 1962, George Shaw played for the Denver Broncos in the American Football League, and then retired after that season. George came back to his hometown of Portland, Oregon and went into the investment business, working several years for the June S. Jones Investment House.

In Jack Patera's senior year, he was All-PCC tackle and played in the Hula Bowl, East-West Shrine Game and College All-Star game. He was inducted into the Oregon sports Hall of Fame in 1982, and the University of Oregon Hall of Fame in 2000. He was the fourth draft pick of the Baltimore Colts. He played seven years of pro ball with the Colts, Cardinals, and Cowboys.

He was assistant coach for the Rams, Giants, Vikings and head coach of Seattle Seahawks for seven years.

Chapter 3
(1955-1957 Seasons at Oregon)

1955
Overall record 6-4

Date	Home Team	Score	Visiting Team	Location
Sat. 9/17/5	Utah	14 – 13 (W)	Oregon	Salt Lake City, UT
Fri. 9/23/55	USC	42-15 (L)	Oregon	Los Angeles
Sat. 10/1/55	Oregon	19-7 (L)	Washington	Portland, OR
Sat. 10/8/55	Oregon	13-6 (L)	Colorado	Eugene, OR
Sat. 10/15/55	Oregon	21-0 (W)	California	Portland, OR
Sat. 10/22/55	Arizona	46-27 (W)	Oregon	Tucson, AZ
Sat. 10/29/55	Oregon	25-0 (W)	Idaho	Eugene, OR
Sat. 11/5/55	Wash St	35-0 (W)	Oregon	Pullman, WA
Sat. 11/12/55	Stanford	44-7 (L)	Oregon	Stanford, CA
Sat. 11/19/55	Oregon	28-0 (W)	Oregon St	Eugene, OR

Season Recap

On September 1, 1955, Oregon State's new coach, Tommy Prothro, had 26 returning Lettermen. UCLA's Hardiman Cureton was voted team Captain by their 23 Lettermen, becoming the first black player chosen team captain.

On September 8, 1955, Oregon was having closed practices because the Utah game was only six practice days away. Bruce Brenn, a transfer from Boise Junior College, was still injured. He was advised to allow six weeks to heal. A scholarly man, Brenn would go on to a successful business career running the International Department of Citibank.

They called Him Cas

Player Profile: Jack Crabtree, 1955-1957

Jack Crabtree was raised in Lakewood, California, played at San Bernardino Junior College, and was recruited by Johnny McKay. He worked in the oil business on Signal Hill in Long Beach, California during the summer after his freshman year. Working on oil wells was hard physical work. At the end of the summer, he decided to ride up to Oregon and look the school over. If he didn't like it, he would travel up the road to OSU, Washington, or WSU. Those schools were all interested in him.

On the first night in Eugene, he stayed in a motel in Glenwood. He met Cas for the first time and liked him very much. Between meeting Cas and McKay, he decided he wanted to play for Oregon, and stayed in Eugene. He ended up playing quarterback for 3 years. He was a year younger than Tom Crabtree (no relation). Tom was brought up in Coos Bay, Oregon. Tom and Jack shared the quarterback duties together for two years, then Jack started in 1957. Jack showed more ability to throw, and possibly run.

Crabtree made a big difference in that ball club. He had a passing arm. Prior to that time, we were not a very good passing team. When George Shaw was playing quarterback and I was a sophomore playing part time, I caught 19 or 20 passes. That is more than I caught the next two years after George left. His influence made us more than a one-dimensional team. Jack was a junior when I was a senior.

"Cas and Me" by John Robinson

"Cas was all things to me. I received a scholarship to Oregon when I lived in the San Francisco Bay Area. My father was ill and he died my freshman year, so Cas was like a parent and mentor to me. He was a disciplinarian and imposed rules and standards to live by; not only for me, but everyone on the team.

We could brush off the full effect of Cas's influence, but if we accepted it, it was a blueprint for what we could do and where we could go in life. Speaking of his influence is, for me, personal. He cared about whether I was going to church and going to class. He would call my mother. He had a special touch for that kind of thing,

Chapter 3

and it didn't matter whether someone was a great athlete. He treated everybody the same. He was one of the most significant people in my life.

He modeled the way we should treat other human beings. And his players noticed. I hurt my hand badly during fall camp my sophomore year. It was swollen and painful. I had also injured some ribs. Emotionally, I was pretty low and not doing well. I was ready to go home and attend a different school.

I went into his office after the morning practice and told him I was quitting. He got up from his desk and asked me to go with him. We got in his car, not talking about the subject at all. I wondered if he was taking me out to the country to kill me, but instead he took me to his house. He walked me in and introduced me as one of his players to his wife. Then he took me to the back yard. It was sunny and warm and he asked his wife to make me lunch. Then he said he was going to come back for me after practice.

There I was, sitting in his backyard enjoying a sandwich that Cas's wife had made; relaxing and looking at the swimming pool. This gave me time to think about things. Our team was out on the field practicing and I thought, 'What the hell is going on in my head?' Just like that, my mood changed and I was embarrassed by my attitude. By the time practice was over, I figured I was tough enough to stay and be a regular team member. Then Cas came back and said, 'Are you okay?' I said, 'Yes.' And he said, 'Good, we will go back to the school and have dinner at the training table.' And that was that.

His responses to players were not routine. Some people who get in authority have a script they go through when you come to them with a problem. There were times I wished he would leave me alone. I was not the best player and thought he paid too much attention to me. But it felt fabulous.

It wasn't to his advantage to keep me since I was not going to be a great player. He knew that, but he had my long-term best interests at heart."

They called Him Cas

Win Over Utah, 14-13

The morning of the game, Cas had the team do a little sightseeing in Salt Lake City and had the bus stop at the Mormon Tabernacle.

Oregon scored a touchdown after a 29-yard effort by Jack Morris of Medford and Shanley of Coos Bay. They played well, but the old pro, Dick James, racked up 91 yards on the ground. Jack Morris of Medford, and Jim Shanley of Coos Bay, played exceptionally well. Sophomore linebacker, Norm Chapman, stopped Herb Nakken on the 5-yard line with inches to go. Head coach Jack Curtice of Utah would later become head coach of Stanford.

Loss to USC, 42-15

On September 23rd, the team played to a crowd of 37,470 in Los Angeles. Game highlights included John Arnett's four touchdowns and a record 90-yard punt return for a touchdown. This became a USC record for number of scores in one game. Jim Shanley had a 72-yard run in the second quarter. USC had a huge line. This was thought to be the best USC team in 75 years.

Loss to Washington, 19-7

In this game, Tom Crabtree passed to Jim Shanley for 48 yards, and Phil McHugh threw a key block to make the play a touchdown.

Loss to Colorado, 13-6

The heavily favored Colorado won in a tight game in Eugene. Dell Ward (He grew up on a farm in Lexington, Oregon, and played at Oregon State) said afterward that Colorado was lucky to win the game. Oregon's offense had six fumbles and lost them all. Cas took the blame for the fumbles. He said he had the players too keyed up to win after losing two in a row.

Chapter 3

In spite of the loss, the Ducks were showing improvement each week. On offense and defense they were expecting better results to come.

Win Over Cal, 21-0

This was a night game, and Cal's worst loss since 1917. His players carried him off the field.

Oregon's defense was impenetrable, holding Cal's offense scoreless. Cas moved up on Pappy Waldorf in his personal feud going back to Santa Clara days. It now stood at 6-6-1.

This was the biggest scoring spree for Oregon in seven years. From Jack Crabtree to Phil McHugh, the plays materialized. Jack Morris' 51-yard George Slender pass interception led to a 51-yard touchdown. Jack Morris' 17 carries for 136 yards produced two scores. Jim Shanley had 10 carries for 48 yards. Jack Crabtree was 4-4, passing 72 yards.

Phil McHugh recovered James' fumble in the end zone for a touchdown.

At this time, Herm Meister Sr. was an assistant coach at Cal. After the game at mid field, Herm Meister Jr. went up to Cas and congratulated him with tears running down his face because his dad was now a Cal Bear assistant coach. Herm, by now, was in high school. It was hard to nudge in there and for Herm Jr. even to get Cas's attention. Cas not only said hi to him, but within about ten days, Herm Jr. got a handwritten letter from Cas saying how nice it was to see him, and how he hoped everything was going well for him. This was an incredible personal touch.

Win Over Arizona, 46-27

The Oregon Ducks were explosive on offense. Jack Morris ran for a 51-yard touchdown. George Slender took a pass interception and scampered 55 yards for another. The victory was Oregon's highest scoring performance since opening the 1948 season with a 55-7 decision over Santa Barbara in Eugene.

Jack Crabtree completed three straight passes in the last two minutes, and Leroy Phelps heaved a 33-yard pass to Phil McHugh

They called Him Cas

for the touchdown with 1:10 remaining in the period. Jack Morris had 125 yards rushing and scored two touchdowns. Jim Shanley had five touchdowns and George Slender had three. Tom Crabtree went 1-7 in passing and Jack Crabtree was 4-4.

Win Over Idaho, 25-0

Oregon held a slim 7-0 margin at halftime and went on to beat the Vandals, 25-0. Sophomore halfback, Jim Shanley, scored twice on 6 and 30 yards runs. Norm Chapman, the sophomore from Medford, performed well blocking and as a linebacker.

Win Over WSC, 35-0

Oregon scored two touchdowns each in the first two quarters, and one in the final quarter. This became the most convincing victory over the Cougars in history. Oregon was becoming explosive on offense and stingy on defense. They were morphing into a more formidable team to fear.

The sun was shining, but the temperature was shivering cold this day. The crowd, at 9000, was the smallest attendance in five years. Player standouts included Phil McHugh whose defensive play and blocking was outstanding as usual. He recovered a fumble by Dick James in the end zone for the opening score. Jack Crabtree passed to end Bill Tarrow for another TD. In the dressing room following the game, Cas said he thought his Webfoots played an exceptionally fine first half, but a terrible second half. He failed to mention he used just about everybody but manager Don Sullivan during the skirmish. Oregon used 33 players. Capt. Lon Steiner injured his shoulder during the first half, and didn't play in the last two quarters. Harry Mondale pulled a leg muscle.

Jim Shanley, fourth in the PCC and 15th in the nation in ground gains, collected 82 yards to bring his aggregate to 516 yards.

Chapter 3

Loss to Stanford, 44-7

Brodie's air game riddled the Duck defense as Oregon lost, 44-7. It was an embarrassing defeat for a team that did not play in the same class as Stanford that day. Tom Crabtree went 1-5 in passing for only 9 yards. John Brodie went 12-18 for 122 yards. Harry Johnson went beyond the call of duty and had a personal high game.

Win Over OSC, 28-0

Seniors Dick James, Harry Johnson, Jim Potter, Art Weber and captain Lon Stiner handed OSC their worst whipping since 1899. Dick James had 114 yards. There was a surprise no-huddle offense with Tom Crabtree at quarterback.

After McHugh came the rest of the happy Ducks in small groups of four or five merrily congratulating each other on their finest football moment. Finally, after nearly the entire squad was in the room, coach Casanova ducked in the doorway. For a moment there was a silence; one that would have made a bystander believe this was not the winning team at all. Then suddenly the Duck players, led by Captain Lon Steiner, rushed en masse and grabbed their startled mentor, carrying him to the shower room on their shoulders. When they were through with Casanova, they rushed back and gave assistant coach Jack Roche the same treatment.

Cas hesitated to name any of his Duckplayers for special commendation, but he was high in his praise for backs Dick James, Jim Shanley and linemen Lon Steiner, Renous Cochran, Spike Hillstrom, and Harry Johnson. When questioned whether he might face an appendicitis operation in the near future, Casanova blurted, "I'm so happy right now I'd be willing to take the operation without an anesthetic." Oregon State had beaten Oregon five straight years. Cas had not beaten this team since arriving in 1951. No wonder he was happy.

Capt. Steiner summed up the Ducks feelings as he trudged for the shower room and said, "This is just wonderful." Yes, it must have been wonderful for Lon to win against OSU, his old hometown he grew up in. The college where his dad coached for so many years

They called Him Cas

and was sadly fired, his old hometown. A lot of emotion. His last chance to get a win in the Civil War game, his own civil war game.

The Hoffman award went to Dick James that year. Upon receiving the award he said, "This is the greatest honor I will ever have in football." Dick went on to play in the East-West Shrine Game later that year in San Francisco. Dick would then go on to enjoy a long professional football career as the last athlete to play both ways. Phil McHugh was selected captain for next year.

Bill Bowerman introduced coach Casanova. Bowerman was never one to over compliment someone. If he complimented you he really meant it. This was the 5th season he was around Cas. He had personally watched as Cas took a football program from nothing, to having just completed Oregon's 2nd winning season in a row. This also included a big win over Oregon State for the first time. "I have been associated with the University of Oregon since 1929. I feel that we have the finest football coach and leader of young men in the history of the school." This brought a standing ovation.

Moments like these highlighted what Cas was all about. He obviously wanted the most talented kids to play at Oregon. But there was so much more to his vision. He wanted them to do well in class. He wanted them to find a way in life and become great citizens and leaders in their communities. People could not help but love Cas as an individual and head coach.

The speaker for the banquet was an ex-Duck football player from 25 years earlier, Dr. Don Zimmerman, Dean of the US Air Force Academy in Colorado.

Dr. Zimmerman recalled growing up in Eugene and seeing Oregon play Washington one rainy day. Late in the fourth quarter, the score was tied at zero and there was a lake of water in the middle of the field. The other part of the field was mud and sawdust. A Washington punt landed, then floated into the lake on the field. Johnny Larson picked the ball out of the water and ran for a touchdown. As he slid across the goal line, it sent Oregon on to the Rose Bowl and led to a victory over the Pennsylvania Quakers in Pasadena in 1916.

Five seniors said goodbye to Oregon: Dick James, Harry Johnson, Art Weber, Jim Potter and team captain, Lon Steiner. Phil McHugh would be team captain the next year.

Chapter 3

Cas also paid tribute to his coaching staff saying they were the best he ever had since becoming a coach in 1928. The staff consisted of Jerry Frei, John Mc Kay, Jack Roche, and Bill Hammer.

Cas was then given a 24-pound turkey basket as an appreciation gift from Duck supporters. The Duck season had ended by Thanksgiving. Today the Ducks' seasons run well into January.

1956
4 Wins, 4 Losses, 2 Ties

Date	Home Team	Score	Visit Team	Location
Sat. 9/22/56	Colorado	35-0 (W)	Oregon	Boulder, CO
Sat. 9/29/56	Oregon	21-14 (W)	Idaho	Eugene, OR
Fri. 10/5/56	UCLA	6-0 (L)	Oregon	Los Angeles, CA
Sat. 10/13/56	Washington	20-7 (L)	Oregon	Seattle, WA
Sat. 10/20/56	Oregon	21-7 (L)	Stanford	Eugene, OR
Sat. 10/27/56	Pittsburg	14-7 (L)	Oregon	Pittsburgh, PA
Sat. 11/3/56	California	28-6 (W)	Oregon	Berkeley, CA
Sat. 11/10/56	Oregon	7-7 (T)	Washington St.	Eugene, OR
Sat. 11/17/56	Oregon	7-0 (W)	S. California	Portland, OR
Sat. 11/24/56	Oregon St.	14-14 (T)	Oregon	Corvallis, OR

Season Recap

In 1956, everybody was thinking the Oregon Ducks would go to the Rose Bowl. There were several close games and two ties as the team went .500 for a 4-4-2 record. This was a disappointing season; one in which Cas was hung in effigy.

Oregon has hopes of getting off to a faster start than the last year, when they lost three of the first four games.

The Ducks had 20 returning lettermen. With Jim Shanley as halfback, Jack Morris, fullback, and Tom Crabtree at quarterback, the backfield was returning. Jack Brown, Hank Lumena, and Charlie Tourville were scheduled to fight it out for the job left vacant by the graduation of Dick James. The regular linemen from last year

They called Him Cas

included Captain Phil McHugh at right end and Spike Hillstrom at right guard, returning men from last fall, and Remus Cochran at left guard, a three-year veteran.

Several Korean War Veterans returned to school when the War ended in July 27, 1953. Some played part or all of the 1955 season. In 1956, they were adjusting to being students again and working on blocking and tackling. The talent on the squad was adding up. Cas was known to smoke up to three packs of cigarettes a day. He was at a function and with several players around him. He asked, "Hey, does anyone have a cigarette?" He was not thinking about the fact he was surrounded by student athletes who should not be smoking. Three or four players whipped out cigarettes in instinctive obedience to their coach. The rules were a little gray at that point, with veterans coming back and adjusting to college life after having put their lives on the line and defending their country for several years.

On September 16th, 1956 coach Casanova announced that Jerry Frei, freshman coach, would swap duties with Hammer for the season, and that both Frei and Hammer would handle most of the scouting assignments. Assisting Hammer with the freshmen would be Lon Steiner, former Oregon captain and tackle last year, who was going to law school at Oregon.

The Webfoots completed their second full week of practice Saturday afternoon and had the advantage of near-perfect weather conditions. Much time was spent on defensive work designed to stop Colorado's varied single wing.

Nineteen lettermen, including six two-year veterans, provided Casanova with a solid aggregation and fairly well rounded team. Oregon's offense, basically a running attack the previous year, was expected to be more balanced with two veteran quarterbacks on board. The team also had a promising newcomer in Jack Daniels who transferred in from Southgate California.

A thirty-seven-man roster went to Boulder, Colorado. It was a big win with 444 yards. There were five touchdowns in the last two quarters. A record crowd of 40,500 fans showed up in the remodeled Stadium. Thirty-seven players saw action in the fourth straight opening game triumph for the Ducks. Boyd Dowler was wide receiver for Colorado. He went on to play for the Green Bay Packers and Washington Redskins.

Chapter 3

Shanley had 16 carries for 71 yards, Morris, 17 carries for 84 yards, Miklanics, seven carries for 64 yards, and Brown, eight carries for 39 yards. Shanley also had two catches for 76 yards, and Stover had a one pass for five yards.

Idaho, 21-14

Jerry Kramer, future offensive guard for the Green Bay Packers, played for Idaho. This was one of the greatest defensive games in years.

Jack Crabtree scored and off tackled the right keeper to win the ballgame. Phil McHugh threw a key block for the touchdown. With 451 yards, it was one of the most potent offenses in the PCC. Harry Mondale had a stiff neck and a minor leg injury according to trainer Bob Officer. Jim Shanley ran for a touchdown only to have it called back for clipping. Oregon's defense was ranked 5th in the nation and number one in the PCC.

Loss to Washington, 20-7

The scouting report was given by Bill hammer. Casanova and his staff had gone to work immediately making preparations for the big game.

Oregon ended up with five fumbles. Washington had the 4th best ground game in the nation, so their performance was not a surprise. Morris did get off a 70-yard run aided by Chuck Austin who threw a key block. Jim, "The Shadow," Shanley was knocked out during the game. However, Dr. George Guldager, team physician, did not believe Shanley suffered an injury. Times have changed.

After the loss, John McKay did not give any particular reason for the team's case of butterfingers. He did say, "No one back was particularly at fault. They were consistent in that all of them fumbled."

McKay's quick wit made him quotable and his best lines began to show up in the newspaper. Here are a few of his classic lines over the years:

Bemoaning the 51-0 loss to Notre Dame in 1966: "I told my team it doesn't matter. There are 750 million people in China who don't

They called Him Cas

even know this game was played. The next day, a guy called me from China and asked, 'What happened, Coach?'"

Following a game in 1967 in which O.J. Simpson received over 30 handoffs, McKay was asked "Why are you giving the ball to Simpson so often?" He replied, "Why not? It's not heavy, and he doesn't belong to a union."

On recruiting his son, J.K. to play football at USC: "I had a rather distinct advantage. I slept with his mother."

After a series of questionable calls helped Notre Dame tie top-ranked USC in 1968, McKay was asked about the officiating. He answered "I'm not surprised. The referee is a fine Catholic fellow by the name of Patrick Murphy."

When asked his opinion of the NFL, he said, "I've seen what they do in the professional ranks and it's not anything different than what we do here." McKay also did not understand the huge amounts of drama the league built around games, stating, "What's so different between losing in the NFL and losing in college? You win, you put a check mark next to the game on the schedule list, and when you lose, you put an X next to it."

When the media asked about McKay's coaching skills in the NFL, McKay replied, "You guys don't know the difference between a football and a bunch of bananas." In the next interview, members of the media left bananas for McKay. He then replied, "You guys don't know the difference between a football and a Mercedes car."

Cas said the team looked like they were doped and couldn't do anything right. The Huskies were coached by Darrell Royal. Royal and Jim Owens both played for Oklahoma and played against Santa Clara in Kezar Stadium when Cas was coaching at Santa Clara in the 1940's.

Oregon now had three straight losses due to fumbles. But this is the fastest backfield in the land and good things were on the horizon.

Loss to Stanford, 21-7

John Brodie and Paul Wiggin, All-American tackle, were team leaders. Brodie shined for Stanford, and they rushed for 200 yards. John Brodie went on to play quarterback for the San Francisco 49ers. Paul Wigginwould play many years as defensive tackle for the

Cleveland Browns. He would retire and become defensive line coach for the 49ers while John Brodie was still playing quarterback. Wiggin became head coach of the Kansas City Chiefs. Both Tom Crabtree and Jack Crabtree were both sick and couldn't play, so Roger Daniels was the quarterback. He struggled throughout the day due to his lack of experience. Brodie was 11-21 for 91 yds.

Loss to Pittsburgh, 14-7

The loss to Pittsburgh was Oregon's fifth straight loss. Tom Crabtree called the ground game. Leroy Phelps and Charlie Tourville played well. Harry Mondale, at 5 ' 7," 206-pounds, was the toughest lineman Pitt had faced that season, according to pit coaching staff. Harry came from Elizabeth, Pennsylvania, 17 miles from Pittsburgh. He had nearly 50 friends and family members at the stadium that Saturday and went all out for them.

Win Over California, 28-6

Oregon led 23-0 at halftime, the biggest margin in 30 years. Leroy Phelps had a 40-yard touchdown. The defense thwarted every scoring threat. Oregon led, 21-0, at halftime. The Bears did not look like the two-touchdown favorites the experts predicted.

Crabtree looked better, but the Ducks still fumbled 3 times. LeRoy Phelps, had a 40-touchdown run in the 1st quarter. Fred Miklancic had a touchdown, and Jim Shanley scored the final one. Joe Kapp, known more as a basketball prospect than a football quarterback, kept the Bears from a worse beating. Joe went on to play for the Minnesota Vikings, eventually entering the Hall of Fame. Casanova said, "It was our best offensive game of the year."

Washington State, 7-7

There was a deadlock on the fog-bound Hayward field that Saturday. The Webfoots threatened four times following a second-quarter touchdown. However, they failed to break up the tie in the last 40 seconds when Jack Morris missed a field goal attempt from the

They called Him Cas

Washington State 27-yard line. Tom Crabtree had a 43-yard run that set up the Oregon touchdown. Crabtree scored on a two-yard dive play. Jim Shanley threatened to give Oregon two touchdowns in the third quarter, but it was to no avail. Oregon's defense, one of the best in the conference, gave ground on passing, but held back the rushing defense by allowing Washington State only 96 yards. The Webfoots had allowed 167 yards per game previously. Tom Crabtree completed 10 out of 16 passes for 93 yards. Spike Hellstrom dropped Bunny Aldrich for a 13-yard loss on a critical third-down play.

Oregon State, 14-14

This game, played in Corvallis, came down to a tie. And in the end, Cas was hung in effigy.

At the annual football banquet at the Eugene Hotel, Senior Phil McHughSr. was awarded the Hoffman award and got at least one vote for the Heisman Trophy.

Bob Blackburn, veteran and popular sportscaster from Portland who worked nearly all of Oregon's games that fall, was guest speaker. Blackburn paid tribute to a team that fought all season, despite ups and downs. He also mentioned coach Casanova was recognized as one of the great coaches of the game, and a man many would like to have their sons play for.

Bob Perkins was Master of Ceremonies and was assisted by his wife, from Coos Bay. She had a very entertaining mind-reading performance that enthralled the crowd.

The annual banquet was always a first class event with an emcee, popular guest speakers, and awards. Cas announced that next year's captains would not be announced until after spring practice.

Graduating seniors included Tom Crabtree, Nick Markulis, Fred Mikleic, Reannous Cochrane, Chuck Austin, and Bill Tarrow. Bill would coach the linebackers for many years at Oregon under Rich Brooks and Mike Belotti.

Chapter 3

Player Profile: Phil McHugh, 1954-1956
6'0,"186 pounds (Varsity)

Phil McHugh played high school ball at Central Catholic in Portland. He played tight end for Oregon and was considered one of the all-time best. Phil had a total of 37 catches for 468 yards and one touchdown. Phil also played on the basketball team for three years. He was the football team's captain the 1956-57 season. A tough competitor both offensively and defensively, Phil played in the East-West Shrine Game with quarterback John Brodie.

Phil was also a high-ranking officer in ROTC and was awarded the Emerald Athletic Trophy, signifying the best all around student athlete in 1957. Phil carried a 3.26 GPA and went on to coach at Oregon under Casanova

Letter from Cas

Cas wrote a letter to my parents after I accepted the offer to play for the Ducks. In it he promised them he was going to make sure I behaved and that if I needed anything, I could always come to him and talk it over. He lived up to that promise as long as I attended. Having the opportunity to join him later as a coach was an unimagined bonus.

Cas had an honest attitude. He would not fake it for anyone. He did not tell anybody else what he was doing. He would just take care of a kid if he had a problem. Cas was always there to help them. He also had an ever-present sense of humor that grounded him.

1957

Overall record 7-4

Date	Home Team	Score	Visit Team	Location
Sat. 9/21/57	Idaho	6-9 (W)	Oregon	Moscow, ID
Sat. 9/28/57	Oregon	3-6 (L)	Pittsburgh	Eugene, OR
Sat. 10/5/57	Oregon	21-0 (W)	UCLA	Portland, OR
Sat.10/12/57	Oregon	26-0 (W)	San Jose St.	Eugene, OR
Sat. 10/19/57	Wash. St.	13-14 (W)	Oregon	Pullman, WA
Sat. 10/26/57	Oregon	24-6 (W)	California	Eugene, OR
Sat. 11/2/57	Stanford	26-27 (W)	Oregon	Palo Alto, CA
Sat. 11/9/57	Oregon	6-13 (L)	Washington	Multnomah, OR
Sat. 11/16/57	S.Cal.	7-16 (W)	Oregon	Los Angeles, CA
Sat. 11/23/57	Oregon	7-10 (L)	Oregon St.	Multnomah, OR
Wed. 1/1/58	Ohio St.	10-7 (L)	Oregon	Rose Bowl

1957-58

Overall Record, 7-4

By now, the Korean War had ended and several players had come back to school to replenish the depth of the squad. Oregon

Chapter 3

actually had a winning season in 1957, then again in 1958. They had gone 4-4-2 in 1956. The guys who returned were now seniors. Jack Morris and Harry Mondale were appointed two of the four captains. So Oregon had vets and then the younger regular student athletes who were about four years younger. Everyone wanted a good season. Oregon was brimming with talent and speed. The team knew they were good. They just needed a taskmaster to show them the way.

In the summer of 1957, Cas wrote a letter to all four of us: Harry, Jack, Morris, Jim Shanley and me. He told us that a popularity contest had developed among the coaching staff. It was determined the four of us would be co-captains through the year. This was in the summer after spring practice was over. So the four of us came into camp in the fall and shared co-captain positions. It was two older guys, Morris and Mondale, and the two of us younger guys, even though we were all seniors. So we went into the season that way. We alternated-two of us were captains for one game, then two the next.

They called Him Cas

This would be Jack Crabtree's third and final year playing quarterback. Most of the time Tom Crabtree—one year older than Jack—would start, but both would play and do well. Since Cas had come to Oregon, the quarterback position had always been demanding. The quarterback had to be a leader first, and then be able to throw, run, and hand the ball off. If one was lacking in any of those areas the whole team would suffer. When the quarterback was a sophomore and just learning the complexities of the passing game, the whole team would suffer. Jack added value with his passing prowess this year. Jack did not have great speed, but he did run the quarterback option effectively. These two small things aided the Oregon offense in the 1957 season.

Jack felt Johnny McKay was an offensive genius. Jack's goal was to try and get inside McKay's brain and think what play he would want him to run. An accurate passer, he would lead the Ducks to a tie for the Pacific Coast Championship with Oregon State.

Player Profile: Jack Morris, 1955-1957 (Varsity)

Jack came from Medford, Oregon where he was a multi-sport standout. Jack also had a brother named Frank who also ran track and coached for the Oregon track team. Jack came from very humble beginnings in Medford. Bob Newland Sr. was his track coach at Medford, and on a certain occasions, Jack and his brother were actually homeless and Bob Newland housed them.

Jack spent four years in the Air Force during the Korean War. Upon completion, he went to the University of Oregon and excelled both in football and track. He played fullback on offense and linebacker on defense. He could play every position. He played blocker, receiver, tackler, punter, and place kicker all in the same game. As a sophomore, Morris set the Ducks' single season scoring record of 68 points, also setting another school record by having a string of 23 consecutive extra point kicks. In 1956, as a junior, he led the team in rushing with 519 yards. As a senior, he rushed for 212 yards against USC. This became the single game rushing record. It still ranks eighth among all-time single-game efforts over 50 years later. He ranked third in career points when he finished.

Jack excelled as a sprinter, running the 100-yard dash in 9' 6." He also ran the 220 and was on sprint relay teams.

Jack played professionally with the Los Angeles Rams in the 1958- 1960 seasons. During his rookie season in 1958, he had six interceptions, which led the team. He also played at Pittsburgh in 1960, and Minnesota in 1961. We again have that Oregon connection with norm Van Brocklin. This was his rookie season as head coach.

Jack was inducted into the Medford Sports Hall of Fame in 1985 and the University of Oregon Hall of Fame in 2005.

They called Him Cas

Player Profile: Jim Shanley, 1955-1957
5'9," 174 pounds

George Shaw had graduated. He was the bonus draft pick in the pros, everybody's All-American, and the nation's leading passer. But instead of there being vacuum, in stepped Jim Shanley. He picked up any slack in the offense over the next three years by running the ball with extreme proficiency. He would later conclude his career at the pinnacle of the sport by leading Oregon to two Rose Bowl appearances, and scoring the Ducks' only touchdown. Jim was brought up in Coos Bay Oregon and played for Marshfield High School. He established himself as all-time ground gainer as starting halfback, an accomplishment that stood for 14 years. He was selected to the All-Pacific Coast Team in 1957— one of only 11 players — and earned All-American recognition. As a sophomore, he ranked 10th in the nation in rushing, with 711 yards, and completed his career with 1,837 yards overall. This warranted Oregon's first ever postseason All-Star invitation to play in the Senior Bowl.

Jim Shanley won the Hoffman award as Oregon's upsetting football player 1957. He was drafted by the Green Bay Packers and played for them in the 1958 season. Jim would coach at Highline High School in Burien, Washington from 1960-1963. He later coached at Washington State University from 1964-1970.

The football players at Oregon at that time were teammates in every sense. They were congenial and got along well. There was no backstabbing. It was a supportive team. It was an environment fostered by the coaches. We all felt like we could not have had a better coaching staff.

I always thought John McKay was the smartest football coach around. I wasn't around Cas as much as a player. He would growl at you, but always treated you well.

Cas expected the assistant coaches to do their jobs well. John McKay was the offensive mind, and Jack Roche, the defensive guru. They were the only assistants in those areas and they each bore sole responsibility for their group. I spent most of my time around John McKay and witnessed his commitment up close.

Chapter 3

Robbie and I were very close. Although we were not roommates, we were in the same dorm together. Then we joined the same fraternity. So we were close all the way through school. Robbie was one of those guys that did not bitch about not getting to play. One would think he was one of the coaches. He knew what every position was doing on different plays. A player would come out of the game and he would be right there saying, "Good job!" He was a cheerleader on the sideline to the guys on the field, regardless who was playing.

Jack Morris was probably the best candidate for professional football because of his size and speed. He played a number of years with the Rams and the Minnesota Vikings. He had the ability to cover players one-on-one and he was fast and tall.

Player Profile: Harry Mondale, 1951 and 1957
5' 6"

Harry Mondale became an All-PCC guard at Oregon. He came in from Elizabeth, Pennsylvania in 1951 where he played high school ball at Elizabeth High.

He was a shirtsleeve relative of Johnny McKay, and somehow found his way out to Oregon. He was a good offensive guard and defensive tackle for the Ducks.

He was in Oregon in 1951, and then had to go to the Korean War. He returned to Oregon for his senior year, and the 1957 season.

Sadly, he injured his foot in the first series of downs in the Rose Bowl, the greatest game he would ever play. Joe Sheffield took his place for the remainder of the game.

Harry was very effective as a blocker and as a defensive player. He would go on to serve for 30 years as line coach at Phoenix High in Southern Oregon. He was also head wrestling coach.

While Harry was involved in several state championship teams on the football field for Phoenix, he was a legend as a wrestling coach. The wrestling teams were perennial state champs. He was widely known in the coaching world.

They called Him Cas

Norm Chapman, 1955-1957
6'0," 199 pounds

Norm Chapman came to Oregon from Medford, Oregon where he played football for Fred Spiegelberg. He played both ways; center on offense and linebacker on defense.

Norm would be one of four captains chosen by the coaches for the Rose Bowl-bound team in the summer of 1957. He broke his leg against Washington State but was well enough to suit down and go out and perform his captain duties at the Rose Bowl.

Norm went into coaching after graduating from college. He coached football and taught at Springfield High. Then from 1961-1965he coached at Willamette University as assistant coach. From 1966-1971, he was an assistant coach at University of Oregon, coaching the freshman team and then coaching the linebackers on varsity.

Chapter 4
(Rose Bowl, 1958)

University of Oregon Vs. Ohio State University

It is not the critic who counts; not the man who points out how the strong man stumbles, or where the doer of deeds could have done them better. The credit belongs to the man who is actually in the arena; whose face is marred by dust and sweat and blood; who strives valiantly; who errs and comes short again and again, because there is no effort without error and shortcomings; who knows the great enthusiasms, the great devotions and spends himself in a worthy cause; who at the best, knows in the end the triumph of high achievement, and who, at worst, if he fails, at least fails while daring greatly; so that his place shall never be with those cold and timid souls who know neither victory or defeat.

Teddy Roosevelt, April 23, 1910

The Ambassador Hotel was located on Wilshire Boulevard, not far from downtown Los Angeles. Rich in history and one of the city's high-end hotels, it attracted A-list Hollywood stars and those who made a living entertaining them. During the Duck's stay, pianist and showman, Liberace, was the nightly headliner in the ballroom. It was a whole new ball game for the Ducks, as well as a venue befitting potential 1958 Rose Bowl champions.

The team enjoyed several outings in Southern California: Visiting the Walk of Fame in Hollywood, going to Disneyland, and dining at famous restaurants. Married players were allowed to bring their wives along on this game trip; from Christmas Eve through New Years' Day festivities and practices that led up to the big game. It was a great adventure, and once-in-a-lifetime experience for the players. Offensive lineman, Tom Keele, had never been on an airplane before he played football at Oregon, and his wife had not flown before the Rose Bowl trip.

They called Him Cas

    A Christmas party at the Ambassador kicked off the week's festivities. Ray Bolger danced at the party. Two decades before he played the Scarecrow in The Wizard of Oz. It seemed incredible to the young men and women from small-town Oregon that they were being entertained personally by stars normally seen on the silver screen. A weeklong whirl of Hollywood—its studios, stars, and restaurants—followed. Norm Van Brocklin, former Oregon quarterback, and now All-Star quarterback of the Los Angeles Rams, made it to some of these events. He especially enjoyed getting together with Oregon's offensive coordinator, John McKay, his old Oregon teammate and favorite passing target. Another team favorite, Walt Disney, occasionally dropped by the team's temporary office at the hotel. Ten years earlier, in a handshake deal with Athletic Director Leo Harris, he had given the University of Oregon permission to use his cartoon character, Donald Duck, as its mascot.

    Best of all, the Oregon Ducks, coached by Cas, along with creative offensive and defensive coaches John McKay and Jack Roche, had practiced hard. This after winning the seven regular season games that confounded the experts and earned them Oregon's first trip to the Rose Bowl in almost forty years. Still, the Duck's seven wins and three losses would not have earned them the Pacific Coast Conference's 1958 Rose Bowl berth had it not been for the conference's "no repeat" rule. It prevented the Oregon State Beavers from taking a second straight trip to Pasadena, even though they had prevailed over the Oregon Ducks in their annual Civil War rivalry game. Despite the Beaver's claim to the PCC championship, it was the Ducks who went south to Pasadena.

    The Ducks' 1957 road to the Rose Bowl was anything but smooth. At the beginning of the season, sportswriters predicted the team would finish seventh in the conference. During the season, nearly every game had been a close battle; some involved odd circumstances and down-to-the wire finishes. In a game during the second week of the season, Oregon led Pittsburgh, 3-0, with 20 seconds left. Quarterback Jack Crabtree gave up a long touchdown pass that resulted in a heartbreaking 6-3 loss. At the time there was little confidence the team would factor into the PCC season's standings.

Chapter 4

In the game against Washington State, a dog ran onto the field just as the Cougar kicker was about to hit the game-winning field goal. Distracted, the kicker sent the kick wide right resulting in a 14-13 Oregon victory. After that, big wins over UCLA, San Jose State, and Cal were balanced by a string of nail-biters against Idaho, Pittsburgh, Stanford, Washington, USC, and OSU. Oregon won most of its games, but it wasn't pretty; it was a messy, by-any-means-necessary, scrapping for tough victories and close losses. Then suddenly, it was over. Cas's team, led by quarterback Jack Crabtree, faced Coach Woody Hayes' top-ranked Ohio State University Buckeyes in the Rose Bowl.

Special Collections & University Archives, University of Oregon Libraries

Beating the Buckeyes was considered impossible. Hanging with the top-ranked team in the Rose Bowl would be considered a great accomplishment in itself. Almost no one thought Oregon had any chance to win. Yet Oregon's 21-0 shutout over UCLA and the 16-7 victory over USC (where fullback Jack Morris had run for 212 yards), were impressive. Ohio State was ranked number one in the coach's poll and number two in the AP poll behind Auburn. The Tigers were on probation due to recruiting violations and were not eligible to participate in postseason play. The Buckeyes were stacked with a roster of All Americans and future NFL Hall of Famers and were widely considered the top team in the country. They had names like Jim Marshall, Dick LeBeau, Jim Shafrath, Jim Houston, Bill Jobko, Galen Cisco, Bob White, and Joe Cannavino. Oregon may have been lacking in superstars, but they had made a collective effort as they struggled to earn victories. Their sheer will came to define the 1957 Webfoot blueprint that also defined Oregon for decades to follow.

Coach Len Casanova was upset about—indeed, truly incensed at—the lack of respect the Los Angeles-area sportswriters gave his Ducks before the game. They called it one of the biggest mismatches in the history of the Rose Bowl. Little thought had been given to the unlikely possibility that Oregon had any chance of defeating Ohio State. The Ducks were 19-point underdogs, and the Los Angeles Times had picked Ohio State to vanquish Oregon, 48-14. The way the game started, Cas later allowed, with the Buckeyes driving down the field, reporters looked like they knew what they were talking about. He said, "But after that, we settled down and gave them quite a ball game." Perhaps the persistent media pessimism regarding the Duck's chances made a positive impression on the team. Perhaps the coach who believed in his team, his staff who believed in their head coach, the team and his players, made a conscious decision to prove the pundits wrong. One thing is certain: Cas had been the underdog before—at Santa Clara, at Pittsburgh, and since arriving in Eugene—and this was nothing new to him.

Everybody woke up on New Years' Day ready to play a football game. At eight in the morning, a bus arrived at the Ambassador Hotel to pick up Coach Casanova and the other coaches and players who chose to attend a pre-game Mass at a local Catholic church. Attending Mass before a game was something Cas had done since his playing days at Santa Clara in the 1920s. He had made it his mission to do so when dealing with the loss of his younger brother.

"On Sunday mornings, one of the biggest challenges was trying to figure out what Mass he would attend. If you went to a different service, he would challenge you the same day and say you weren't at church. We would say, 'Yes I was, Cas. I was at the 10AM!' And he would say, 'No you weren't.' I would drive by his house to see if his car was there during 9 AM mass. If his car was gone, then I would run as fast as I could to get in the back of the church." John Robinson

Chapter 4

Cas's Rose Bowl Prayer

"Father God, I just wanted to thank you so much that Oregon is able to play in the Rose Bowl. It has been a while, several years as you know, since the Orange Bowl. Thank you that I have the opportunity to coach these men. I am so proud of them. I believe in these guys so much. I know that they are going to have a wonderful game today, and I just want to ask that you be with them and the other team and our coaches. Thank you for Jack Crabtree. He has matured so well this year. Thank you for my four captains: Jack Morris, a wonderful athlete and veteran, Jim Shanley, the other runner who will do Coos Bay proud. Thank you for Harry Mondale, another veteran. Norm Chapman, a great player and leader from Medford. I also thank you for all the players that have come down here to wage this exciting battle this afternoon. Father we have been humiliated down here, and I just pray that these players play the game of their life. Amen."

Attending church helped him come together with the other coaches and the team members in a solemn way, to pray, and get right spiritually before the heat of battle. The battle was just five hours off.

Cas believed his Oregon Ducks were going to win the Rose Bowl. After all, he had John McKay as his offensive coach; he was the mastermind who had created effective game plans and had a track record of wins. And seven years before, he had beaten Kentucky at the Sugar Bowl under similar conditions. Cas had been the underdog before.

Coach Len Casanova and his Ducks showed up early and made their way out onto the field nearly two hours before they were scheduled to go through warm-ups. They had left early—much too early, as it turned out—after grossly miscalculating the traffic they would encounter as a result of Pasadena's annual Tournament of Roses Parade. Not quite sure what to do, Cas told his assistant coaches to relax their respective position groups. By the time the team returned to the locker room for pre-game preparations, Cas saw how loose and ready everyone was. That's when he asked his team to go and "make me proud today."

They called Him Cas

The legends of sports broadcasting were at Rose Bowl Stadium in Pasadena to cover the big game: Keith Jackson on the radio, Mel Allen and Chick Hearn on television, for a national audience. Although they tried to remain impartial, even they couldn't help but subtly predict the slaughter everyone—well, almost everyone—expected.

At one o'clock, the team captains met the game officials in the middle of the field. Among them was Norm Chapman, who had broken a leg earlier in the season. Cas was particularly thrilled Chapman was able to suit up and join his co-captains for the coin flip. Oregon lost the flip and Ohio State chose to receive. The 1958 Rose Bowl Game was under way.

The Ducks kicked off and the Buckeyes ran the ball out to the 21-yard line. Then came a 79-yard drive kept alive with a pair of key third-down conversions that quickly positioned them on the Duck's one-yard line. From there, quarterback Frank Kremblas dived over his center to score. Ohio State took an early seven-point lead in what proved to be the Buckeye's only touchdown of the game.

Oregon took a costly hit on the third play of Ohio's first-quarter drive when Harry Mondale, one of Cas' two All-PCC players that 1957 season, was injured. This forced backup guard Joe Schaffeld into the lineup. Just a few days before, Schaffeld had rolled his ankle in practice. He had Dr. Guldager tape it tight, and then Guldager shot

Chapter 4

it with Novocain. According to Darrell Aschbacher: "I could not believe that Joe could play the way he did! He played the whole game and did a great job. After the game, he kept the tape on for days. He couldn't have stuck his foot into a wastepaper basket it was so swollen."

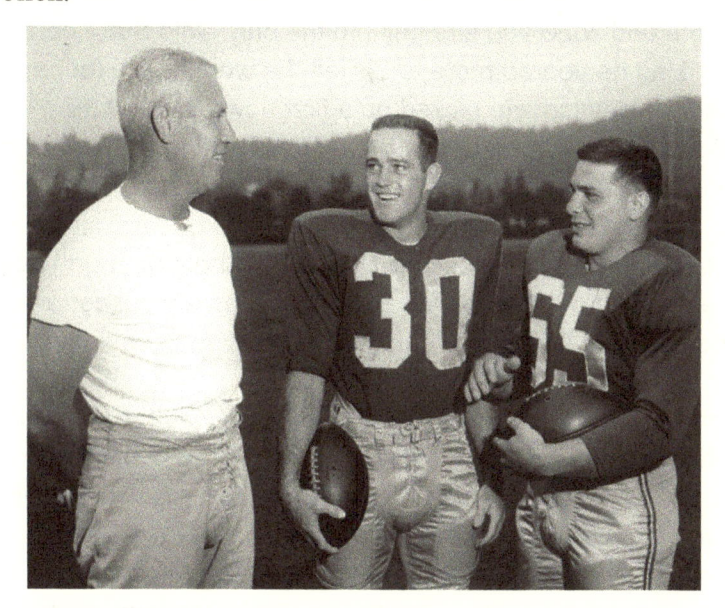

Oregon followed receipt of Ohio's kickoff and pulled off a surprising no-huddle offense for ten plays. Quarterback, Jack Crabtree, called the plays he felt Offensive Coach John McKay wanted him to call; indeed, he felt as if he were inside McKay's brain and calling exactly what McKay would call. Oregon was all over the field; halfback option passes, deceptive quarterback fake jump pass draws, option plays, and even a triple reverse pass that had Oregon marching downfield. But the Duck's drive stalled midfield, and Jack Morris had to punt the ball to surrender possession to the Buckeyes.

In the second quarter, the Ducks tied the game by again driving 80 yards in ten plays to the Buckeyes' five-yard line. From there, halfback Jim Shanley ran five yards into the end zone. Oregon had been able to advance the ball thanks to the passing of Jack Crabtree, the hands of Ron Stover, and the running of both Shanley and Jack Morris. Morris had speed and was able to outrun some of the Buckeye defenders. Halfback Willie West also proved very effective, going three for three on halfback passes for 42 yards.

They called Him Cas

    Another chance for Oregon to score came and went with one of the strangest fluke plays in the history of the Rose Bowl. A pass from West was deflected by an Ohio State lineman into the hands of Oregon offensive tackle Tom Keele. Standing up after being knocked to the ground, Keele suddenly found the ball in his hands. He ran toward the end zone and straight into the only Ohio State defender in his way. Had he veered more to his left, he would have found a wide open lane to pay dirt. He picked up a first down, but not the touchdown that might have been. That touchdown would have put Oregon in the lead and possibly given them the game.

    Toward the end of the first half, Ohio State once again drove close to Oregon's end zone. The Ducks held them on fourth down as Crabtree leaped over a receiver to bat down an almost certain touchdown pass. The score remained tied seven to seven well into the second half.

    Fans at the Rose Bowl, and millions more watching on television and listening on the radio, were stunned at the 7-7 halftime score. Almost nobody expected the Oregon Ducks to hang with the national champion Ohio State Buckeyes. But Oregon's extremely impressive defense and innovative offensive had set Ohio State's players—and most game spectators—back on their heels. Each team had scored with short touchdown runs, but Oregon was the far more impressive team. They racked up hundreds of yards on long plays, while Ohio State slowly ground out gains in short bursts punctuated by an occasional big run or run-action pass. The Ducks were playing above and beyond anyone's expectations or predictions.

    At half-time as Jack Roche came into the dressing room, tears were streaming down his cheeks. The other coaches, Frei and McKay, were also deeply moved. This was the number one team in the nation and Oregon was tied with them. The coaches were so proud of their players.

    The score remained tied well into the second half. With five minutes and 20 seconds remaining in the third quarter, the Ducks had another chance to take the lead. But Jack Morris' 34-yard field goal attempt hooked to the left. Both teams went scoreless during a third quarter that ended in the 7-7 tie with which it began. But before the end of the quarter, the Buckeyes gained 56 yards in 14 plays to set themselves up for an early fourth-quarter score.

Chapter 4

Jack Morris

In the first minute of the fourth quarter, Ohio State's Don Sutherlin, attempted a field goal kick from the very same spot on the field at which Morris had attempted his third-quarter field goal kick. Sutherlin's kick was good, and the Ohio State Buckeyes retook the lead by three points. Oregon still had a few chances to tie or win the game. On their next possession, the Ducks drove hard to the Buckeye's 24-yard line. In the next play, Stover caught a pass but was hit hard and fumbled the ball. Oregon continued to hold off Ohio State efforts to score. But the clock was Oregon's other foe, as Oregon State moved the ball down the field.

    The Ducks got the ball back in the game's final minute, and had one last chance to tie or win. One long pass could put them in scoring position. From such a position, they could attempt a field goal to tie, or a touchdown to win. Crabtree's fourth-down pass from Ohio State's 43-yard line to wide receiver, Ron Stover, was caught, but Stover was stripped of the ball as he went to the ground and fumbled. With 47 seconds remaining in the game, the Buckeyes held on to win, 10-7.

They called Him Cas

Ohio State won the 1958 Rose Bowl by three points. The 21-pointdrubbing the pundits predicted never materialized. Such was Oregon's pride that day. Ohio State had won the game on the scoreboard, but Len Casanova was the one being carried off the field by his players in celebration. Despite the 10-7 loss, the Ducks had done everything their coach had asked of them. Cas's boys had made him proud.

Dan Hafner of the Los Angeles Examiner said it best: "Ohio State won the football game, but scrappy little Oregon won all the other honors in yesterday's grueling Rose Bowl classic, including the lasting respect of those who came to scoff." The statistics backed him up. The Ducks outgained the Buckeyes 351 to 304 yards and made 21 first downs to the Buckeyes' 19. Crabtree completed 10 of 17 passes for 135 yards, while Ohio State quarterback Kramblas completed two of six passes for 59 yards. Stover's 10 receptions and 144 receiving yards set a new PCC record. Most of the other statistics reflected Oregon's superior playing. Oregon quarterback, Jack Crabtree, became one of the few losing team players to win the game's most valuable player (MVP) award, and one of only two to win the award without sharing it with a member of the winning team. It was four turnovers—two fumbles and two interceptions—that kept the Ducks from winning the game.

Good sportsmanship reigned. Ohio State players congratulated the Oregon team for the way they had played, and the mass of Ohio State fans cheered the Oregon team as they left the field.

The Buckeyes retained their No. 1 UPI ranking, and Coach Woody Hayes was named college football coach of the year. One award Hayes would not have won, had it existed, was a coach's

Chapter 4

personal sportsmanship award. As the story goes, Andy Casanova, Cas's youngest daughter and a young teen, was watching the game from a seat just above the Ohio State bench. She wore a nice dress her mother had picked out for her to wear to the big game. When she saw near the very end that Ohio State was going to run out the clock, she decided to leave her seat and walk over to the other sideline to meet her father. As she walked just behind the Ohio State bench, just before the ending gun went off, she heard the gruff voice of Hayes, who had met her before: "Hey, young Casanova, the right team won!" Like a mature adult, she just walked on.

After the game, Casanova unloaded on the Los Angeles media. "Nobody can be humiliated like our guys were and take it," he said at the time. "They were denied by everybody, but they showed up. My parting words to them as we left the clubhouse were, 'Boys, just make me proud!' and I certainly was proud of them after the game." Another story had it that Cas locked all the Los Angeles sportswriters out of the locker room after the game because they had been so awful to his team. Cas was furious and refused them interviews. Those sportswriters took notice and admitted they were wrong.

Yet another story holds that as John Robinson left the locker room, sportswriters mistook him for Jack Crabtree, whom they wanted to interview, and said, "Nice game!" "Yeah, thank you, I thought so, too," Robinson responded.

There's a funny story about John Robinson who was a member of the Duck Rose Bowl team. As the clock was winding down with 43 seconds left in the game and with victory out of reach, Cas called for Robbie on the bench. Robbie had a raincoat with metal snaps on and they were rusty. He couldn't unbuckle them because of the many times they had been in the rain. Cas told Robbie to get in there, and Robbie jumped up from the bench. He was struggling to get his jacket off. He was bent over trying to get the snaps off and someone started pulling them off from the bottom up, pulling them over the top of his head. After struggling for a couple seconds, Robbie finally came flying out of this thing, grabbed a helmet and ran out on the field. Told to go in for Robinson, he realized he was the only Robinson on the team. So he turned and came back to the bench and Cas said, "Good job, Robbie." That was his experience in the Rose Bowl.

They called Him Cas

Players Who Went Pro
Ohio State 1958

1. Joe Cannavino: 1960-1963, Oakland, Buffalo, Hamilton Tiger-Cats
2. Galen Cisco: 1961-69, Pitcher for Red Sox and KC Royals
3. Don Clark :1958-1962, Chicago Bears, Ottawa and Montreal
4. Jim Houston: 1960-72, Cleveland Browns
5. Bill Jobko: 1958-1968, Rams, Vikings, Falcons
He played with Van Brocklin on the Rams, and Van Brocklin coached him on the Falcons and the Vikings.
6. Dick LeBeau: 1959-72, Detroit Lions, 1973-present, coach in the NFL
7. Jim Marshall: One year with Saskatchewan. Nineteen years with the Vikings, coached by Van Brocklin. Played with Bob Berry
8. Dick Schafrath: 1959-71, Cleveland Browns
9. Don Southern: New York Giants and Canada
10. Aurelious Thomas: Steelers
11. Bob White: Houston Oilers: Academic All American
12. Russ Boermaster: Cleveland Browns

Response to the Game

"The score of 10 to 7 was a complete moral victory for the underdog Ducks from Eugene who had been predicted to lose by three touchdowns. They lost, but at day's end, there weren't many fans who were willing to concede that the better team had won."Braven Dyer, Los Angeles times, who had picked Ohio State to win by a 48 to 14 score.

"Len Casanova undoubtedly performed the greatest coaching feat of the season for the Rose Bowl classic. There couldn't have been a bowl team anywhere in America yesterday that dazzled with more spectacular finesse. After the Rose Bowl, Cas was honored as the season's most highly recognized football coach in the country. Humble County, also proud of its nationally acclaimed hero, honored Len Casanova and his wife, Dixie, at the Redwood Acres Fairgrounds in Yreka, California, where over 500 gathered to pay

Chapter 4

tribute to America's most famous coach on January 14, 1958."Vincent Flaherty, San Francisco Examiner

After the Rose Bowl, Casanova and the players directed some words to the Los Angeles sports writers who had written before the game that Oregon was hopelessly mismatched. Cas said, "To you Los Angeles writers, I want to say thanks. You helped us a lot. No one can be humiliated the way we were down here and take it. We were derided by almost everyone, and then those kids went out and played like the champions I knew they were. For my money, they are absolutely tops."Fullback Jack Morris said, "Ohio State's good, yeah, but this team has more guts than anyone could ever imagine." Casanova added, "Personally I thought we looked a little better when we trimmed UCLA. I just told them all I wanted was to be proud of them when the game was over. And I am real proud. We're going home with our heads high," he said.

"For a tremendously protracted spell it seemed as if the condemned man was going to throw the switch on the executioner yesterday in Pasadena. But the executioner, after a frightening ordeal, escaped with his life as Ohio State narrowly defeated gallant Oregon." Vincent Flaherty, San Francisco Examiner

"There wasn't a member of this vast throng, upon leaving, that didn't go away convinced Oregon deserved no worse than a tie…There couldn't have been a bowl team in America yesterday that dazzled with more spectacular finesse…There was nothing phony about Oregon's great showing. Take the game play by play and quarter by quarter and Oregon battled Ohio State on even terms and sometimes better than even."

Oregon Homecoming

On Thursday night, an enthusiastic crowd gathered at Mahlon Sweet Field in Eugene, Oregon to welcome the Ducks home. A searchlight picked up the United Airlines charter plane shortly before 9:30 PM as it passed over the Eugene field. As soon as the motors stopped, the crowd surged around the ramp to cheer the debarking team.

The first man off the plane was coach Len Casanova. He was greeted at the bottom of the ramp by Governor Robert B. Holmes:

They called Him Cas

"It's wonderful to have you back with this great team," Holmes said. "The boys and you, Cas, gave us a wonderful game. It meant a great deal all over the country for the state of Oregon."

Casanova expressed his thanks for the welcome and added, "The boys did themselves proud, their school and the state."

One of the first people off the plane was tackle, Tom Keele. Approached by a young person seeking an autograph, Keele readily complied and cautioned, "Don't go selling it."

While Oregon wouldn't be back in the Rose Bowl for 37 years, there were Oregon players & coaches that day who would make many return visits as head coaches at USC. John McKay brought his USC Trojans to the Rose Bowl seven times and John Robinson took his USC team three times. For their Rose Bowl Game coaching accomplishments, Cas, McKay, and Robinson were inducted into the College Football Coach Hall of Fame.

So much had changed in a year. 1957 was a different story. In the custom of the day, Oregon became the host school as the PCC representative, and many of the duties of administering the game fell to North Ritchie, a rookie U of O event manager, who, at 24, was younger than Oregon starting fullback Jack Morris.

Ritchie later became Director of Athletics at Oregon, serving from 1970 to 1975. Still missing Eugene, he recalled that to stage the Rose Bowl Oregon he had to purchase office equipment they didn't have, including a postage and sorting machine to handle the 90,000 plus tickets. With a 21,000-seat field as its home venue for football, Oregon staff members' tradition had them sorting tickets by hand.

Oregon's travel budget for the game was $80,000. The network TV payout was $500,000. Richie, who received the check in the mail recalled, "I'd never seen so many zeros in my life." In Ritchie's view, the 1958 Rose Bowl gave Oregon a national image and recognition that endured for a decade or more.

Game Highlights

- Kramblas: Six passes and 2 completions for 59 yards
- Willie West: Three for three in passing for 42 yards
- Bob White: Twenty-five carries for 93 yards
- Clark: Fourteen carries for 82 yards

Chapter 4

- Jim Shanley: Eleven carries for 59 yards
- Jack Morris: Eleven carries for 57 yards
- Charlie Tourville: Two receptions for 27 yards
- Ohio State passing: Two for six for 59 yards
- Fumbles lost: Two for Oregon
- Interceptions: Two for Oregon.
- Turnovers: Four for Oregon
- Attendance: 98,202.

Player Profile: Tom Keele
1957-1959
6'2," 203 pounds

Tom Keele is an interesting story. He played football for Jefferson High School in Portland, Oregon. He was good enough to be invited to play in the East-West Shriner Game the summer after his senior year. It was to be the last football he played for quite a while.

He continued to live in the same neighborhood in Portland where he worked as a box boy at a grocery store. He later married and had two kids. Cas's daughter, Margot, lived in that same neighborhood because her husband was in the Army and was assigned to the headquarters in that area. Margot did her shopping in the grocery store where Tom worked and they often talked football. Margot encouraged her dad to look into talking to Tom.

Cas gave Tom a call and asked him to come down and have lunch with them in Eugene so they could talk about football. Tom Keele came down to Eugene to meet Cas. After talking a while, Cas offered Tom a full-ride scholarship. Tom was overwhelmed by this gesture and accepted it. He was 23 and had not played football for four years.

He went up to Portland, rented his house out, picked up his family up and moved down to Eugene and registered. Tom would be the first one in his family to attend college. Tom played in the Rose Bowl his second year at Oregon as a 6' 2," 210-pound offensive tackle. He would almost be the hero of the game. A pass was deflected right into Tom's hands and he ran right at the defensive back rather than the open field to his right. Veering off just a little, he could have run for the winning score. But he made a first down.

Tom Keele In His Own Words

My first days at Oregon....'56 was my freshman year. I was 23-years old, married and had two children and working in a grocery store. I graduated from Jefferson High School and the guy that I worked for—a German Grocery store, Repp Brothers in Portland—he had gone to Oregon, and Cas's older daughter shopped there. I used to deliver groceries. That's one of the things I did; in a truck. And I delivered groceries to a family by the name of Wells. I delivered groceries to them and Cas's son-in-law, my boss, was kind of a talker and he said, 'Hey, I got a good football player working for me, so Cas's son-in-law told him that, and that I played in the 1951 Shriner Game. I don't know how that went. I wrote a couple letters because I wanted to get an education. So I wrote to Cas and he told me to come down, and bought me a sandwich and said I'll put you on scholarship. And that was it. I was 23, so I just quit my job. I had bought a house when I was in Portland, so we rented that out, and my wife and I and our two kids went off to Eugene and that was the beginning of that deal down there.

How many coaches would give a guy who hadn't played football for that many years a scholarship? So I'm certainly so thankful. I was a small guy. I think the most I ever got was 210 pounds.

As for what I thought of Cas, I always thought of him as a very kind of distinguished guy. And as you meet people, just said what he meant and meant what he said. And I always remember, I grew up in a small church in Portland. In fact, probably the most famous guy at the church was a guy named Jim Elliot. He got killed by the Auca Indians. A little church called the Grace and Truth Bible Church. It was on Knott Street. It was what they called a Brethren Church that really taught the Word, but it was run by part-time pastors. They didn't have any full-time pastors. I think those Brethren Churches kind of ran themselves with a couple of leaders and stuff like that, kinda like an elder-run church. It was a neat old church because that was when I was 10-years old. Actually looking back to that's when I was saved, but I didn't exactly walk the walk and talk the talk until years later.

The one thing about Cas, when we'd go to games he'd take all the Catholic kids to Mass, so I would also go. I wasn't Catholic, but I'd just go along and sit in the back of the church on game days. I also remember how well he treated his assistants. Of course Jack Roche was really good. Cas very seldom said anything gruff, but Jack would smooth things over when he did. Jack Roche was like his son and he would say, "Oh yeah, we can do this or do something." Jack was great. When Jack would mimic Cas it was out of love. It was just pure love, you could tell that. And you could tell he wasn't doing it out of spite. He was doing it to be funny—in his quiet way. Jack was a funny guy.

Chapter 5
1958

Overall Record, 4-6

Date	Home Team	Score	Visit Team	Location
Sat. 9/20/58	Oregon	27-0 (W)	Idaho	Eugene, OR
Sat. 10/4/58	Oklahoma	6-0 (L)	Oregon	Oklahoma, OK
Sat. 10/11/58	Oregon	25-0 (W)	Southern California	Multnomah, OR
Sat. 10/18/58	Oregon	6-0 (L)	Wash. St.	Eugene, OR
Sat. 10/25/58	California	23-6 (L)	Oregon	California
Sat. 11/1/58	Wash.	6-0 (L)	Oregon	Seattle, WA
Sat. 11/8/58	Oregon	12-0 (W)	Stanford	Eugene, OR
Sat. 11/15/58	UCLA	7-3 (L)	Oregon	Los Angeles, CA
Sat. 11/22/58	Oregon State	20-0 (W)	Oregon	Corvallis, OR
Sat. 12/6/58	Miami	2-0 (L)	Oregon	Miami, FL

    1958 was a frustrating year for Cas. Ten months earlier the country saw his team come within a few points of defeating Ohio State. They saw him claim his team was best in the country. His 1958 team's defense was one of the best, but his offense failed to materialize.

    Jack Crabtree graduated and a new rookie, Dave Grosz, became quarterback. He needed seasoning and time to develop and become familiar with his targets. Another strategic necessity was that Grosz got an incredible added receiver by the name of Cleveland, "Pussy Foot," Jones. But that would not be until next year. Unfortunately, the result was a 4-6 season. Only 50 points were scored on Oregon all season. Oregon was second to Oklahoma in defense for the year. The Ducks played five teams ranked in the top ten in 1958. In 1959, Grosz led his team to an 8-2 record and in the 1960 season, another bowl appearance. Oregon made two bowl appearances in three years. Dave Grosz had an incredible last two years and went on to play pro ball in Canada. Then he became a college coach in Southern California for 18 years. Dave could run, throw, and handle the ball well. 1958 would be John McKay's last

They called Him Cas

year at Oregon. He had been at Oregon playing or coaching since 1947. He helped develop George Shaw, Jack Crabtree, Dave Grosz, Jack Morris, Jim Shanley, and Willie West. He went on to USC as an assistant, then head coach.

Win Over Idaho, 27-0

On Monday, September 15th, 1958, coach Len Casanova closed the gates as the Oregon Ducks started a 5-day grind in preparation for their opener against Idaho's Vandals at Hayward field on Saturday. Casanova's biggest problem was offsetting a huge Vandal line that averaged 214 pounds per man.

On September 20th, 1958, perfect weather conditions prevailed and there were a number of plays as brilliant as the sunshine. One was a 15-yard run by fullback Marlan Holland on the sixth play of the game. It was nullified by a 15-yard penalty. Then Oregon's first score came on a 9-yard run by Don Laudenslager, junior halfback from Gresham. Will Reeve, senior guard from North, tackled the fullback in Idaho's end zone. Charlie Tourville, senior right halfback, scored inside the four-yard line on a pitch in the fourth quarter. A 61-yard pass play was tallied in the final four minutes. Then came a pass from Paul Grover to Herman McKinney. Oregon won, 27-0.

Loss to Oklahoma, 6-0

The gallant Ducks scared the Sooners in a 6-0 loss. A crowd of 61,700 fans sat under sunny skies and 74 degrees in Norman, Oklahoma. The number-one ranked Oklahoma Sooners had to fight for their lives before nosing out the Ducks, 6-0. Despite the fact Bud Wilkinson's Sooners were 21-point pregame favorites against an Oregon team ranked only 4th in the Pacific Coast Conference. The defensive effort was even greater than the one against Ohio State the past January 1st. In the first half, Dave Grayson missed a reception that would have been a touchdown.

Cas had served with Bud Wilkinson during WWII and they knew each other. Under Bud Wilkenson they had just set a NCAA record, winning 47 consecutive wins. Bud knew Cas from being in the Navy together during WWII. Bud came into the dressing room after the

Chapter 5

game and mentioned to Darrell Aschbacher that he was the best defensive tackle he had ever seen.

Win Over USC, 25-0

The Ducks scored a touchdown in the opening two minutes of play on a Saturday night and added a field goal in the second period. They scored two touchdowns in the fourth quarter to complete a 25-0 route. Following a brilliant defensive performance against Oklahoma the previous Saturday, Oregon showed a sparkling running and passing attack that rolled up an amazing 469 yards.

"McKay, was really funny. I was from Kent, Washington, and every time I would screw up he would run me to Kent. And whenever Paul Grover screwed up he would run him to Anaheim. It was funny though. If he did something wrong, he took us around the field and it was how he coached. I had good memories of him. I really liked him. He was one of my favorites." Dave Grosz

Loss to WSC, 6-0

A crowd of 22,000 braved inclement weather for the Oregon game against WSC. Bobby Newman, WSC quarterback, tallied a touchdown from within inches of the goal line. Phil Steiger, one of several WSC halfbacks, provided much of their offensive and defensive feats. Oregon ranked among the top 10 in the nation in both total offense and defense prior to the game. Oregon was inept in both departments that Saturday. Oregon's homecoming theme was a new look at Oregon, but the real new look was a football team that showed an inability to perform up to expectations for the old grads. Had the game been played at Pullman, the theme would have been pluck the Ducks, which is exactly what the Cougars did.

Loss to Cal, 23-6

Joe Kapp, All-American quarterback candidate, collected All-Star support on an alternately sunny and foggy Saturday afternoon. The Cal Bears defeated the Oregon Ducks, 23-6, before 47,000 fans.

They called Him Cas

Coach Pete Elliott's Split-T Formation Bears, after winning one game last year, had won four straight. They were now ranked Rose Bowl contenders in the last Pacific Coast Conference campaign.

Oregon was looking much better than during the previous week's 6-0 loss to WSC. But they still didn't have consistency either on offense or defense against a team that led the PCC in total offense; the team that must have been underrated defensively. Cal's defense was tough in the clutch, although allowing 125 yards in passing.

Casanova held Joe Kapp in highest regard saying he was, "Darn good." Oregon had to stop him, but couldn't. The Ducks lost Bob Grottkau, co-captain with Ron Stover, and starting guard and center Bob Peterson, early in the third quarter with Cal up by only two points. Oregon had been a two-point favorite, but the three injuries were extremely costly for a club without bench strength.

Jack Roche had planned on doing a recruiting appointment before the start of the game in Berkeley, near where the bus would be traveling. Cas told Jack to take a cab to the athlete's home and wait at such and such a street. He told Jack the team bus would pick him up on the way to the stadium. But someone forgot to look for Jack and the bus did not stop. It went all the way to the stadium. The game was getting closer to starting and Jack showed up in the dressing room. Cas said, "Where the hell have you been?" and Jack said, "What do you mean, I have been waiting for you for an hour." They went back and forth and settled down. Everything was back to normal. Jack had hailed a cab to get to the game.

Chapter 5

Loss to Washington, 6-0

It was Oregon's third straight loss in as many weeks. About 32,000 people sat under overcast skies to watch the Ducks falter at the goal line on four different occasions. They also missed a first quarter field-goal attempt by John Clark. The turf, protected by a tarp throughout Friday's daylong rain, still did not provide a good footing for the players.

Saturday afternoon could have been a hangover from Friday night. There must have been a lot of goblins around to carry on the jinx the Huskies held over coach Casanova. He had now lost seven of eight games in the inter-state rivalry. Six seemed to be a jinx for Oregon any day, let alone Halloween weekend. Oregon had also lost, 6-0, to Oklahoma and WSC.

The veteran Duck boss said, "I hate to say anything about the game until we see the movies," speaking almost inaudibly. "I don't want to condemn anyone without a better look."

Win Over Stanford, 12-0

Oregon broke its three-game losing streak on a rain-washed Hayward field on a Saturday afternoon. They defeated a much-beaten Stanford football team, 12-0, on the strength of third and fourth quarter touchdowns.

A crowd of 13,500, smallest of the year, saw the stubborn Stanford Indians hold the 12-point favorite Ducks scoreless in the first half after being in Oregon territory three times in the first two quarters. The game, however, featured a 23-yard pass from Dave Grosz to Pete Welch; the longest pass of the day. The longest run from scrimmage was 11 yards by Bernie Dowd, 210-pound sophomore fullback for Stanford, and a 13-yarder by Breyer. Touchdown 20—a practice maneuver coach Casanova devised the previous week—paid off. This, after being held to six points in three games.

Dave Grosz, Oregon's talented sophomore quarterback, scored the first touchdown by sliding off his right guard from the one-yard line in the final six minutes of the third quarter, climaxing a 64-yard drive.

They called Him Cas

Loss to UCLA, 7-3

The PCC died Saturday afternoon on a sour note as the underdog UCLA Bruins scored a 7-3 victory over now ex-rivals, Oregon Ducks.

Apparently, few people cared whether the ex-rivals were here to settle more than a football dispute, because only 22,297 fans turned out in perfect Southern California football weather. Although the lights were turned on in the third quarter, the skies were clear most of the afternoon and the temperature was around 60 degrees. Most California fans were wrapped in blankets, the men in topcoats.

Oregon failed to show the scoring punch they put together in a 12-0 victory over Stanford the last week as they faltered on a 68-yard drive in the first quarter.

It looked like Dave Powell, Junior fullback from Eugene High, was Oregon's answer to that missing punch in the fourth quarter. He personally gained 80 yards on 10 running plays to move the Webfoots to a first down on the UCLA 11-yard line. Three running plays by Willie West and Charlie Tourville lost a net one-yard and made Clark's second field goal of the season necessary to end a scoreless tie.

Win Over Oregon State, 20-0

A record crowd of 27,574, sitting under cloudy skies, watched the superb Oregon defense stop cold Tommy Prothro's hard-running Beavers. OSC had only 87 net yards rushing, four first downs, and no yards gained in 0 for 10 passes. Oregon, held to three touchdowns in its last five games, completely dominated the game offensively and defensively. Dave Powell, junior fullback from Eugene High, blasted out 80 yards and 21 carries and scored the first two touchdowns. Oregon's final touchdown came with four seconds to play; a 7-yard pass from quarterback Paul Grover and Fred Siler. A possible shot at Iowa in the Rose Bowl went with the annual Civil War game at one point. It looked like the Beavers still might be in the running for a visit to Pasadena on January 1st.

It had been a long season for Casanova as he thought back to his last ride off the field after the USC game where Oregon won, 25-

Chapter 5

0. The Webfoots had not wasted a second before picking up Casanova and his assistant. He said, "It was a hell of a defensive job. I was pleased we could contain Nub Beamer." He said Oregon used four different defenses and "thought it would be a battle of the lines and we beat them up front." He praised the entire forward wall of the Duck 11, but heaped special praise on guard, Bob Grottkau, and tackle, Darrell Aschbacher. He named quarterback, Dave Grosz, and fullback, Dave Powell, as the backfield standouts, but was quick to add Grayson, the reserve halfback who started his first game.

Loss to Miami, 2-0

On Saturday, Oregon ended its most frustrating season on the same note. As 22,898 fans watched in the stands, and millions watched on TV, the Miami Hurricanes eked out at 2-0 victory over the Webfoots. It was a game of breaks, penalties and mistakes, and all went against coach Len Casanova's Webfoots. They saw two touchdowns called back by the officials and had three other scoring opportunities go to waste.

The Ducks ended the year with only 50 points scored against them for all of 1958. This ranked them second to Oklahoma who had given up 49 points all year as the stingiest defensive team in the country. Much of the credit went to Jack Roche, defensive genius, who came up with the right defenses each week to whatever offense they faced. He was an invaluable asset to Cas for 16 years at Oregon.

Graduating seniors were Greg Altenhofen, Roger Daniels, Gerald Gibson, Tom Keele, Eldon Kimbrough, Don Laudenslager, Harry Needham, Bob Peterson, Dave Powell, Fred Siler, Jack Stone, Willie West, John Wilcox, and John Willener. The Hoffman Trophy went to Bob Peterson, All-PCC center.

Guest speaker at the annual banquet was Pappy Waldorf, Cal head coach for several years, and close friend of Cas. He had been in college coaching for 32 years with a record of 170-94-22. He had quit coaching to run the scouting department for the San Francisco 49ers.

They called Him Cas

Pappy had many good seasons at Cal, and many good players. One was Ray Solari, a lineman from 1948-50. He went on to Cleveland with Otto Graham and then into coaching.

Ray was head coach of Menlo College for several years. Mark Speckman, who became head coach of Willamette University for several years, wrote a book called, "Figure it Out."

"It was before my first game at Menlo that I realized I had really earned my spot on the defense. All during camp I had watched as Ray Solari, our head coach, had pushed everyone to the limit-physically and mentally...I had decided as long as I had gear on I was going to go as fast as I could and that was going to make it so Coach Solari never had to show me anything remotely physical. Still, after three weeks of grueling practices, Solari's perspective on the game didn't fully crystalize for me until he gathered us together in the locker room, minutes before kickoff.

'Booth get up here.'

Booth, our captain, stood up from among the kneeling and approached the Coach Solari. The two faced each other there was a glimmer in both of their eyes and a febrile intensity to their jaws. It reminded me of two heavyweights waiting for the referee to finish his pre-fight instructions.

'Give me a shot sir!'

Coach Solari wound up and slapped Booth across his face.

My jaw dropped. What the hell was going on? I looked around at the crowd.

Some of my fellow freshman were doing the same. The sophomores reacted with an expectant murmur.

'Give me a shot!'

I watched as Booth hauled off and slapped coach Solari.

'Yeah!'

'Yeah!'

'Let's go!'

I felt myself swept up in the moment and charging into the bouncing mass, allowing my body to be carried out in a sea of emotional momentum even as my mind swam ina sea of uncertainty. I still remember the one thought that was going through my mind as I prepared to take my first collegiate snap: What the hell just happened?"

Chapter 5

Cas talked about the season saying it was tremendous, unfortunate, and hard luck. Len Casanova called 1958 his most disappointing season of the 16 seasons he coached at Oregon.

According to Dave Grosz: "When McKay left, he called me into his office. He said he was leaving to go to USC to be an assistant coach and talked to me two or three times telling me to hang in there. He said I was going to do just fine. He was very positive, but believed he couldn't turn the job down."

1959

Overall Record, 8-2

Date	HomeTeam	Score	Visit Team	Location
Sat. 09/19/59	Stanford	28-27 (W)	Oregon	Stanford, CA
Sat. 09/26/59	Oregon	21-6 (W)	Utah	Eugene, OR
Sat. 10/3/59	Oregon	14-6 (W)	Wash. St.	Eugene, OR
Sat. 10/9/59	San Jose	35-12 (W)	Oregon	San Jose, CA
Sat. 10/17/59	Oregon	20-3 (W)	Air Force	Portland, OR
Sat. 10/24/59	Oregon	12-13 (L)	Washington	Portland, OR
Sat. 10/31/59	Idaho	45-7 (W)	Oregon	Moscow, ID
Sat. 11/7/59	Oregon	20-18 (W)	California	Portland, OR
Sat. 11/14/59	Wash. St.	7-6 (W)	Oregon	Pullman, WA
Sat. 11/21/59	Oregon	7-15 (L)	Oregon St.	Eugene, OR

This would be the best season Cas ever had, with an 8-2 record. The team, however, would not be invited to a bowl game. There were only seven bowl games.

The transition of Dave Grosz, going from rookie to an experienced quarterback, was dramatic. Several talented players were still on the team. 1959 was a wonderful year for Oregon.

It is mind boggling that Oregon did not go to a bowl game. Cleveland Jones, from San Diego, would become a favorite target of Grosz, and make unbelievable catches. A great receiver with a capable throwing quarterback helped the offense ignite. Johnny McKay would be gone. Max Coley would replace him. Max came from San Jose State where he last coached the offense. It was a familiar area for Cas to choose from, being very close to Santa Clara. No doubt a trusted friend recommended him.

They called Him Cas

Dave Grosz said, "We had a pipeline from San Diego. We had some great guys: Dave Grayson, Cleveland Jones and Alvin Kimbrough. All those guys played. I don't know if they all went to the same high school, but they were really good people and really good."

Grosz & Pussyfoot Jones

Win Over Stanford, 28-27

What a difference a year made. By now Dave Grosz was a confident veteran field general for Oregon, throwing two touchdown passes. The new exciting runner and receiver, Cleveland Jones, was a great addition. Grosz had Needham, Altenhofen, Jones, and Grayson. Riley Matson caught a tackle eligible on a two-point conversion attempt to win the game. Grosz was effective and did the punting also. Dave Grayson took the ball away from the Stanford receiver on a clutch play on the goal line to assure Oregon's win. The Ducks were showing signs of good things to come.

Dave Grayson came from Lincoln High in San Diego California; another San Diego guy. He came to the University of Oregon in the

Chapter 5

1958-1960 academic year and played offense and defensive halfback. He was a superb receiver and an excellent defensive back.

He was vital and often made key plays in games, especially in 1959 and 1960. He had a very successful pro career from 1961-1970. He was All Pro four years as a defensive back.

His last team was the Oakland Raiders, where he played from 1966-1970. He was a respected defensive back, widely considered one of the best in the NFL when he was playing. His son, David Lee Grayson, also played football at Fresno State and then five years in the pros.

Win Over Utah, 21-26

Dave Powell, senior fullback from Eugene, scored on short gainers in each of the first three quarters. Oregon's Webfoots defeated Utah, 21-6, at sunny Hayward field on a Saturday in front of an opening day crowd of 15,200. This was the Webfoots' second game of the season as the underdog Redskins from Salt Lake were playing their inaugural game for 1959. Dave Grosz, with a three-touchdown performance, was impressive on offense as the Ducks moved the ball. Defensively, Oregon was vulnerable, especially in the closing minutes of play. Ken Vierra, the slim senior quarterback from Hayward, California, completed seven passes for 80 yards. But time ran out for coach Ray Nagel's Utes on the Oregon 13-yard line.

Bob Peterson, outstanding senior center for Oregon, blocked a quick kick in the opening seven minutes of play. This gave Oregon possession on the two-yard line from where Dave Powell scored. The second Oregon touchdown came mostly as a result of a triple play. It was a pitch out from Grosz to Willie West and Ducks' half back pass to Dave Grayson; a 32-yard play that gave Oregon first down on the Utah 37. The third quarter score came after Eldon Kimbrough recovered the loose ball on the Oregon 20-yard line.

Win Over WSU, 28-27

A sun-drenched crowd of 16,800 sat in the warmth of a 77-degree Indian summer day. On this day, pass interceptions led to Oregon touchdowns. Alden Kimbrough picked off one of Melon's passes on the Oregon 31-yard line in the opening period, and Powell scored 19 plays later.

Dave Grayson was pass defense against Stanford in the opener. He provided Oregon with a 28-27 victory and came up with one even more spectacular in the fourth quarter Saturday.

Win Over San Jose State, 35-12

Much of the Oregon scoring came as a result of San Jose mistakes, plus aggressiveness and alertness on the part of Oregon. Dave Powell recovered a San Jose state fumble while West eventually scored from five yards out.

Cleveland Jones scored from the seven-yard line. Mickey Bruce, one of the Nuggets who became a fullback only Monday night, intercepted a Washington pass and returned it 30 yards to the San Jose 36-yard line. Willie West scored from the seven. Greg Altenhofan blocked a Lee punt. Alden Kimbrough picked up the ball and ran like a demon for 40 yards. He looked like one of Oregon's halfbacks cutting in and around and streaking to the goal line once he saw daylight.

Since the game was played on Friday night in San Jose, the team went to the Cal versus Notre Dame game the next day across the Bay in Berkeley. Of course, Cas and Jack Roche were familiar with the Bay area. What a weekend of football that must have been for each player. They flew home on Saturday night. Arrangements like that were not easy to coordinate, and today, are unheard of, if not illegal. It must have been great fun to do. Oh yes, Oregon did play Cal later on in the season and did win that game.

Win Over Air Force, 20-3

Nationally ranked Air Force Academy, sporting a record of 14 straight games without defeat, fell before a harder charging Oregon line and a superb pass defense that scored a 20-3 decision over the flying Falcons. The reversal rocked gridirons in every section of the land.

Coach Casanova's new spread formation which made the Air Force Falcon linebackers vulnerable to down-the-middle drives and off-tackle slants, scored twice in the second. This, after a first-quarter Falcon field goal. Then they salted the game away with a touchdown in the final frame. It was a team triumph and 34 Webfoots had a part in it. Oregon posted their fifth straight triumph of the season.

Cleveland, "Pussyfoot," Jones, 5'3, 148-pound junior transfer from San Diego, stunned the sundrenched spectators and the Air Force defense with a 40-yard plus pass play from quarterback Dave Grosz, a 31-yard pass and a 19-yard run.

Loss to Washington, 12-13

Dave Grosz threw a 12-yard pass to Greg Altenhofen in the second quarter. Bob Schloredt, one-eyed junior quarterback from Gresham, looked like he had 20/20 vision in both eyes as he recovered an Oregon fumble. Then he intercepted a late fourth-quarter end zone pass to keep Oregon from a comeback triumph.

Win Over California, 20-18

With five minutes to go, Grosz scored with a pass to Jones. Cleveland, "Pussyfoot," Jones' courageous comeback netted the seventh win of the season against one loss. 20,000 fans sitting through 55 degree temperatures had just about given up until Jones took Dave Grosz's 35-yard fourth down score pass. Grosz passed to Willie West for an 18-yard score. Then another Oregon touchdown came after West intercepted a Wayne Crows pass. Alden Kimbrough intercepted another Crow pass. Roger Daniels kicked both extra points.

The loss of All-Coast center, Bob Peterson, who suffered an ankle injury on the third play of the second quarter, was costly. A Grosz to Jones 50-yard pass secured the win.

Win Over WSU, 7-6

Casanova's comeback kids delivered a 7-6 victory over WSU in cold weather on frozen turf. Cleveland Jones made the key block. Gail Cogdill sprung Willie West into six-point territory. West caught

They called Him Cas

the Grosz pass on the 15-yard line and he was knocked out of bounds on the 4-yard line. Only 11 seconds remained when West, in basketball shoes, almost tiptoed into the coffin corner to make the catch. Grosz also wore tennis shoes.

Oregon acquired their basketball shoes in Spokane Friday night after learning the Ducklings were unable to move with football shoes Friday afternoon. Roger Daniel's 19th extra point placement of the season provided the victory. The sub senior quarterback was wearing a football shoe on his kicking foot and a sneaker on his left foot.

Powell, West, and Grosz did most of the gaining. Gail Cogdill later played many years as split end for the Detroit Lions and then the Atlanta Falcons. He was an outstanding receiver.

Loss to OSU, 7-15

The week of the Civil War game was known as Hell Week back then. Flood lights were on all night at Hayward Field to prevent the Beavers from tampering with it. This year if Oregon won, they could be invited to the Rose Bowl. A lot was riding on the game.

Oregon scored first. Grosz pitched the ball to Cleveland Jones who passed it to Willie West for a touchdown. OSU's Don Kasso came back and scored. Dainard Paulson made a run for a two-point conversion, but failed. In the fourth quarter, Dave Grayson attempted a halfback pass to Willie West, but was intercepted by Amos Marsh. Here were three players who went on to have successful pro careers.

Jim Stinnette scored a Beaver touchdown to win the game. Despite the loss to OSU, this would mark the third most wins in a season in Oregon football history.

Dink Templeton spoke at the annual football banquet. He competed in the Olympics as a high jumper and also played football and rugby at Stanford. He also went to law school at Stanford. He then became head track coach at Stanford for 19 years. He had many insights into athletics and higher education. He was very positive on Oregon and felt the University had a great future in college athletics and that college life was very attractive in the relatively small town of Eugene, Oregon.

Willie West and Tom Keel were co-winners of the Hoffman award. This was West's third and final varsity year at Oregon. He

Chapter 5

played in the Rose Bowl in the 1958 season, and now ended it sharing the Hoffman Award.

Willie went on to play nine years of pro ball, becoming an All-Star in 1963 and 1964. He taught school, worked for department stores and sporting goods stores as a buyer, and manager for several years throughout the country. He came back to Eugene where he has a real estate company managed by his son.

He also coached football at Marist High and coached for the University of Oregon under Rich Brooks.

"Cas was a great man. He is one of the few people that comes along every 25 years that make such a great impact on the people around him, and the program or his directives to the program that he is running. He was just a very impactful person. He was such a warm person. He was always concerned about your welfare. He would come and talk to you or call you into his office and you think you had done something wrong, wondering what he wanted. He just wanted to say hi. 'Willie, I see you every day on the football field', or this might even be in the off-season. He'd say, 'I haven't seen you around a while, I just wanted to talk to you.' And I was saying, 'What's wrong? What's the matter coach?' Then he would say, 'I just brought you in to talk to you and see how you're doing.' And he would sit there and talk to me not even about football or anything. He'd call you in there and he'd say, 'Hey, Willie, I just talked to your folks yesterday. We had a nice conversation. I let them know that you are doing okay. I just wanted you to know I'd made contact with them, and we had a nice conversation,' and then talked about this and that. It was nice.

Football was important to him, but it wasn't the most important thing. He was more concerned about the individual, how the individual was developing. He was about church and community. He was just an overall person. He was not just a typical athletic administrator." Willie West

John Wilcox, Bob Peterson, and Alden Kimbrough would play in the East-West Shrine Game. Bob Peterson and Ed Kaohelaulii would play in the Hula Bowl. The 1959 team had a better record than the 1957 Rose Bowl team, and the 1948 Cotton Bowl team.

Player Profile: Dave Powell, 1957 – 1959

Dave Powell was raised in Eugene and played at Eugene High School, later renamed South Eugene High. As a sophomore in 1957, he was on the second platoon notoriously known as the Ugly Ducklings. In 1958 and 1959 he was a very successful fullback for the University of Oregon.

Early in his career he ran the run and shoot offense and compiled a record of 67-26-1 at South Eugene High. He would later coach at Hillsboro High and take the place of Mouse Davis, father of the run and shoot, who went on to become head coach at Portland State.

Cas was active in the Fellowship of Christian Athletes. Each summer he would attend the summer camp held at Southern Oregon

Chapter 5

University in Ashland, Oregon. Dave Powell would do the same thing. He would have a "huddle group" at his campus and would help send several athletes to the camp each summer. He loved seeing different former athletes of his throughout Oregon and listening to some of them preach on Sunday, as some of them became pastors, others businessmen and leaders in their communities.

1960

Overall Record 7-3-1

Date	Home Team	Score	Visit Team	Location
Sat. 9/17/60	Oregon	33-6 (W)	Idaho	Eugene, OR
Sat. 9/24/60	Michigan	0-21 (L)	Oregon	Michigan
Sat. 10/1/60	Utah	20-17 (W)	Oregon	Utah
Sat. 10/8/60	Oregon	33-0 (W)	San Jose	Eugene, OR
Sat. 10/15/60	Oregon	21-12 (W)	Wash.	St. Eugene, OR
Sat. 10/22/60	California	20-0 (W)	Oregon	California
Sat. 10/29/60	Washington	6-7 (L)	Oregon	Seattle, WA
Sat. 11/5/60	Oregon	27-6 (W)	Stanford	Portland, OR
Sat. 11/12/60	Oregon	20-6 (W)	West Virginia	Portland, OR
Sat. 11/19/60	Oregon St	14-14 (T)	Oregon	Corvallis, OR
Sat. 12/17/60	Oregon	12-41 (L)	Penn State	Liberty Bowl

The 1960 season was affected when Dave Grosz broke his right arm working on a summer job for Peter Kiewit and Sons construction in late June. The question was whether he would be able to play by early fall. But have no fear, the infamous Dr. George Guldager said he would be ready for the first game.

Dave had been working for Peter Kiewit and Sons on a bridge construction job between Springfield and Eugene. He fell head first 35 feet. The first person they called was Cas. Not Dave's wife, nor his parents, but Cas. Incredibly, he performed well his senior year, in spite of the accident. He was not only lucky to play, but lucky to be alive. It was miraculous that Dave led the team to another winning season and an appearance in the Liberty Bowl; the second bowl game in two years.

"At school there was stability. The coaches have all been there for a long time and he'd been there a long time and that's probably part of my problem. When I went into coaching, I was at Cal Poly 14 years. Other than the University of Oregon, those guys have been there for 20-something years, but usually guys that are a few years, like Orson Wells. But it was a great family-type program and Cas was the head of it. You got to know his life and he was really special people.

We had a pipeline from San Diego. We had some great guys: Dave Grayson, Cleveland Jones, and Aldan Kimbrough. All those guys played—I don't know if they all went to the same high school—but they were really good people and really good players. So the recruiting field they had, they just did a good job and now he's got a few guys from the State of Washington, but it was a good staff and it was a good place to go.

I think that's probably a big part of it because I was really fortunate that I got to play all five years and he was the head guy. And I think his principles, and he affected so many people, guys that played under him, and they still speak highly of him, and considered him a great coach and a great person."   Dave Grosz

The 1960 season record was 7-3-1. Then came the Liberty Bowl.

"I can remember Johnny McKay, who was known for his love for cigars, would walk down to the field, and the large laurel hedge that surrounded the field. Johnny would be smoking a cigar, and he would delicately put it on a laurel branch leaf for practice. And he would pick that up at the end of practice, light it up, and keep smoking it. He was an environmentalist." Dick Arbuckle

Cas cared as much about the players and their off field life as much as he did about their playing on the field.

When he would recruit down in southern California, he would stop by and visit my mom. He didn't have to do that. It was just something he did.

The guys I played with were young and immature. Cas went the extra mile to keep them squared away and on the team. They turned out to be very, very successful adult men.

Cas would come in and say, "What's the score?" And all the players would echo, "nothing to nothing." Which is a great way to say that the half time score didn't mean a thing. We got to go back out and play the second half. We would have been really shocked and disappointed if he hadn't come in and asked us that question.

Chapter 5

When you look at the lack of facilities or their age, it is incredible to think Cas was a successful coach for 16 years and took his team to three bowl games. With modern equipment and training facilities, the Ducks would have probably gone to many more bowl games.

Win Over Idaho, 33-6

Oregon beat Idaho once again to start the 1959 season. Idaho had not had a winning season since 1938.

Loss to Michigan, 21-0

September 24, 1960: Oregon loses to Michigan, 21-0, at Ann Arbor. Michigan head coach, Bump Elliott, was Pete Elliott's brother. He was a coach at the University of Illinois and both played at Michigan.

The team played like they were drugged. This game became famous because Mickey Bruce was offered money to throw the game. He declined, and immediately told Cas about it. Mickey Bruce's association with the underworld became famous, and he was interrogated on the witness stand by the United States government. Ironically, Mickey became an attorney in San Diego, like his father.

"We were playing at Michigan. I don't think he travelled with us. He came later because his wife was ill. Then we had a team meeting because some gamblers had approached a couple of our players. So he got all the players together to make sure that the gamblers wouldn't hit on anymore of the players, because they were still in the proximity of the hotel. And we knew, of course, that Cas was really struggling with his wife's health and issues and so forth. He was there with us. We didn't play particularly well. We lost back there at Michigan. It was great to have him with us under all the circumstances. First of all, playing at Michigan, and the distractions. He brought us all together and he was very much a calming influence on the whole situation. We respected him for being there and being with us, in spite of the family difficulty." Dick Arbuckle

They called Him Cas

Win Over Utah, 22-17

This game ended with a double reverse with Dave Grayson and Cleveland Jones involved.

Win Over San Jose State, 33-0

On October 8, 1960, Oregon took on San Jose State. It was a convincing win at 33-0. Dave Grayson, Cleveland Jones, Mickey Bruce, and Roscoe Cook all had good games.

Jack Imitates Cas

"One day the players were together waiting for a meeting to start. They were sitting in chairs like a large classroom and Jack Roche started mimicking Cas on the proper hitting position. He was showing how to bend the knees, keep the head up and the butt out. He went on and on. Suddenly, there was a loud comment from Cas in the back of the room. Jack jumped to attention and said, "Yes sir!" and got the meeting going."   Dick Arbuckle

Win Over WSU, 21-12

It was Homecoming, October 15, 1960, and Oregon was playing WSU. 18,500 fans watched Oregon win, 21-12. Grosz's passes were off during the day. He hit Burnett for a touchdown. WSU was ranked first in the country in passing. Keith Lincoln, future San Diego Charger, and Hugh Campbell, future Canadian All Star, were wide receivers.

Chapter 5

Win Over Cal, 20-0

October 22, 1960

Dixie

Dixie Casanova passed away on October 17th. Cas did not coach that week because of family obligations. It was the second death of someone close to him relatively early in his lifetime. His younger brother, in 1928, now his wife of 30 years. Cas was still only 55 years old. It would be a great loss to him.

Cas buried Dixie on Friday and then flew down to Berkeley to be with the team. He would eventually meet and marry Margaret Pence Hathaway three years later.

He hadn't coached all week so he let Jack Roche continue to be the head coach in this situation. The Ducks won and Cas asked Jack if he had any aspirations of becoming a head coach someday. His reply was, "Are you kidding, I couldn't get a wink of sleep all night, I worried about the game so much."

Loss to Washington, 7-6

October 29, 1960

Win Over Stanford, 27-6

November 5, 1960: Oregon versus Stanford. Oregon wins, 27-6, in Portland. 18,727 fans watched the game. Stanford lost its eighth game in a row. Cleveland Jones drew praise from Stanford's coach, Jack Curtis, who said he had done it all year. Fullback Bruce Snyder suffered a knee injury. Grosz did a superb job of quarterbacking. Cleveland Jones gained 91 yards on passes. Bruce Snyder made the first score on a one-yard run. Jones also was kicking the extra points. Grosz had a 45-yard run.

They called Him Cas

Win Over West Virginia, 20-6

On November 12, 1960, Oregon played West Virginia in front of 11,000 people in Portland. The Ducks won, 20-6. Cleveland Jones had a 50-yard spectacular run in the fourth quarter. It was a close game until the last four minutes. Dave Grosz' seven-yard quarterback sack loss was a key play in the game. Grayson had an interception.

Tied With OSU, 14-14

On November 19th, 1960, Oregon tied OSU, 14-14, in Corvallis in front of 27,000 fans. Terry Baker was a sophomore. Groszto Kent Peterson passing was effective. This was the first year Tommy Prothro was head coach for Oregon State. He would call plays from the press box as he did all season. Cleveland, "Pussyfoot," Jones can be credited for the comeback tie with his catches and running.

Loss to Penn State (Liberty Bowl), 12-41

Oregon played Penn State at the Liberty Bowl on December 17th, 1960. Although Penn State defeated Oregon, 41-12, the Liberty Bowl was special. One reason was that the wives got to make the trip. Cas had a special meeting with them to educate them on the proper way to tip a waiter. There were six wives who went, and they ate separately from the players. They ordered food off the menu in the dining room and the waiters complained because they didn't get a tip. Cas explained what a proper tip would be, and let them know it was covered by the athletic department. Soft touches like that showed the love and care of Coach Casanova.

The weather was terrible. It had snowed the night before, and during the game. There were mounds of snow on the sidelines. Robbie was the defensive backs coach and in pregame warmups, Robbie supposedly slipped and got lost in a pile of snow for a while.

Cleveland, "Pussyfoot," Jones, biggest little man in college football, didn't have a chance to show the Philadelphia fans and pro scouts what he could do. He was kneed in the back on the first play from the line of scrimmage. Jones said he had never been hurt before. Mickey Bruce came in as substitute and performed well.

After the game, there was an awards dinner and dance for the players and their wives. They danced to Bobby Darin songs, among other festivities. The couples really enjoyed this part of the program.

Dave Grayson got the back of the game award and replaced Jones in the All-American game. Dave Urell got an invite to the East West Shrine game.

This time around, Norm Van Brocklin was playing for the Philadelphia Eagles. They won the NFL Championship and beat the Green Bay Packers. Norm was bestowed the title of NFL player of the year. Aschbacher and Wilcox were rookies on the team with another friend who would one day be well-known in football: John Madden. The head coach was Buck Shaw. Cas coached with him at Santa Clara several years before.

Player Profile: Riley Mattson, 1958-1960
6'4," 248 Pounds

Riley was born and raised in Portland, Oregon and went to Grant High School. He was All-PIL (Portland Interscholastic League) and played in the annual East-West Shrine Game. In 1961, he was drafted in the 11th round by the Washington Redskins. He did rally play for the Redskins from 1961 to 1964, and played tackle for the Chicago Bears in 1966.

They called Him Cas

Chapter 6
Oregon Football
(1961-1964)

Overall Record 4-6

Date	Home Team	Score	Visit Team	Location
Sat. 9/23/61	Oregon	51-0 (W)	Idaho	Eugene, Oregon
Sat. 9/30/61	Utah	6-14 (L)	Oregon	Utah
Sat. 10/7/61	Minnesota	7-14 (L)	Oregon	Minnesota
Sat. 10/14/61	Oregon	6-15 (L)	Arizona	Portland, OR
Sat. 10/21/61	Oregon	21-6 (W)	San Jose	Eugene, OR
Sat. 10/28/61	Oregon	7-6 (W)	Washington	Portland, OR
Sat. 11/4/61	Stanford	19-7 (W)	Oregon	Stanford, CA
Sat. 11/11/61	Washington St.	21-22 (L)	Oregon	Pullman, OR
Sat. 11/18/61	Ohio St.	12-22 (L)	Oregon	Ohio
Sat. 11/25/61	Oregon	2-6 (L)	Oregon St.	Eugene, OR

The 1961 season was the rookie season for Doug Post and Mel Renfro. Oregon lost Dave Grosz, Dave Grayson, Dave Powell, Cleveland Jones, Dave Urell, and Riley Matson. Matson went on to have a 6-year pro career with the Redskins and Bears. Oregon lost several starters, and several talented athletes replaced the graduating seniors. It proved difficult to replace the veteran quarterback, the key player in the creative triple-threat quarterback offense led by offensive coordinator Max Coley. The rookie year for a quarterback is always the toughest. The transition in the quarterback position had also occurred in 1955 with Shaw leaving and in 1958, with Crabtree graduating.

The recruiting class which Mel Renfro was in was quite large with 26 players. They were now sophomores. There was excitement that Renfro would play on the varsity squad for Oregon. He ran and showed his exciting talent, and Oregon beat Washington. Mike Gaechter also had an outstanding season and almost singlehandedly won the Washington game.

They called Him Cas

On July 2, 1961, The Eugene Register Guard wrote that sophomore quarterback, Bob Berry, would take a 6-month tour of duty in the army in the summer and return in the fall of 1962. He would not play again until the 1962 season.

Another player, flanker Paul Burleson, almost didn't make it back also. He came to Oregon from a junior college in Southern California. After spring ball, Paul didn't think he would make the team, so he packed his bags and headed to the train station. While he was sitting there, Cas showed up out of nowhere. He came and sat next to Paul. They talked with each other for over an hour. Cas spoke about the importance of staying with something, commitment, and facing challenges that seem bigger than you can handle. Paul said, "He caused me to realize that a part of my character was being developed in this decision. Cas saved me that night, and it had a profound effect on the entirety of my life." Paul would go on and have a very successful career at Oregon as we will see.

Cas had his normal "Campus Camp" for kids in the summer, before football started. About 77 kids showed up for the 1961 camp. All the coaches helped out on the week-long endeavor. Every kid got more than his money's worth, and several still have fond memories today. One such camper, Ross Crook, remembers Cas coming into the dining room on Sunday morning and saying, "Ok who wants to go

Chapter 6

to church with me?" He jumped up with several others and said, "I do." He wasn't a Catholic but thought it was a great idea to be able to ride with some other kids in Cas's car. They all had fun.

There was a pre-season Canadian football game held in Seattle where the BC Lions, led by Washington's Bob Schloredt, played the Saskatchewan Rough Riders, led by Oregon's Dave Grosz. Dave would play a few years in Canada and then coach college ball for 20 years.

The highlight of 1961 was that Oregon beat Washington, 7-6. It would not have been possible without the effort, talent and determination of Mike Gaechter. This was the only season he lettered. In track, he ran a 9.4 second 100-yard dash, but he was also physical. Even more renown, the Oregon track team won the National Championship that spring in Eugene, Oregon for the first time. Mike Gaechter, Mel Renfro, and Jerry Tarr, all football players, were key. Oregon track sprinter Harry Jerome was also on the team. They won the 440-yard relay race and broke the world record while doing it. Renfro and Tarr added points in other events. Jerry Tarr, an end, won both the 120-yard high hurdles and also ran his leg on the 440-yard relay team. Renfro came in second in the 120 low hurdles, and placed 3rd in the broad jump as well as running his leg on the 440-yard relay team. These men were great all-around athletes.

Doug Post, sophomore, became new quarterback for the Ducks.

Win Over Idaho, 51-0

Oregon defeated Idaho, 51-0, on a Saturday afternoon. An enthusiastic crowd of 17,800 watched the 1961 season opener. The old gridiron rivalry, playing itself out for the 47th time, had never attracted this many fans. The offense shattered the previous record of 502 yards with a 544-yard performance. Most of the Oregon fans were especially anxious to see Mel Renfro in his first varsity college football game. The halfback touted as the greatest prospective back in Oregon history did not disappoint. The 190-pound Portland sophomore played briefly, but well. Renfro romped 80 yards for the opening touchdown with less than five minutes into the game. He only carried the ball three other times for an additional 42 yards. He caught one pass for 20 yards. Other scores were passed from Ron

They called Him Cas

Veres to Lou Bayne, a 32-yard run by Mike Gaechter, a 14-yard pass from Doug Post to Bayne, and a 37-yard pass from Veres to Paul Burleson.

Loss to Utah, 6-14

September 30, 1961: Oregon at Utah. Oregon lost, 6-14.

Mel Renfro was injured in the game, chipping a bone in his foot. It was unknown when or if he would play again. Fullback, Duane Cargill, sustained a badly bruised right hand. Mickey Bruce, defensive back, was considered for offense with Renfro out of action. Battered, but well, Mike Gaechter had two black eyes from the game.

Loss to Minnesota, 7-14

Oregon scored 36 seconds before intermission. Sophomore, Doug Post, went all the way at quarterback and played almost flawlessly. He passed to half back, Mike Gaechter, 6 yards into the end zone. Sandy Stevens, starting senior quarterback for Minnesota, spoiled everything. He scored a go-ahead touchdown in the last three minutes of the third quarter and his pitchout to Jim Cairns made it 8 to 7. Jim Cairns scored again with eight minutes remaining in the ball game.

Minnesota had been favored before the game by two touchdowns. Coach Len Casanova said after the game, "Youth and inexperience hurt us at key times in the second half. I never saw anybody play a better game than Mickey Ording. And that includes both offense and defense. He was simply great out there today. I thought Steve Barnett, Rich Dixon and Ron Snidow played very well, and Doug Post was outstanding at quarterback. He was calling automatics on most of the key first half plays and doing it very effectively, and his passing was good too." The Ducks lost Dick Schwab with a broken collarbone midway through the second half.

The team stayed overnight and watched the Minnesota Vikings play the Dallas Cowboys. Then they flew home Sunday night with the arrival scheduled for around 10 PM.

This was a bit unusual and incredibly exciting. To go all the way back to Minneapolis, play a game one day, and then watch the

Chapter 6

fledgling Minnesota Vikings play the Dallas Cowboys the next. Norm Van Brocklin was coaching the Vikings, Jack Morris, was defensive back, and George Shaw, starting quarterback. That is until Fran Tarkington got in a pre-season game.

Before the NFL game started, the University of Oregon team was introduced on the PA system. It was quite a highlight for the team. Oregon was really moving up in the world.

Loss to Arizona, 6-15

It was an Indian summer evening and the temperature was 70 degrees. The only problem was Oregon lost; crippled at the halfback position with Mel Renfro injured. Casanova said after the game, "It was our own mistakes that killed us." Three Oregon offensive backs were injured. Casanova singled out fullback, Duane Cargill, for his hard-hitting running in the second half which helped keep the Webfoots in the ball game. He said, "I didn't think we played a bad game at all defensively, but the young boys still have a lot to learn. They are learning with each game however."

Win Over San Jose State, 21-6

On October 21st, 1961, Oregon played San Jose State, winning 21-6. The game was in Eugene in front of a crowd of 10,200. Defensive giant, Ron Snidow, grabbed a fumble recovery for a 16-yard touchdown pass interception. Kent Peterson made effective receptions and Larry Hill, penetrating runs. Steve Barnett did well as offensive and defensive tackle, and Lou Bayne played well at fullback. Buck Corey did the PAT's. Post threw a touchdown to Mickey Bruce. Rich Dixon, Bill Swain, sophomore, Lou Bayne, and Monty Fitchett all looked hopeful.

They called Him Cas

Win Over Washington, 7-6

This was only the second win Cas would have over the Washington Huskies. Mike Gaechter stopped quarterback Ohler short of the goal line and had a phenomenal defensive game. Great plays included diagnosis of quarterback Pete Ohler's bootleg run around Oregon's right end on a fourth and six for a hopeful touchdown. Gaechter's tackle just short of the goal line on the one-yard line was probably the most important defensive play of the game and the year. No one else was in reach of the Husky. Ron Snidow did well too as did Mickey Ording, Lou Bayne, Bill Swain, Rich Dixon, Greg Wilner, Kent Peterson, and Steve Barnett.

Ron Veres gave his best quarterbacking performance of the season while under pressure. Doug Post was benched with an injury. Ron passed to Kent Peterson for clutch passes and Jim Josephson started and had a good ball game.

Win Over Stanford, 19-7

Renfro played well in this game and there were many memorable plays. Gaechter had a 65-yard interception, Lou Bayne ran four yards for a touchdown. Mel Renfro ran a 94-yard kickoff return. And Steve Barnett and Mickey Ording did well at the tackle positions. Jack Curtis said Renfro was the best back he had seen this year. Mel Renfro scored twice, while limping. Mike Gaechter and Lou Bayne both added to the offense as did Larry Hill. Paul Burleson grabbed a 39-yard touchdown throw. Casanova said, "Thank God for Renfro."

Loss to WSU, 21-22

A WSU rally nipped Oregon, 22-21. Washington State Cougars, after building up an early 10-point lead, came from behind in the final six minutes on a Saturday to upset the Ducks. A shivering crowd of 10,500 homecoming fans braved 30-degree temperatures to watch the Cougars make use of the battering ram running game. The game was windy, cold, hard fought, and another close one to add to the long list of close Cougar -Duck contests.

Oregon closed the gap to 14-16 early in the third quarter. They went ahead, 20-16, early in the fourth quarter on touchdowns by Jim Josephson and Mel Renfro, respectively. Quarterback, Ron Veres, did a double reverse to Mel Renfro that was very effective.

Loss to Ohio State, 12-22

It was sunny and cold on Saturday when Casanova's Webfoot warriors, apparently awed by a gigantic crowd of 82,073, settled down after trailing 15-0, and came back with touchdowns in the second and fourth quarters. Mel Renfro had a 24-yard run and played with a sore ankle. Ohio State had the all-American fullback, Bob Ferguson, and head coach Woody Hayes. It was the 26th straight game with a crowd of 82,000 or more.

Oregon controlled the ball more than Ohio State in the final three quarters, running 63 plays from scrimmage versus 41 for the Buckeyes. The Ohio State line outweighed the Webfoots by an average of 10 pounds to the man. Mickey Ording was involved in most of the tackles as was the case in Oregon's loss to Minnesota. The 4-5 record to date was incredible in view of the number of injuries suffered.

Loss to OSU, 2-6

Rain and snow greeted Homecoming week. The Homecoming bonfire almost wouldn't start because the wood was so wet the night before. Game-time temperature was 35 degrees. Once again, Prothro was up in the press box calling the plays. At a critical time in the game, the player going with the play from the sideline got tangled up in the cord and almost dragged the assistant coach with the earphones on to the field.

The OSU goal-line stand stopped the Ducks on the 1-yard line. The field was covered by several inches of snow Friday morning but was in exceptionally good shape for the game and the footing was reasonably good. Three Duck passes were intercepted and two fumbles lost. Five turnovers almost always equal a loss.

They called Him Cas

Homecoming 1961

Oregon 2, Oregon State 6

Chapter 6

Homecoming featured a speech at halftime by Arthur Fleming, new President of the University of Oregon. He said the game was an example of the great American spirit at its best. A student from the stands cracked a comment, "Yes, and pass the cranberries, please." This got several laughs from the crowd. Arthur Fleming had been the Secretary of Health, Education and Welfare in the Eisenhower administration. In 1959, he cautioned people about buying cranberries for Thanksgiving because of a possible danger of aminotriazole, a weed killer shown to cause thyroid cancer in rats. Fleming could never live down his association with cranberries.

Once again, awards night came for the football team at the Eugene Hotel. Kent Peterson won the Hoffman trophy. He was speechless and had no idea he would get the award. He went up and said, "I don't know what to say, but I want to thank my coach, Jack Roche." Jack was a quiet guy who hardly ever raised his voice. He was a genius on defense, and was a superb receiver's coach. He would take a player further than he ever dreamed of going. He did it by building them up and making them believe in themselves.

Peterson was invited to play in the East-West Shrine Game. Mike Gaechter received the Clark Award, the most improved athlete award. Gaechter did not letter his first two varsity years, but did his senior year. He would go on to excel in track and pro football.

Buck Shaw was the guest speaker. In introducing him, Len Cassanova credited Buck Shaw, his former boss at Santa Clara, with being the originator of football's multiple defenses and said, "I have patterned my coaching after Buck Shaw."

Shaw was a former Notre Dame tackle who opened holes for George Gip under Knute Rockne. Shaw, who retired from coaching after leading the Philadelphia Eagles in the National Football League title the year before, shared from 29 years of experience in coaching football. He said his 1959 Philadelphia team had three Oregon players on the squad: Darrel Aschbacher, who had great possibilities as a pro player, but returned to Oregon to fly for Delta Airlines, John Wilcox, a defensive end, and Norm Van Brocklin, who he believed was the finest pro quarterback he had ever seen, along with Y.A. Tittle of the 49ers, Shaw said.

Also on that 1959 Eagles team was John Madden. He was Darrel Aschbacher's roommate. Madden was injured for a greater

They called Him Cas

part of the season. He would be in the therapy room and somehow be drawn to the film room next door where he often saw Norm Van Brocklin. He would go in and watch the films with Norm and they would talk about what Norm was seeing on the film. John said he picked up insights from those times that greatly aided him later on in his coaching career. He said Norm was a master at finding out tendencies of a team by watching film. He was drafted out of California Polytechnic by the Philadelphia Eagles, but wrecked his knee in training camp. He said, "I had to come in early for treatments and there was always one other guy there, Norm Van Brocklin, watching game films. I'd sit in the back waiting for him to tell me to get the hell out." Instead, the great quarterback talked strategy with the banged-up rookie, and Madden decided to be a coach.

Shaw said 80% of success in coaching was material, but that some coaches got more out of their players like Rockne and Casanova. As a parting message, Shaw said, "There is plenty of room at the top, but there is never room there to sit down."

John Robinson, Oregon freshman football coach, did an outstanding job as master of ceremonies for the banquet that attracted a near-capacity crowd.

Mike Gaechter

Mike was brought up in Lancaster, California and went to Antelope Valley High School. He attended the University of Oregon and played football from 1960-1961. He also competed in track in the long jump, the 100-yard dash, the 220-yard dash, and low and high hurdles. He was also a member of the relay team. In 1961, he earned his re-acceptance to the University of Oregon. That year, during a track meet at the University of Washington, he recorded his fastest time of 9.4 seconds in the hundred-yard dash. In 1962, Mike, along with teammates Mel Renfro, Jerry Tarr, and Harry Jerome, ran the third leg on the University of Oregon's world-record-setting team in the 4 x 1, 10-yard relay. Mike did not become a starter in football until his senior year, as the right halfback, and he was voted the team's most improved player.

The Dallas Cowboys signed Mike in 1962 as an undrafted free agent and he became the starting left cornerback as a rookie. Mike had a 100- yard interception for a touchdown. Mike's interception return was a franchise record for 48 years. Mike had a track background and he was a punishing hitter as well. He was switched to strong safety in 1963 where he played in the same defensive backfield on Dallas with Mel Renfro, both from Oregon. He played with the Dallas Cowboys from 1962-1970 as strong safety.

Ron Stratten
1961-63

Stratten grew up in San Francisco and attended Lowell High School, where he played linebacker and fullback. He became the first black student body president at Lowell High, an almost all-white student body. He played college football for the University of Oregon from 1961 to 1963, and was the Ducks' defensive line coach from 1968 to 1971. Ron was the first black assistant coach hired in the Pac-8. He became head coach of the Portland State Vikings college football team from 1972 to 1974. He compiled an overall record of 9 and 24 in three seasons. Stratten was one of the first black head football coaches at a university with a majority white enrollment. And the first black head coach at NCAA Division II college level. Ron then worked several years as a Vice President of the NCAA and lived in Kansas City, Missouri. He currently operates his own company, StrataSoles, out of San Diego, California.

Ron Statten recalled, "Cas was a classy guy. He was an educator, he believed in our education. He told my parents that. They believed it, and I believed that. I had Jerry Frei as a position coach between those two guys. They molded me into the person I am today. Cas was a beacon. So many of the things he said as I became a coach are meaningful. From, 'Every meal is not a banquet,' to, 'Every trip is not an excursion,' to, 'The human body can endure a lot of punishment.'

As Jerry Frei would always tell me, 'Don't worry about Cas coming around. You're playing for me. And you're not going to see the field unless you perform on the practice field for me, not for Cas."

They called Him Cas

1962

Overall Record 6-3-1

Date	Home Team	Score	Visit Team	Location
Sat. 9/22/62	Texas	13-25 (L)	Oregon	Texas
Sat. 9/29/62	Oregon	35-8 (W)	Utah	Eugene, OR
Sat. 10/6/62	Oregon	14-0 (W)	San Jose	Eugene, OR
Sat. 10/13/62	Rice	31-12 (W)	Oregon	Rice
Sat. 10/20/62	Air Force	35-20 (W)	Oregon	Colorado
Sat. 10/27/62	Washington	21-21 (T)	Oregon	Seattle, WA
Sat. 11/3/62	Oregon	28-14 (W)	Stanford	Portland, OR
Sat. 11/10/62	Oregon	28-10 (W)	Washington St.	
Sat. 11/17/62	Ohio St.	7-26 (L)	Oregon	Ohio
Sat. 11/24/62	Oregon St.	17-20 (L)	Oregon	Corvallis, OR

    Bob Berry was back in 1962. Sadly, Doug Post injured his knee the first day of the season and was out the entire year. As a result, Berry took over the quarterback helm for the next three years. They were all winning seasons, with great talent on the line coached by Jerry Frei, and a superb backfield led by Mel Renfro and nicknamed, "The Firehouse Four." On top of that, a top notch wide receiver and tight end group led by Rich Schwab, Paul Burleson, and Dick Imwalle, the tight end. The passing game went up a notch and Larry Hill, Lou Bayne, and Mel Renfro came out of the backfield. They were all excellent receivers and were so powerful; not to say anything about their excellent running ability. Timing, precision, and good throws by Berry made the passing game very effective. This receiving corps would be together for the next two seasons.

    The talented group of players that came in with Renfro were now juniors, except Berry who was now a sophomore ready to play his first year of varsity at Oregon.

Chapter 6

Bob Berry: A Unique Man

"Bob Berry, he was unbelievable. I mean everybody on offense was scared of him. I don't care how big you are. He had a stern look about him and if he told you to do something you did it. I mean, even linemen were scared of him. They didn't want anything to do with him when he got mad. How did he do when he went to Minnesota? He never changed. He was always the same. Everybody knew he was a leader, nobody talked back to him, and nobody said anything to him. He knew the big guys. They knew they'd get their ass kicked if they backed off a little bit. He was tough. He didn't stop. He was like a Van Brocklin, basically." Bill Swain

When you go into the huddle it was never kind of a casual gathering. It was a high-intensity gathering every time. He would holler, 'Get your ass in here,' or something like that. Whenever it was. You knew when you got into that huddle, he might just call your play. It might be a simple process of calling F89 or something like that. But when he wanted emphasis, he would do that. And he'd reach over and grab a helmet, a facemask, and he'd twist it. He would turn it so your neck would kink a little bit. He was making a point. He did that.

He did it with me on F 88 and an F89, which was a bootleg quarterback option with a single pass route. And it was specifically to the split end. That was me. And so I remember those. After he would call the play he would say, 'Run the hard route. Run the hard route.' He said, 'You've been setting this guy up. Get ready. I'm getting the ball to you.' And so that was it. I mean there was no way I was going to let him down. It was like are you kidding me? It's like letting Cas down. Run the hard route! I'd run as hard as I knew how to run. Bob would say, 'Schwab, this F89 is critical!' Oh, man. My butt would pucker up, and I was thinking, wow, this is critical. He just told me it was. And then when I would catch the pass. Then after the completion I would look over at him and he'd give you that smile, you know that kind of a sneaky smile like he had just gotten away with something. Boy, was that a powerful deal.

It's kind of like Prefontaine. No one taught Prefontaine to be Prefontaine. All the parts and pieces were there, and no one taught Berry how to be that way. In fact, people worked hard to try to take some of the rough edges off of Bob, and I think they did the same

They called Him Cas

thing with Prefontaine. You don't take those edges off. That comes in the package. And part of Bob's success was his toughness and quick to ignite kind of technique. That's what he was all about.

If he had an injury and could move his legs or stand on one leg, he was going to play. There was never a question about his toughness in that regard, ever, ever. He played a couple games where he limped to the huddle, and limped out of the huddle, and limped when he ran. That's what he was going to do.

If you want to describe the Firehouse Four or the Sun Bowl team, Berry was the motor. However you want to describe it, he was the guy that made everything happen. So there's no question about that. And certainly Mel Renfro was the best athlete. No question about his athletic skills and what they were like."Rich Schwab

"Yeah, it's a team sport. I can't throw if you can't block. If we all work together, we'll win. I learned that from my father. He's the one that taught me the leadership stuff. I knew football when I got there. I knew routes and where they're supposed to be and what's going on. It was probably an advantage having a dad for a coach. Some of the intricacies of the whole game.

I was going to games since I was a little kid, sure. My dad, he's the first guy who taught me to throw and get the ball up over my ear. A million times I heard that, 'Get that ball up. Throw it over.' No side arm preps. He taught me the mechanics and then just by osmosis I think the football stuff came easy."Bob Berry

Chapter 6

Loss to Texas, 13-25

The first game of the season was played in Austin, Texas, state capitol and home of the University of Texas. The team flew in with 35 players. They get off the bus and checked into the hotel. They went down to the dinning room for dinner where the staff refused to serve black players like Mel Renfro, H.D. Murphy, Ron Stratten, Lu Bain, and others.

Cas got on the phone with Darrell Royal and said, 'If Afro-Americans cannot eat at the hotel, we are flying back to Oregon tonight and there will be no game tomorrow." Suddenly, the hotel served everyone.

"We went down to play Texas in 1962. The South was still segregated at that time. The blacks couldn't get into restaurants. They wouldn't serve the football teams because we had blacks on our team. Cas said we'll fly back tonight. This was typical Cas, even in those days when you wouldn't think that a coach would step up and say, 'What can I do here?' he stepped up and didn't stand for it. When the conventional wisdom would have been to say, 'Okay, the Afro-American guys will go over here,' because that's what they did in the South. He wasn't going to allow that." Dave Tobey

On that trip to Texas they went outside and they thought they were still in Eugene, and that you could go anywhere. They walked into a place and the first guy talks to Milt Kanahe, who is a full-blooded Hawaiian, says, 'You can't come in here. You blacks can't come in here.' Milt says, 'I'm not a black.' They looked at him like he was crazy and said, 'Yeah, you are.' The guys came back and told me what they said. We were quite naïve to what was happening in the rest of the world. Ron Stratten

This was an Oregon football team that gave a splendid account of itself, and must be considered King of the Northwest until proven otherwise.

Casanova was pleased with our flip-flop defense. We made too many mistakes at crucial times. Cas said, "You can't make the defensive errors we made tonight. I thought Barry played well. Renfro did a terrific job, and Greg Wilner and Snidow both played outstanding games in the line. Our kids got a little tired out there. We couldn't rest our first unit as much as we wanted, and that didn't help

They called Him Cas

us any. Our kids gave it all they had. They came to play. Texas has good depth, no question about it." Darrell Royal who was forced to use his regulars in the fourth for only the third time in two seasons said, "I have mixed emotions about this one." Texas, the second ranked team in the nation, won 25-13. Larry Hill, Junior right halfback, galloped 38 yards for an Oregon touchdown in the opening four minutes of the game. At the start of the game, the temperature was 80 degrees and the 65,000 capacity stadium had an estimated crowd of 52,000 that Saturday night. At the end, coach Darrell Royal's Texas Longhorns were serenaded by the traditional, "The Eyes of Texas."

The mighty Texans were whipped soundly the first half and part of the third quarter by the rampaging Ducks, led by Mel Renfro and Bob Berry. Texas trailed 13-3 until they suddenly caught fire near the end of the third quarter. Cas said, "We made too many mistakes at crucial times. You don't make the defensive errors we made tonight and still win. I thought Berry played well. Renfro did a terrific job." This was a closer game than the score showed. Oregon was ahead going into the 4th quarter. Oregon came with 35 guys. Texas suited down 120. Berry remembered the cannon going off with every score as being very loud and Bevo, the Bull Mascot, just behind the visitor's bench, coming out and running around after a score. Bevo required four guys to control it. Later on, Oregon would also deal with injuries.

In 1970, USC played the University of Alabama in Alabama. USC was the first integrated football team to play in the State of Alabama. Undoubtedly, McKay had memories of playing in the Cotton Bowl in 1949. One of the conditions Oregon insisted upon accepting the Cotton Bowl bid was that three of its players who were black, Chet, "Cool Papa," Daniels, Woodley Lewis, and Win Wright, would be allowed to play in the game; the second team to do so in history. Keep in mind that the Cotton Bowl was to be played in the southern State of Texas where Jim Crow laws were enforced. Daniels, Lewis, and Wright would not be permitted to stay in the same hotel as the rest of the players and coaches. They would stay with a prominent black physician and his family. They were, however, allowed to dine with their teammates in a private dining room in the hotel. The three players were also the first black players permitted to attend a post-game awards ceremony held in a private club. This was

Chapter 6

the peak of success for Al Aiken and this was also the very best team that Oregon had ever assembled. The 1948 record is the best season record to that date, despite the 21-6 bowl loss to SMU.

No doubt McKay thought back on this game when Bear Bryant called and asked him to play with Alabama in Tuscaloosa, Alabama on September 12, 1970. At that time, Alabama football was all white and so was the SEC. By this time, McKay was known for having an integrated team with such famous running backs as Mike Garrett and O.J. Simpson who were also Heisman Trophy winners and on National Championship teams.

Darren Everson in his Wall Street Journal article is quoted as saying, "Mr. Cunningham was able to do more to integrate Alabama in 60 minutes than Martin Luther King Jr. did in 20 years." Supposedly, after the game Bear Bryant brought Sam Cunningham over to his locker room and introduced him to his players and said, "Now this is what a real athlete looks like."

No doubt Johnny McKay was pleased to win the game but, more importantly, to have everyone stay in the same hotel, eat in the same dining room together as a team, and to not make race an issue. He was happy to help make a difference in this regard.

USC had had an integrated team for years with such outstanding backs as Mike Garrett, O.J. Simpson, and in that year, 6' 3," 235-pound Sam the Bam Cunningham who gained 125 yards on 12 carries. Sam went on to play 10 years for the New England Patriots.

Win Over Utah, 35-8

The Webfoots gave the game football to Mel Renfro. Forty-three players took part in the victory including senior Captain, Steve Barnett, and Ron Snidow, and honorary game Captain, Greg Wilner. They picked Renfro, the junior half back as their big boy. A crowd of 18,800 watched the seventh straight winning home opener. Ray Nagel, Utah coach, said the Ducks were the best football team in the nation. Coach Casanova was pleased, but the mistakes took some of the joy out of the triumph. This despite the fact Oregon beat a team from the Western Athletic Conference by 27 points.

Renfro contributed most to the spectacular show. He went 38 yards for a touchdown the first time he handled the ball rushing. The next time he went 59 yards with a pitch out around his right and behind tight end Dick Imwalle's screen block. It was "Katie bar the door," but he stumbled on the Utah 14-yard line. Renfro tallied two other scores on a 7-yard slant in the second quarter and on a one-yard smash in the opening minutes of the third. Renfro retired after a total of 110 yards rushing in the first half. This made Renfro a sure thing for a school record. But he played only about 25 minutes, and Jack Morris had the record, 212 yards, against USC in 1957.

Forty-two Ducks saw action. Roche smiled when asked about third string center, Oliver McKinney. He was a demon on defense from his left linebacker spot, after he finally got into the game late in the second quarter. He said, "I knew he could play defense. We just gotta give him more work on offense. He's got good mobility, he is smart and you saw, he's a good tackler. Snidow, Ording, Barnett, all of them, we force them to pass." Cas said Jack Roche, designer of most Webfoot defenses, had diagnosed the Redskins so well that by halftime he said they wouldn't even call defense the next half unless they got down on the goal line and he wanted the goal-line defense.

Win Over San Jose State, 14-0

One word could aptly describe an Oregon football team that almost put 15,700 fans to sleep Saturday at Hayward field: Unimpressive. Oregon blanked San Jose state, 14-0, despite a performance that, at times, left the onlooker wondering whether the Ducks knew how to block or tackle. "I don't know if anybody played a good game," said Casanova, "and I'm irritated enough not to give anyone any credit."

A 50-yard touchdown pass play from halfback, Mel Renfro, to halfback, Larry Hill, put the Ducks on the scoreboard the second time they had the ball. A 79-yard drive in the second quarter culminated when Renfro went less than a yard and made it a two touchdown advantage.

Win Over Rice 31-12

A night game against Rice in Rice Stadium in Houston led to the first Oregon grid victory in Texas or against a Texas team in the

Chapter 6

history of the school. Mel Renfro was much better than the weather, at 78 degrees with 78% humidity, as he ran through and around a Rice defense.

Renfro, who was twice given a surprising ovation when he left the field, tallied the only opening touchdown in the first 11 minutes of the game. But that was just a minor incident. The run was for only one of the 141 yards he had rushing. He returned 65 yards on a pass interception, returned a kickoff of 25 yards, and caught two passes for 17 yards. Mel had a great game, saying it was one of the most fun college games he played, because he had 15 relatives watching him. His grandfather—who he smiled at as he came off the field—made the night even more enjoyable. Final score was 31-12.

Earlier in the season, Rice had tied LSU, 6-6, and lost to Penn State, 18-7. This was Rice's Homecoming celebration.

Rice Stadium had been a whites-only facility prior to the Ducks' visit, but university officials allowed Renfro's family to enter and sit in a special section of the stadium near the 35-yard line. According to a contemporary account in the Eugene (Oregon) Register-Guard, when Renfro left the game, he was given a loud and appreciative ovation by the Rice crowd. An Oregon sportswriter asked a Houston counterpart in the press box if an African-American had ever received such an ovation by a predominantly white crowd. The Texan enthusiastically replied, "We've never seen any player that good!" The morning after the game, a Houston paper headlined, "Renfro Runs Rice Ragged."

"What every one sees as the engagement of college, we didn't have that as black students. Every time we would break off, and everyone would go to their fraternity parties and do all that stuff, and have all that fun, we were by ourselves. We would have a party of our own, that's about it. The girls would come down from Portland. For the most part, the undergrad young ladies who were of Afro-American descent numbered two or three when I was going to college in Eugene. They were dating the seniors. We were freshmen, sophomores, and juniors. Very little there. You might meet someone in the dormitory who is white. That might be somebody you could go out with, but that was about it."Ron Stratten, 1961-63

They called Him Cas

Win Over Air Force, 35-20

Teams tallied eight times. Berry passed for 32 yards to Dick Imwalle in the end zone. There was a Berry to Renfro pass. Larry Hill ran a trap play. Renfro dove over right guard for two, and Berry scored. Defensive coach, Jack Roche, found the answer to the Air Force double wing attack and stopped the wide runs and cutbacks off the tackles by the time the second half started. Adjustments took the sweeps away from the Falcons offense, and then Oregon rolled for three straight touchdowns. Larry Hill had a nearly 50-yard sweep. Then Renfro, Bayne and Hill had a 35-yard double reverse that set up the final Oregon score. Mel Renfro, Larry Hill, and Jim Josephson rolled up 302 yards between them. Cas said, "Washington has a fine team. They are strong defensively and very hard-nosed. It should be a real battle."

Bob Berry had special praise for Mel Renfro's blocking on Larry Hill's 50-yard third-quarter touchdown romp: "Mel threw a fine block at the line of scrimmage, got up, ran down the field, and threw another block at the goal line."

Tie With Washington, 21-21

The Washington game was tough. It was more than a game. As Jack Roche said, "This is not a game it is a full scale war." Jack was a WWII vet and did not mince words. Two years before, Cas was walking down the long runway to the stadium from the locker room and was knocked down by Husky players on the way out to the field.

Chapter 6

You had to button your chin strap before a Husky game. Everyone who played the Huskies, especially in their own stadium, knew and experienced incidents of rough, dirty, illegal play, and had stories to that effect.

The Ducks came prepared for a tough fight on a sunny Saturday afternoon. However, hopelessly behind, 21-13, with less than three and a half minutes remaining, coach Casanova's comeback kids staged a brilliant aerial game. It brought them a touchdown and tying two-point conversion with only two minutes and four seconds remaining.

A crowd of 55,500 was electrified by Oregon's determination to take the fat out of the fire against a nationally-ranked Huskies team looking for their third Rose Bowl bid in four seasons. This great Oregon comeback came as the result of Larry Hill's touchdown run of 18 yards and a great two-point pass play from Bob Berry to Dick Imwalle.

With six seconds left, Oregon had the ball midfield. Berry threw one last pass 58 yards to Hill in the end zone. Larry was open but the crowd had streamed onto the field early. Hill was completely surrounded by the Husky student body and the ball was knocked down by the students. Cas commented, "You can't run a very good pattern with 1800 kids on the field." Such was the end of another close Husky game. There were complaints filed with the League office of the Pac-8, to no avail.

Win Over Stanford, 28-14

The bus ride up to Portland went well. Oregon beat Stanford soundly, 28-14. The offense was working and so was the defense.

"They came at us as though they were going to a picnic ," Stanford head coach Jack Curtice said. They took a battering in Portland only to face USC next week. Jack Curtice said, "Coach Len Casanova told me that Oregon has the best team this year that it has had in his 12 years here."

After this week's game, the Cotton Bowl announced it was eyeing 11 schools; one of them was Oregon. It is nice to be doing well and being so successful on the scoreboard you are wanted for a bowl game.

They called Him Cas

Win Over WSU, 28-10

Oregon had another good game in Portland at Multnomah Stadium. The offense was working and Mel Renfro was dazzling, and the Firehouse Four were alive and well. Oregon's offense both sputtered and exploded and the closest thing to a sustainable drive was on the second touchdown that went 67 yards in seven plays. The first touchdown came on a homerun pass play from Bob Berry to Mel Renfro for 76 yards. Renfro scored two touchdowns and Berry ran for another touchdown.

Forty-three net rushing yards were allowed by the defense; the third time in the season the Oregon defense held a team to less than 100 yards. Probably the most consistent performances by the Oregon line this season were from tackles, Ron Snidow and Steve Barnett. There's no question Snidow was every bit as good as Barnett, a second-team All American the last season and listed as a first-team candidate this season. Snidow was probably more agile and spectacular, but Barnett had done everything they asked of him.

There was a player who was particularly noticeable, especially in the past two games. That was Dave Wilcox, the 6'2," 215-pound transfer from Boise Junior College, who missed spring practice and was just now learning to know his way around.

John Wilcox told his little brother after the WSU game, "You knocked down a few people out there this afternoon." Dave answered, "Yeah, I guess so." John, a 6'4," 221-pound Oregon tackle who was a rookie starter with the Philadelphia Eagles, was now line coach at Milwaukee High School for Mouse Davis. The Wilcoxs came from Vail, Oregon. A few more Rimrock Savages were also in the Oregon dressing room Saturday after noonalong with ex-Oregon linemen, Joe Schaffeld, line coach at Roseburg, and Tom Keele, Head Coach at Oregon city. Renfro led the Webfootsin all-time scoring with 12 touchdowns and 72 points with two games remaining. He also led the Webfoots in aggregate yards in rushing, passing, receiving, punt returns, kickoff returns, passing and interception returns, with 1,236 yards. He was followed by Larry Hill, 718 yards, Greg Wilner, 251 yards, Jim Josephson, 243 yards, H.D. Murphree, 191yards, and Lou Bayne, 176 yards.

Chapter 6

Joe Schaffeld

Joe would eventually find his way back to Oregon and coach the defensive line for a record 25 years. He was known for inspiration, toughness, and glory for Oregon. His players loved him.

Loss to Ohio State, 7-26

Coach Woody Hayes brought a cloud of dust offense on this wet and drizzly Saturday; The first bowl bubble of the Oregon Webfoots. The final score was26- 7and the game was played before a crowd of 72,828. Oregon was still in the game at halftime after scoring a late second quarter touchdown that left a 14-7 halftime margin. Casanova said, "We couldn't get our hands on the ball and you can't expect to score if you don't have the ball. They were powerful. They really came at us." Hayes commented on Renfro's play, "Renfro is a strong running back." Ohio State went on to score 12 more points in the second half and won the game, 26-7.

Loss to Oregon State, 17-20

The Beavers trailed at halftime, 17-6. Oregon was unable to score any points the second half. Terry Baker, on fourth and three, threw a touchdown pass to Vern Burke in the end zone away from defender Larry Hill for the winning touchdown. OSU defeated Oregon, 20-17.

As far as large-shouldered, deliberate talking Tommy Prothro was concerned, there never was really much doubt that Oregon State would upend Oregon again Saturday. As he said after OSU's win Saturday, "This is definitely the best team we've had since I've been at Oregon State." In his eight years as coach at OSU he's lost to Oregon only twice."

The Ducks missed so many blocks at crucial times, said Casanova. The defensive work of Dave Wilcox, Oregon's Junior transfer, was an exception in the second half. He was a demon.

Terry Baker and Mel Renfro had been teammates at Jefferson High in Portland. They were state champs in football in

They called Him Cas

1958. Terry was at quarterback, Raye Renfro at fullback, Mickey Hergert at halfback, and Mel Renfro at halfback. Raye was 6' 3," 210 pounds, and would win the 100- yard dash in 9.7 at the state championship in track. Raye and Mel—more or less—won the state track title for Jefferson High. Terry Baker went on to win the Heisman Trophy, then play in the final four in basketball. He played back-up quarterback for the L.A. Rams and went to law school at night while with the Rams. He became a very successful lawyer in Portland for many years. Mickey Hergert would play at Lewis and Clark, coach baseball there, and go into the insurance business.

Casanova told his team before the game that Baker would be key to Oregon State's attack. Stop him and you stop the Beavers. Terry had not been stopped very often, and he wasn't stopped Saturday.

The Wednesday night banquet slated Jack Curtis, Head Coach of Stanford, as guest speaker. It was held at the Eugene Hotel at 6:30 PM. Dinner was three dollars. Jack Curtice was known to be a very humorous speaker in his day, and a well-sought-after speaker in the off season.

However, this was a very unusual situation. Stanford decided to fire Curtice just days before he spoke at the Oregon banquet. In his speech he said that football coaching is a very cruel profession. Curtice went on to say that there are four things that cause people to lose their job: Carelessness, laziness, dishonesty, and not getting along with co-workers. He compared those issues to playing on a football team and felt that being on a football team helped nurture the opposite effect. This was a conclusion he had arrived at during his 32 years of coaching.

Cas summed up the season by saying, "It was successful but disappointing."

Ron Snidow won the Hoffman award, and Larry Hill won the Clark award or most improved player.

Bill Swain, 1960-1962
6'2," 230 pounds

He played for the Los Angeles Rams in 1963, Minnesota Vikings in 1964, New York Giants from 1965-1967, and the Detroit Lions from 1968-1969.

"I was being recruited by Oregon State, Washington State, the University of Washington, Stanford, and Oregon. Len Casanova came to my house, personally, to see my mother. My mother was a widow at that time; my father had passed away years before. And being that my mother, she had a lot to say on where I was going to go. So Cas found out that my mother was a Catholic. And Cas looked at her and said I will promise you that your son will go to church every Sunday. I will have him in mass every Sunday of the year, and that's what happened. He made damn sure that I went to church every Sunday. Mother said you can go to Oregon.

Cas was a great guy and I really enjoyed being around him, playing for him. I went to Oregon because my mother said, 'That's where you're going.'

I was always considered a hard hitter. One time I hit a guy so hard in a game, somewhat of a cheap shot, Casanova took me out of the game, put me on the bench, and told me never to hit a guy like that again. He said 'You're hitting them way too hard.'"

They called Him Cas

Mickey Ording, 1960-1962
6'0," 225 pounds

Mickey Ording played at St. Mary's High School in Berkeley, California. He was an outstanding player and was recruited to several colleges. He decided on Oregon mostly because of the personal recruitment of Len Casanova. Mickey played on the freshman team in 1959. He played several minutes in 1960 and started from 1961-1963. He was named All Coast in 1963.

Upon graduation, Mickey was drafted by the Canadian Football League. He had a tryout with the Saskatchewan Roughriders. It did not work out. He went on to become a football coach at Santa Clara High School and for the next 30 years he was a high school football coach. The passion of his life was rugby. He played for several years and was on the USA team which competed all around the world. He was known as Mr. Rugby in America and his picture was on the front page of Sports Illustrated.

Ron Snidow, 1960-1962
6'3," 250 pounds

Ron attended San Rafael High School in California, where he played football and basketball, and went to the state championship in discus. He went to the University of Oregon and was a standout for three years as an offensive and defensive tackle. In 1960, he played in the Liberty Bowl against Penn State. He was known as the gentle giant in high school. He was named All Coast in 1962, played in the East-West Shrine Game in 1962, and played in the Hula Bowl in 1963.

Ron was drafted in the third round by the Washington Redskins in 1963; 35th pick overall. He played five years as a defensive lineman and was traded to the Cleveland Browns in 1968. He played there until he retired in 1972. He was first-team All-Pro with the Browns in 1969. After retiring from the NFL, Snidow worked as a commercial real estate broker in Irvine, California until he retired in 2008. Snidow was diagnosed with Lou Gehrig's disease, and died a year later on May 17, 2009.

Chapter 6

Bob Berry, 1962-1964
5'11,'" 185

Bob was born in San Jose California. His father was a high school football coach in the San Jose area. His younger brother played at San Jose State. He was also a quarterback. His younger sister went to the University of Oregon and now resides in Bend. Bob was a three-year letter winner under coach Len Casanova. Berry teamed with future Pro football Hall of Famers Mel Renfro and Dave Wilcox. Berry led the Ducks to three consecutive winning seasons and the 1963 Sun Bowl, at which Oregon beat Southern Methodist, 21-14.

Berry guided Oregon to three consecutive winning seasons; The first time the school was over the .500 mark three years in a row in 30 seasons.

Berry was named first team All American after senior year and Hoffman Award his senior year. He played in the East-West Shrine Game and the Hula Bowl. In 1985, Berry received the University's Distinguished Alumnus Award. He was a University of Oregon Hall of Fame inductee in 1992.

Berry signed with the Minnesota Vikings in 1965. He played for the Vikings three seasons, 1965-1967, the Atlanta Falcons from 1968-1972, the Minnesota Vikings again for four seasons, from 1973-76, and he was the backup for Fran Tarkenton. He retired from football in 1977.

Berry was selected to the Pro bowl in 1969 and played in Super Bowls VIII, IX, and X as a member of the Minnesota Vikings.

"The only thing my dad ever said to me about where I might go is that he just wanted me to do him one favor, and that was to go visit Cas at the University of Oregon. It became the biggest favor he ever did for me.

I loved the Northwest. I first visited on a spring day when it was beautiful. I think it was Mothers' Day weekend. The sun was shining. I fell in love with it. I loved the area. I loved the people I met. Of course, Cas was a legend. I look back my whole football career, from high school on up to college, and then 12 years in the pros, and he

They called Him Cas

stands out as the one guiding light. This guy was great. He cared about the individual.

Cas was a football coach, but he was a teacher and a mentor and a father figure to so many guys including myself, that it's kind of hard to explain. You have to have played there for him to understand what I'm talking about.

He led by example, sure. He was devout Catholic, Yet he never flaunted his religion. He promised the mothers of the guys who were of the Catholic religion that he would make sure that they would go to mass and they'd observe all the religious properties. If you weren't Catholic, there was no burden on you. Like I said, he never flaunted it. Guys appreciated that. He was just him. He was just so natural.

One time Cas and I spoke at a banquet in Pendleton. I thought I might go out after dinner, but Cas booked us in a single room. So we're sharing a room. I stayed with Caswe went upstairs to the room. Cas, he's just the greatest guy. It's hard to explain. I just went to bed and read for a while.

I heard Cas rustling around, I roll over to see if he is okay. The next thing I know he's saying his prayers. He's on his knees at his bedside.

Anyway, I just adored him. What a guy. He was just a true believer. You gotta appreciate people like that. I'd follow that guy anywhere. To me, having known my father, he was like my second father. What else can you say.

He was always in his teaching mode. It was more than criticism. It was a learning time for his players. If you screwed up or made a mistake or did the wrong thing, he was always trying to improve these kids as human beings."

Chapter 6

1963

Overall Record, 8-3

Date	Home Team	Score	Visit Team	Location
Sat. 9/21/63	Oregon	7-17 (L)	Penn State	Portland, OR
Sat. 9/28/63	Stanford	36-7 (W)	Oregon	Stanford, CA
Sat. 10/5/63	West Virginia	35-0 (W)	Oregon	Morgantown, WV
Sat. 10/12/63	Oregon	41-21 (W)	Idaho	Eugene, OR
Sat. 10/19/63	Arizona	28-12 (W)	Oregon	Tucson, AZ
Sat. 10/26/63	Oregon	19-26 (L)	Washington	Portland, OR
Sat. 11/2/63	Oregon	7-13 (L)	San Jose	Eugene, OR
Sat. 11/9/63	Washington St.	21-7 (W)	Oregon	Pullman, WA
Sat. 11/16/63	Oregon	28-22 (W)	Indiana	Portland, OR
Sat. 11/30/63	Oregon	31-14 (W)	Oregon St.	Eugene, OR
Tue. 12/31/63	Oregon	21-14 (W)	Southern Methodist University	

155

They called Him Cas

On August 17, 1963, Len Casanova married Margaret Pence Hathaway. This got the season off to a great start and the team had a great year. The talented team performed to an 8-3 record. With a little more luck they would have been National Champions.

Margaret Casanova
Marriage: August 17, 1963

"Well, I met Cas at my sister's. I had a sister that lived here in Eugene and I was very close to her. A friend and I drove up one night to go to a basketball game, and Cas had parked in her driveway. So he was there after the game, waiting to get his car out. And that's when I met him.

Our first date was in Grants Pass. Cas was at a football banquet at the high school. He thought that it would be over at 10:00 PM, which was fine. Well, 10:00 came; 11:00 came. My sister said, 'I'm going to bed,' so here I was sitting up for him. I didn't really know him at all. I guess it was after 11:00 when he did show up.

So we sat and visited a little bit and he said, 'Is there any place we could go and dance?' and I said 'Go and dance? Well, there might be one hotel down here that does have music.' So anyway, we drove down to this hotel. We went in and they did have music, and we danced. He loved to dance. We both loved to dance.

And we just hit if off right there. He was a good dancer and he said that I was a good dancer. So we danced and had a lot of fun. I don't know what time we finally left. I let him off at the motel and I went on home. And that was just the way he did things. He just thought about nothing else but the here and now. We were dancing and having fun and he was oblivious to time, or where he was. He was just having fun dancing.

We used to dance every time we'd go up to Portland. We'd go to the Hilton and there was this orchestra and this man in there was in the orchestra always. When he saw us coming, he played Oregon for us. And then he played all of our favorite songs. He knew them all. So we had a lot of good dancing times up at the Hilton in Portland. We loved to dance. Margaret Casanova

Chapter 6

Oregon went 8-3 in 1963. They went to their third bowl game in five years. They lost to Penn State the first game in a tough battle, then barely lost to Washington, and then San Jose State. Because of injuries, neither Berry nor Renfro could play in the San Jose State game. At this point, Oregon was just an injury away from vying for being one of the best teams in the country, and receiving an invitation to a major bowl game.

Loss to Penn State, 7-17

The Ducks' leading ground gainer was Larry Hill, with 91 yards. Third- string tackle Pat Matson threw to Liske for an eight-yard loss as he tried to pass. Passes were thrown to Rich Schwab and Mel Renfro. Renfro was held to 44 net yards rushing, and caught four passes for 12 yards. Barry completed six passes on 12 attempts. This came as a surprise to Penn State's coach, Rip Engles, who said happily after the game, "I just didn't think we'd win the game, really. I was afraid we'd be too slow. We were scared to death of that."

Cas said, "We just couldn't handle the guy on Renfro's side. We could handle the guy on Hill's side." Lou Bayne didn't carry the ball at all until only two minutes and 44 seconds remained in the game. He was used as a blocker because the Lion defenders played him rather than quarterback, Bob Berry, on the quarterback fullback option plays.

Pete Liske completed 11 of 12 passes for Penn State, the other one was dropped. Casanova said, "I think we made a lot of mistakes defensively. We were a little slow getting to where we wanted to get, but Oliver McKinney played a hell of a game."

Win Over Stanford, 36-7

Bob Berry threw for two touchdowns and ran for a third score as the Webfoots massacred Stanford's Indians, 36-7, Saturday afternoon.

Some 31,000 paying fans in Stanford's cavernous 90,000 seat stadium expected fireworks from Oregon's Firehouse Four backfield. They watched the junior quarterback, Berry, pileup 216 yards through the air as he guided the Ducks to their seventh consecutive victory

They called Him Cas

over the red-clad Stanford. Doug Post, second string quarterback, passed and ran for two more touchdowns. Together, Berry and Post amassed 270 yards through the air while Duck runners contributed 230 yards for a grand total of 513 yards.

Win Over West Virginia, 35-0

The whole world was different in West Virginia. It was a segregated community. Something these west coast boys had never seen. The fans were rabid. On the way to the game, the team bus was run into by a passenger car and delayed the team from getting to the stadium.

Game film showed obvious unnecessary roughness which caused costly injuries to Oregon's guards. Casanova said, "I personally didn't think it was a very well-officiated game. I think the first offensive unit was in the second half about five minutes." He liked the way the second and third teams made goal-line stands. He added, "The big thing I liked about it was we got experience for a lot of kids. Lou Bayne ran better this game than he ever has. Mel was used on the final extra point kick to see if he'd be a replacement should Buck Corey get hurt. Renfro has been practicing place kicking. I really didn't believe after viewing the Navy films that West Virginia was that slow, however they really were," Cas said. And he liked the way everyone used their heads when West Virginia got rough, saying, "We let them get penalized."

Win Over Idaho, 41-21

Casanova used Mel Renfro, All-American half back, as a quarterback for a series of plays in the third quarter to the cheers of "Give them hell, Mel." Renfro, who had been a quarterback at Jefferson high in Portland, worked at that position last week. Mel said, "I really like it." Coach Dee Andros was probably the only coach in the nation who shifted into instead of out of an "I" formation.

Renfro said to Berry after the game, "You keep fooling around like that, and you're going to make All American.""Heck," said Berry, "you were running down there and I just threw it to you."

There was the "Firehouse Four" and the second unit was called "The Hook and Ladder." You didn't have to worry when you had Mel out in front of you. All you had to do was watch his hips. He would give you a good block every time, said Lou Bayne. Mel, who the professional scouts were describing as the best running back in college football, since he was a sophomore, was held by the Vandals defense to 35 yards rushing. Bayne was not nearly as frustrated by his inability to score as was Rich Schwab. He had never scored a touchdown in his life in high school or college until Saturday.

He made it look easy when he finally did get a step behind Idaho's Bill Scott, and then gathering in a 39 yard pass from Berry, ran it across the goal line with Oregon's third touchdown of the game. Schwab grinned later, "I knew it would happen sometime." Berry was nine for 11. "You can't ask for a better percentage than that, can you," said Casanova.

A pre-game discipline that Dennis Maloney followed: While still in his street clothes, he would he would make sure that Rich Schwab would see him drop two quarters underneath the goal posts so Schwab would think about picking them up after a touchdown. He never picked up any of the quarters, but he did go on and score several more touchdowns.

Win Over Arizona, 28-12

Oregon's line coach, Jerry Frei, said that Saturday morning, "I hope that Renfro has a big day." Sure enough, breaking loose with his best offensive performance of the season, the Webfoots' fine multipurpose back ran for 113 yards, caught three passes for 24 more, and scored his fifth touchdown in as many games. Oregon ruined Arizona, 28-12, in a football game which wasn't nearly as close as a score showed.

Berry, the nation's third-ranked collegiate player in total offense before the game, completed 13 of 18 passes for 190 yards. He called his plays with such poise that he guided the teams first unit to a touchdown every time he got the ball, except when it ran out of time at the two-yard line just before halftime. Coach Casanova called Berry's play calling "tremendous," saying, "he picked them apart." Rich Schwab got his second touchdown in as many weeks when he

They called Him Cas

took a 19-yard pass from Berry on the three-yard line and dragged the Arizona defender over the goal line. Bayne scored the first time after getting the ball after halftime, when Dick Imwalle, Pat Mattson, and Ron Jones conveniently shoved the right side of Arizona's line out of the way.

Loss to Washington, 19-26

This was a very close, hard-fought game. Renfro was knocked cold and unable to play after returning a kickoff 17 yards and being hit by Junior Coffey in the third quarter with 7:12 left. Mel received cracked ribs from the tackle by Coffey. It kept Mel out of action indefinitely. Milt Kanahe was also injured witha broken fibula in his leg and was in a cast. Hopes were that the 250pounder would be able to play in the Hula Bowl; a contest in which the native Hawaiian had been invited to participate. Bob Berry hurt his right knee and had stretched ligaments. Cas was just about to replace Berry with Renfro when Renfro also got hurt. Cas said Berry going out there on one leg for three quarters showed great courage and what kind a kid he was. Renfro, aching from his shoulder to his hip, spent Sunday morning submerged in the whirlpool bath. He thought he would be ready for Saturday's game at Hayward field.

The question was whether Berry and Renfro would be ready for the next game. Would the next quarterback be Lou Bayne and would Dennis Keller be at left half? Larry Hill, at his usual right half spot, and either of the two reserve fullbacks, Bill Youngmayr and Tim Casey, would be in action.

Loss to San Jose State, 13-7

As bad as Cas felt about losing 13-7 to San Jose State Spartans, the veteran Webfoot coach had to laugh. That is finding something funny about having nearly your entire first unit hospitalized. Actually, neither Cas nor Spartan coach, Bob Titchenal, could say much, but Casanova gave sophomore quarterback, Jack Sovereign, a good shot at running the varsity. He engineered an 86-yarddrive with Lou Bayne collecting the touchdown, but Sovereign's passing was limited.

Chapter 6

There was mixed emotion. Bob Berry Sr. was there to see his two sons in action, but his daughter, Nancy, was probably more disturbed by her dad's 14-0 loss Friday night to heavily favored Lincoln High than he was. Mrs. Mavis Berry admitted she was still shaking with emotion a half hour after the game. "I'm proud of both my boys," she said, and was pleased when Oregon's Bob Berry congratulated San Jose's quarterback, Ken Berry, his younger brother. They had their pictures taken with mom. One of the San Jose papers tried to make a feud about the boys playing against each other, but this certainly was not true.

Bob took over as quarterback on two occasions in the final 10 minutes. He was a pathetic figure. With his right knee swollen and injured in the Washington game the previous week, he couldn't maneuver well enough to make his usual passing motion. Cas said, "He has been our leader all season, regardless if he's healthy or injured, I had to try him." Mel Renfro, All-American candidate, was out of action with a cracked rib. The Greg Johnson tackle was out, as was Larry Hill. The starting right halfback sustained a dislocated shoulder in the opening 10 minutes of the game.

Win Over WSU, 21-7

There were several defensive standouts in the game: Dick Imwalle, intercepted two passes, and Lou Bayne intercepted a pass. Linebackers Oliver McKinney and Dave Tobey did a good job. Both played almost the whole game. Jones, Wilcox, Tobey, Dean and Pat Matson played nearly three quarters of the game going both ways.

The Webfoots, led by Berry, struck with lightning suddenness. Jim Sutherland said, "If Berry had not played well, that might have been the difference. I've got to hand it to the boy, he's got guts and determination. We knew he was hurt and you could tell it, but he still was the key man for them. The Oregon line was just better than ours today, especially Dave Wilcox. We couldn't block him all day. Offensively, we gave them lots of things to worry about, but it just comes down to the fact that they played well, and we gave them too much help. You can't overcome as many errors as we made out there today."

They called Him Cas

Quarterback, Bob Berry, was the savior. Although his right knee was tightly wrapped in tape, and he had been expected to play little, if any, he threw two scoring passes and played almost the entire game on offense for the Webfoots.

Cas said, "We felt we had to start him, the kids have so much confidence in him, that's the thing. I was scared to death, just scared to death," Casanova said.

Win Over Indiana, 29-21

Renfro gave an All-American performance, gaining 81 yards rushing. This included a four-yard touchdown featuring an amazing acrobatic jumping dive for a full first two-point conversion. He caught five passes for 75 yards, returned two kickoffs for 54 yards, and one punt for 25. He was in on several timely defensive maneuvers. Besides Berry's touchdown pass to Murphy and Hill, Berry also hit Dick Imwalle for a six pointer. Those three brought 14 touchdown passes in the season.

Ron Jones shot through the Hoosier line as Indiana tried to punt from their own end zone. Ron didn't block the ball, but his fast charge so shook up the punter that the punt went out of bounds on Indiana's 21-yard line. Berry then passed to Imwalle for the touchdown. Renfro, wearing chest pads underneath his jersey to protect the rib he cracked in the Washington game, said afterwards, "It was my last game in Portland and I had to go out a winner with the fans." He had played at Multnomah Stadium even as far back as Jefferson high school for a total of 7 years. He wanted to go out a winner. He owed it to the fans.

Renfro wasn't even skeptical about Oregon's chances of succeeding. "In the final comeback drive I knew we could do it, we had a minute to go and a new series of downs to score." In that drive, Renfro made a spectacular catch of a Berry pass which had been deflected by a Hoosier defender. It was good for 30 yards. In the huddle Berry said, "If we each do our assignment on each play, we will win the game."

Hill, on a fourth quarter spot appearance, caught a pass from Berry, and shrugged off a couple of would be Hoosier tacklers on a

Chapter 6

37-yard pass to the end zone for a go-ahead duck touchdown. H.D. Murphy scored a two-point attempt; a pass from Berry.

The delighted Hill yelled to team physician, George Guldager, after the game: "I told you I was ready." Hill credited Rich Schwab for a good comeback block on the touchdown run.

Head coach, Phil Dickens, admitted that it was a great pass by Berry and a great catch by H.D. Murphy:"I thought we had it, but they got the ball and marched right down the field and scored a touchdown. Our line generally put a good rush on Berry, but he's a good scrapper."

Win Over OSU, 31-14
The Civil War was all Oregon

If you notice, this game was played 14 days after the Indiana game. It was scheduled to be played November 23rd, a week earlier, but this was the week in history that President Kennedy was assassinated. At that time many events were delayed a week. As a result, the players stayed over in Eugene during the Thanksgiving holiday and continued to practice and prepare for the Oregon State game in earnest.

Renfro was injured with a cut wrist which would bench him for the rest of the year, including post-season games. Dennis Keller took his spot and the Ducks did tremendously. Berry made it all but unanimous as to why the Webfoots whipped the Beavers, 31 to 14, for their first win over OSU in five dreadful frustrating years."We were up for them. We were ready for them," Berry said happily. "We just blew them right out of there, we out-toughed them."

The Webfoots did out-tough Oregon State. At the end of three quarters they had the Beavers down 31-0.

Oregon's defensive coach, Jack Roche, explained that we tried three different kinds of Rushes that presented three different problems. John Robinson, Oregon's defensive backfield coach, yelled after the game, "How about that Murphy! He made a living playing against that guy."

Bob Berry, the 5' 11,"190-pound junior from San Jose, made the difference. His quarterbacking was superb, overshadowing the likes

They called Him Cas

of Rose Bowl quarterback Jack Crabtree, Liberty Bowl quarterback, Dave Grosz of more recent vintage. Grosz said after the game, and Crabtree agreed, "He's the best on the Pacific Coast. I have to give him the nod over the ex-pro George Shaw too, and equal to Norm Van Brocklin, who led the team to the Pacific Coast Conference Championship and Cotton Bowl bid."

Coach Len Casanova feared the loss of All-American halfback, Mel Renfro, would cause a psychological letdown. That was a calculated risk, but Berry, as the leader, overcame the loss of Renfro and provided instead an inspirational All-American effort.

Renfro had contributed a great deal to Oregon football for the past three seasons, but Oregon over the years didn't have anyone who could generate the necessary offense Berry had on one or two legs.

The rush put on Queen by the Webfoots' Dave Wilcox, Dave Toby, and Pat Matson, eventually caused coach Tommy Prothro to replace his regular with Marv Krause. He moved around better, but had never attempted a pass all season. The rush by Oregon's, defensive linemen had put on immense pressure and, as a consequence, four of Queen's passes were intercepted.

Not since 1948, and never in Casanova's reign as coach, had Oregon finished off the season with three straight wins. In the end, it had to be the Webfoots' attitude and desire that won the game. Cas brought them to a peak in the dressing room just before the game:

"I tried to get a little eloquent," he said. "and boy they responded." What did he tell them? "That's the locker room secret," he smiled.

Berry passed for 249 yards. The record for a single game is 272 yards. He had beat George Shaw's 239 yards set in 1952.

There was a wealthy Duck supporter who had a nice, large cabin on the McKenzie River. For a number of years, during the off season in the early summer, he would invite both Oregon and Oregon State's coaching staffs for a weekend of fishing, good food, and being courteous and respectful to each other; even though there was the Civil War each year.

Chapter 6

Prothro had a new assistant on his staff by the name of Jerry Long; a guy that was hard not to like. He grew up in Portland, played at Franklin as a lineman, then OSU. He went into high school coaching for five years. He then coached at Willamette for 6 years, and was finally invited to coach at his alma mater, OSU, by Prothro.

So he was attending this fishing outing on the McKenzie for the first time, and as a rookie coach. He couldn't do anything wrong. Cas spotted him taking a leak near his car outside the cabin. So next week Cas was in his office and typed a letter with a carbon copy back. It was addressed to the President of OSU, and went on about how the fishing weekend was good for coaching and friendship and goodwill. Then he asked, "Why would one of the OSU coaches urinate on my car?" He took the carbon copy and mailed it to Jerry Long as a joke. Nothing went to the President. Anyway, Jerry must have been shocked when he read it, and feared the President calling him on this. Just another great prank by Cas.

The annual football banquet at the Eugene Hotel was held Thursday night. The Hoffman Award went to Mel Renfro. He drove up to the event in a new car; part of his signing bonus with the Cowboys. Gil Brandt, head of scouting for the Cowboys, flew in and signed Mel. Gil Brandt was very conscious of speed, height, and strength. He was aware that Mike Gaechter and Mel Renfro were on the same 440 relay team together in track last season; a team that

They called Him Cas

broke a world record. Mel and Mike played together for years in the same defensive backfield for the Cowboys. They both became All Pro and Mel became an NFL Hall of Famer along with Dave Wilcox.

Dave Wilcox

Wilcox was drafted in the 3rd round by the 49ers. At the football banquet, John Robinson, again, was the master of ceremonies and was quite humorous. He had a book of famous quotations that he pretended to read from: "Beating Oregon State is better than sex, food, or any other damn thing."

Chapter 6

Then he went on to tell about his own great career as a player, which ended when Oregon played Ohio State in the 1958 Rose Bowl. Just like most other games during his three years as a Webfoot, Robinson didn't get to play.

Mel Renfro won the Hoffman Trophy. Dave Wilcox won the Clark Award for most improved player and Lou Bayne got the Tape Can Award. Doctor Slocum, who operated on Mel Renfro's wrist in mid-November, announced that Mel would not be available for any post-game activity.

Lowell Dean

Cas knew that Lowell was married when he came to campus, and he helped them find a job for his wife. Lowell was forever thankful for that.

"I got married before my sophomore year. Cas went down and got my wife a job at one of the businesses in town. He did all these little things that I don't think a lot of people knew about. Townspeople just loved him and Cas would say, 'You know you need to get this young lady here a job,' and they did it. He didn't interfere with his coaches. He let them coach. It was a lot of the off-the-field stuff that I remember and respect him for and honor him for. He never forgot anybody. He would make a point of bringing up stuff; something that had an association with you. He was one of a kind.

Karen, my wife, was pregnant and she worked for Clear Fir in Springfield, as a secretary. They weren't going to let her go to the Sun Bowl Game. We didn't have that many wives, there were probably four or five guys that were married: Burleson, myself, Ron Berg. He went and talked to those people about letting Karen go to the game. Who would envision a major college head coach doing that and just doing a common thing? But that's the kind of character he had. We all thought so much about Cas that it really meant a lot coming from him. To think that he cared about domestic things, little things that other people wouldn't even think about, but he did. I think because he had such a great heart."

They called Him Cas

Win Over SMU, 21-14
Sun Bowl

A 23-yard touchdown pass to Dick Imwalle, a 20-yard end zone pass to Paul Burleson, and several other throws from Berry, were dropped as Oregon receivers developed a tough case of "butterfingersitis." SMU head coach, Hayden Fry, said, "He's not the runner that Staubach is(in reference to Navy's Heisman Trophy-winning quarterback, Roger Staubach), and he's not as accurate as Larry Zeno, (number-one college passer in the nation), but he's a heck of a combination of both. He's definitely one of the outstanding passers in the country."

The Sun Bowl triumph accomplished two important things: Oregon avenged a 21-13 loss to SMU in the 1949 Cotton Bowl in Dallas, Texas. It was also Oregon's first bowl victory since the 14-0 Rose Bowl triumph over Pennsylvania in the 1917 Pasadena classic.

It might be interesting to note: H.D. Murphy, who played so well both on defense and offense during the first half of the El Paso game Tuesday, was one of the two Oregon football candidates for the Bill Hayward Memorial Athlete of the Year award the following month. The other candidate was quarterback, Bob Berry. Murphy's credentials not only included his superb performances in football, but also his play as defensive baseball outfielder and solid hitter.

About the game, Cas added, "It was the longest damn second half I've ever seen." Berry had seen better days. His passing record was only 11 completions and 26 attempts. But he threw two scoring passes; one a 23-yarder to Dick Imwalle, the other a 20-yarder to Paul Burleson.

Singled out for praise was Dave Wilcox who signed a professional contract with the San Francisco 49ers immediately after the game. Also, second unit tackle Ron Berg, who saved the Ducks a couple times. Casanova also had good words for senior halfback, H.D. Murphy, who almost single-handedly wiped out SMU's passing offense in the first half with a pair of timely interceptions. Hurry Doc's most spectacular interception came the second time SMU had the ball in the first quarter and set up Oregon's first touchdown. H.D. leaped high to pick off a long pass from SMU quarterback, Mac

Chapter 6

White, on Oregon's 30-yard line, and raced 49 yards upfield to SMU's 21. Four plays later, Dennis Keller started on an outside sweep, then back and scooted 10 yards for the score.

"I cover the middle, you know, and I go where the ball goes," smiled Murphy, who was a pretty fair country outfielder on the Oregon baseball team during the spring. Murphy said, "As the game went on, SMU wouldn't throw up the middle anymore. Maybe I should have come up."

The Oregon team celebrated New Year's Eve by flying high on the chartered airline which brought the official party back to Eugene at 12:30 AM. Casanova and four players, Larry Hill, Dick Imwalle, Dave Wilcox, and Milt Kanehee, left El Paso separately for a flight to Honolulu, Hawaii for next Saturday's Hula Bowl Game.

The number one star of the game was Berry, whose bullet passes drew rave notices, and whose play won him the games Most Valuable Player Trophy on a vote by the sports writers and sportscasters.

Paul said that Cas was a psychologist and a hard-boiled taskmaster. He said, "Even today, his words ring in my ears, 'Don't let up! Keep scrambling, secondary effort wins the game.' Dick Imwalle said, "Cas was the guy that got us all there, the players and the coaches, because of who he was and how he was. He was a receiver from San Jose who joined his high school buddy, quarterback Bob Berry, in heading to Eugene in 1960. They formed a passing tandem that would pay great dividends for the Ducks in the coming years."

Paul Burleson remembers fondly his performance in the 1963 Sun Bowl: "The greatest moment of that game for me came with less than a minute to play in the half. Berry had called a play in the huddle that flanked me to the left side. I only glanced at the defense as I came up to the line and was looking down to make sure I was lined up onside and was leaning towards the center to hear if there was an audible. Sure enough, Bob changed the play to 'Blue 82' which was my call for a center post. I look up, and low and behold, to my surprise, there was only one man guarding me as their safety had shifted over to the right, leaving the post pattern wide open. 'Good call Bob!' I thought. I ran a Z post, caught the ball thumbs out over

They called Him Cas

my head in the end zone, which ended up being the game-winning touchdown."

Burleson continued, "The fact that this was Casanova's only bowl win made this touchdown catch my way of saying, 'Thanks, Cas, for talking me out of leaving back at the train depot in the spring of '61.'"

Lowell Dean remembers Paul Burleson

"I remember Paul Burleson. We always went back at night and had those meetings in our dressing room downstairs. It was before the time the coaches came in. We were all there, and Paul Burleson got up and started acting like Cas. And he did a fantastic job. And here came Cas in the door behind him and, of course, Burleson wasn't aware of him. He just kept going, and everyone was trying to make hand signals, but he was still going. Cas never got upset, and didn't give him a bad time or anything. Cas had a sense of humor."

Cas was smiling and saying to himself, "Paul, you have really come a long way from that visit we had in the train station that time a few years ago." That's what he was smiling about.

Chapter 6

Imwalle went on work for U of O Development Fund for three years, then Pomona College Development Fund for six years, then the President and CEO of the Development Fund for the University of Arizona for 28 years. He then came out of retirement to run the Hospital Foundation for the Carondelet Hospitals for three years.

When Dick Imwalle was being recruited by Cas, he came into Dick's house in San Jose filled with both hands of a miniature model of Autzen Stadium. So as Dick played his last game in the Sun Bowl, he was awarded Spring Athlete of the Year, and inducted into the U of O Friars Club (Senior Men's Honorary Society) along with Mel Renfro. He still had to wait four more years to see his first game in Autzen Stadium.

The Sun Bowl put the Ducks over the top to be able to build Autzen Stadium. We saved money and were a very austere program at that time. I was the business manager for the department and had a briefcase with a $250,000 check in it that enabled us to proceed to build Autzen Stadium.

So with the $250,000, we had the two and a quarter million dollars that it cost us to build the stadium. We had to have the money

171

They called Him Cas

up front. There was no borrowing from the state at that time. You could not go in debt with the state of Oregon back then. And so we got the money. And that's what the bid was on the stadium: Two and a quarter million dollars. It built 42,000 seats. I think the most Cas made annually was $21,000. Norv Ritchey

1964, 7-2-1

No Renfro, no Hill, No Bayne, just Berry: The Firehouse One.

The 1963 Oregon Ducks had one of the best back fields in the history of the school, if not the very best. It was called, "The Firehouse Four." Just as Notre Dame was known for the four horsemen, Oregon was known for The Firehouse Four. Going into 1964, Oregon had the Firehouse One. The one being Bob Berry. Additionally, 6'0," 190-pound Mel Renfro, the greatest halfback ever to play at the University of Oregon, was replaced by Dennis Keller, a 5' 8," 168-pound player. Keller was a great athlete. He was fast, and a good receiver also. But Renfro was gone. There were no stars, no All Americans. These guys were good athletes, sincere people, smart people. It was a no-name team other than their quarterback, Bob Berry. And what an integral part he would play in the miracle season where the team went 7-2-1.

The Great Escape

Bob had a 250 Honda. He would drive it everywhere. Berry would come to football practice on his bike. He went through the back gate across a muddy or dirt field, and then raced up a steep incline to the Freshman football field right next to our dressing quarters in the basement of Macarthur Court. Going up that steep 15-foot incline, Bob would have to race his bike to make it up, and he would usually get airbound too at the top. What can I say? Each day that he did this, he looked like Steve McQueen in a scene where he was trying to escape on a motorcycle in "The Great Escape." The movie, which came out in 1963, was ever present in any adventuresome kid's mind.

Chapter 6

1964

Overall Record 7-2-1

Date	Home Team	Score	Visit Team	Location
Sat. 9/19/64	Oregon	20-13 (W)	Brigham Young	Eugene, OR
Sat. 9/26/64	Oregon	22-13 (W)	Pittsburgh	Portland, OR
Sat. 10/3/64	Penn State	22-14 (W)	Oregon	Penn St.
Sat. 10/10/64	Idaho	14-8 (W)	Oregon	Moscow, ID
Sat. 10/17/64	Oregon	21-0 (W)	Arizona	Eugene, OR
Sat. 10/24/64	Washington	7-0 (W)	Oregon	Seattle, WA
Sat. 10/31/64	Oregon	8-10 (L)	Stanford	Portland, OR
Sat. 11/7/64	Oregon	21-21 (T)	Washington St.	Eugene, OR
Sat. 11/14/64	Indiana	29-21 (W)	Oregon	Bloomington
Sat. 11/21/64	Oregon State	6-7 (L)	Oregon	Corvallis, OR

Eddie Johns became a full-time coach for Oregon in 1964. He and Fritzi came from San Diego. Fritzi had fond memories of Eugene and their experiences there:

"Ed was working on his doctorate. He already had his masters, but he never got his doctorate because he started coaching there. I just remember how nice Cas and Marg were. How Marg used to have the wives over to watch the games or listen to the games, when Oregon played out of town.... Pat McHugh used to come by and get me, and take me to all those things, because I didn't know anybody. I got to know Cas, really, by being there. Ed thought the world of him. Susie grew up in an Oregon sweatshirt; she still has it.

Ed said that there was really a different staff there than he had ever heard about in any of the other staffs. He knew coaches on other teams before and after. He said there was just a special relationship there because of Cas, because of the type of person he was. They did so many things together as a group, which they don't do on a lot of staffs. FritziJohns

The passing game got completely retooled with Steve Bunker as flanker, Ray Palm, split end, and Corky Sullivan, tight end. These receivers actually do a very good job of performing in the Oregon sophisticated passing offense. Of course, Berry is the key—the

They called Him Cas

motor that has to pull the strings to make all of it go— which he does very well.

Larry Hill, Rich Schwab, Paul Burleson, and Ron Stratten were all part of the coaching staff for the Oregon Freshmen squad and were considered graduate assistants. The head coach was Eddie Johns.

Win Over Brigham Young, 20-13

Counting last season, the Webfoots would win their fifth game in a row; a feat not accomplished by any Oregon football team since 1959. It was a close game no one was happy with. But it was a win. Oregon barely beat Brigham Young. Berry opened up the game with a 12-yard pass to Ray Palm. Then a 14-yard pass to Corky Sullivan sent Dick Winn off tackle three times for 13 yards, and he picked up 8 yards with a run of his own. Dennis Keller caught a pass for the touchdown: 13 plays, 78 yards. Bill O'Toole had a 13-yard gainer on a double reverse 10-yard pass to Ray Palm, and an 8-yard pass to Corky Sullivan. On a number of running plays, Berry ran over for the score, but was negated by a penalty. Three plays later, Berry found Ray Palm in the end zone for the touchdown. Berry put the Ducks back in front for good with a 35-yard touchdown pass to Ray Palm, his second touchdown reception. Three touchdown passes gave Berry 25 for his career at Oregon; two more than the old record of 23 held by Hal Dunham from 1950-1952. Berry passed for 141 yards for a total of 2,811 yards and a career record-breaking effort topping George Shaw's 1952-54 record of 2,676 yards.

Casanova said glumly, "I was disappointed in our tackling, I was disappointed in our defense, we weren't scrambling out there." BYU was led by a tried sophomore, Virgil Carter, who went on to play with the Chicago Bears. Cas said, "I'm glad we got by this one. I'll take this one. I think the kids learned a heck of a lot. We had numerous sophomores and juniors playing without much time in the lineups. You never know how untested players will react until they get into the actual game. They were nervous. They seem to be tight," Cas said as he ticked off some of the reasons why he wasn't smiling. "We seemed slow, that point after touchdown blocked was inexcusable. Our pursuit wasn't good. I don't think we're in as good a shape as we

Chapter 6

thought. Everybody made a lot of mistakes out there." Asked if there was any chance of overconfidence for the upcoming game against Pittsburgh, Cas replied, "I should say not." Mark Richards, Pat Matson, Lowell Dean, and Dave Toby did a good job on defense. Matson and Dean, for example, saw so much two-way duty they ended up playing 48 and 43 minutes, respectively, of the 60 minutes of action.

Nobody had really stopped Bob Berry in two seasons, and the Webfoot quarterback wasn't about to let the Cougars do it. Oliver McKinney intercepted a Virgil Carter pass. McKinney also made a key fumble recovery in the first half. McKinney also made several fine defensive rushes to spill Carter for losses.

Once again, the smaller venue games would be played as planned at Hayward Field on the campus in Eugene. For both teams, the players dressed down for the game in the basement of McArthur Court, the basketball pavilion, and then walked down to Hayward Field, about a quarter of a mile away. For pre-game talk and half time gatherings, both teams went into two very small rooms underneath the stands at Hayward Field. In that small space were a few benches, a chalk board, and a number of power mowers used to cut the grass at Hayward Field. There were also a number of gasoline cans full of gas for the mowers. The gasoline fumes were strong enough to cut with a knife. Most of the coaches smoked and, obviously, did so in that room with the nervousness of the pre-game and half time. Donally said, "I would drop off the sliced oranges and water and get the hell out of there. It was a miracle that there was never a fire explosion from all the gas fumes in the air and all the cigarettes that had been smoked there."

"I told my father after the first game we barely beat BYU, I called my dad. I said, 'We might not win another game this year.' We kept rolling. I think we got to 7-0. Injuries caught up to us. We weren't near the team that we were my junior year with that 1963 class. Wilcox and Renfro and all the Firehouse Four guys. That was a hell of a team. We were doing it with smoke and mirrors my senior year." Bob Berry

They called Him Cas

Win Over Pittsburgh, 22-13

There was Bob Berry, there was Mike Brundage, and there was Corky Sullivan: Oregon's sixth in a row over a two season span. Oregon had not won six straight since 1948. Harry Cartales did a blitz on the quarterback, which hurried the throw, and created an interception by Les Palm. Berry hit Steve Bunker in the end zone for a touchdown. Mike Brundage threw a touchdown pass to Ray Palm. Total offense: 373 yards. Oregon: 230 yards.

Cas thought the kids played well, noting again many of the defensive players lacked experience. There's always a certain amount of luck in any game. It was needed when playing a good team too.

Harry Cartalles recovered a fumble. They started throwing everybody in there at Berry. Cas said it was the same way they tried to stop Roger Staubach last year against Navy. The penalty, which he was thankful for, came with three minutes remaining in the game, and Oregon leading by a razor thin 14 to 13 score.

Keller ran the ball on the next five plays getting the Webfeet to the 18-yard line with a fourth down. This time, with nothing to lose, Berry threw a strike to Ray Palm in the corner of the end zone and the game was Oregon's. Berry hit Bunker for the two-point conversion. Oregon stopped Pittsburgh and went through three plays. Doug Post booted a towering spiral which landed 64 yards away on the Pittsburgh 27-yard line. The ball traveled about 75 yards in the air.

With three minutes and 31 seconds to play, Pittsburgh took over on their own 27-yard line, ready to launch their winning drive. Stewart was jarred loose from the ball on the first play. Mark Richards recovered it. It was first and ten, Oregon, at the 25-yard line. The Webfoots only had to run out the clock, but Berry tossed a pass out to the left flat. Pittsburgh's Eric Crabtree streaked up from nowhere, grabbed the ball, and raced back 80 yards to the end zone. An offside penalty against the Panthers nullified the 80-yard touchdown run and actually gave Oregon a 5-yard gain to the Pittsburgh 20-yard line. As he exhaled smoke from his first after-game cigarette, Casanova said, "That's the only time in my life I've ever thanked God for a penalty on the opponent."

Chapter 6

Keller ran the ball on the next five plays getting the Webfeet to the 18-yard line with a fourth down. This time with nothing to lose, Berry threw a strike to Ray Palm in the corner of the end zone in a game that belonged to Oregon. Barry hit Bunker for the two-point conversion.

Win Over Penn State, 22-14

Casanova wasn't the least bit reluctant about repeating what he had been saying for some time: Berry was by far the best quarterback he had seen. He had seen movies of Staubach and Zeno. Berry was not only a good performer, but a tremendous leader. Bob Berry was drawing superlatives from all over the crowd of 44,600 on that warm, sunny afternoon. He led the opportunistic Oregon football team to a 22-14 victory over old-time nemesis, Penn State, and sent a couple of local traditions to the scrap heap. This was the third straight win of the season and seventh consecutive victory over two seasons; the longest win streak for Oregon since the Cotton Bowl team of 1948. Casanova declined to say that it was Berry's best ever game. Cas said, "I've seen him have several better games," as he puffed on a cigarette, making up for those he didn't smoke on the sideline. Steve Bunker became the father of a daughter on Friday. He caught five of Berry's passes for 86 yards and a touchdown as leading receiver in the game.

Berry completed 17 of 32 passes. Cas praised the following players: 250-pound tackle, Pat Matson, all three of Berry's pass receivers—Steve Bunker, Ray Palm, and Corky Sullivan—plus Dennis Keller, the junior left halfback who gained 66 yards on 16 carries as the Duck running offense gained momentum. He said, "I was real pleased with the kids on defense, all of them, and especially the linebackers." He was especially pleased with Tim Casey, and sophomore, Harry Carteles, who recovered a fumble in the second half as Penn State tried to pass in desperation. Both times were intercepted, first by Oliver McKinney, then by Les Palm. Cas said, "What I like about it is that our kids hit pretty hard out there. They caused some fumbles." This was the first win for Oregon over the former Liberty Bowl Champ of 1960. It took three tries to finally beat Penn State.

They called Him Cas

There were many key roles with jarring tackles. Ron Martin jumped on the ball to get a fumble recovery. Berry completed a 15-yard to Corky Sullivan for the first touchdown two-point conversion. Martin banged into a runner, knocked the ball loose, and defensive end Jerry Parsons recovered on the Penn State 30-yard line.

From the one-yard line, Berry lobbed to Ray Palm in the end zone for a score. Casanova thought the Webfoots were tense in the first half. He said, "I Have never seen them so tense, but they weren't in the second half."

"We were playing Penn State back there. Penn state had some really really big players. It was in those days when it was still one way football and you had to stay in for both offense and defense, this was actually the first year they went to two platoon football but they didn't go completely into it like it is today. Both the offensive or the defensive team might get stuck playing offense or defense for a few plays and then the regular offense or defense would substitute in. So I was playing defensive tackle and if we got caught on the field, and if we had to stay in and play offense, I would play offensive guard and we would run F88 or F89. That's the only thing we were supposed to do, which is a pass or run option by Bob Berry around the right or the left end. We were playing Penn State back there. So Bob calls an F88 in the huddle and then he grabs my facemasks and twists my head a little and said, 'Jack keep number 82 away from me. He has been in my face all day! Get him!'

All I knew when I left the huddle is that I was going to get him. I didn't care if I had to wrap him in a bear hug or cheat—whatever I had to do—I was going to get him.

The Penn State player was a senior. So I go out there and I take him on and I stayed in front of him. After the play, Berry slapped me on the helmet and says, 'Great job, Jack.' So the guy I blocked was Jerry Sandusky. I got the program to prove it. He was playing defensive end. That story reflects how Bob was such an inspirational player to play with. He hung around the linemen more than he hung around the backs. Needless to say, when he said something, we stepped up. He was that kind of a player." Jack Clark

Chapter 6

Win Over Idaho, 14-8

Tim Temple got an interception. Idaho's sensational sophomore fullback, 6'4," 232-pound, Ray McDonald, made his first appearance of the season. He was inserted into the Vandal lineup in the third quarter and gave the Oregon defensemen fits. More importantly, he set the stage for some effective option running by Idaho quarterback Monahan. At this time, Dee Andrus was head coach for Idaho. Ray McDonald was a dream fullback for Dee with his fullback option offense. To this point, Cas had not lost to Idaho, but this became a very close game. Hats off to Dee Andros who would become the new head football coach of OSU the following year. Many believe this close game with Oregon was Andros's selling point on why he should be the next head coach at OSU after Prothro left for the UCLA job. We would see that fullback option offense for many years to come at OSU, led by Dee Andros.

Win Over Arizona, 21-0

Oregon took on Arizona, October 17th, winning 21-0. The game was held in Eugene in front of 18,000 fans. Jack Clark did a good job on the defensive line. Berry threw six passes to Bunker with three receptions to Ray Palm and a Corky Sullivan extra point. Les Palm recovered a fumble and returned it to the Arizona eight-yard line. Corky Sullivan got a touchdown pass.

Cas said afterward, "Darn it, I'd like to have seen that bunch of kids score." For him that was one of the game's high points, the chance he had to get the reserves in and play. He said, "They got a lot of good experience. it's real good for morale of the whole team. Everyone is a part, good enthusiastic football."

Maloney Played center and Dave Fluke, defensive back. Fluke got two interceptions. Cas decided to rest Berry for the remainder of the game. The quarterback's left shoulder was still sore from a bruise suffered in the Idaho game. Besides picking up a fumble, Les Palm intercepted two passes. Palm, a sophomore, spent his spare time studying movies of future opponents. Cas said, "He's a good pass defender. Lowell Dean, Corky Sullivan, and Dick Winn did a good job of blocking. They made our offense go." Berry had three touchdown passes. This gave the Ducks their fifth straight win of the season. Cas said, "I'm really pleased with our defense."

Assistant coach, John Robinson, kept a scoring chart posted on the MacArthur court basement bulletin board. This included: Pass interceptions, fumbles caused, and fumbles recovered. Les Palm now had five interceptions and one recovered fumble. Harry Cartales had one caused fumble and three recovered fumbles. Dave Fluke and Tim Temple had two interceptions and Haggerty, two recovered fumbles. Overall, Oregon recovered two fumbles and had five interceptions. Bob Berry was 12 for 21 for 154 yards and three touchdowns.

Win Over Washington, 7-0

Herm Meister had to go in and get his broken arm re-taped with a pad on it. He was the Oregon field goal kicker. He was sitting next to Bob Berry who was getting a huge shot of Novocain in his shoulder by the ever dependable Dr. George Guldager. Herm remembers a long needle and large syringe. Herm was thinking to himself, 'I'm just kicking the ball and have padding on. Bob is getting this done just so that he can get out there and play in the game.'

He continued, "They just put a hit man on me, and every time I'd hand off or throw the ball, he wanted to hit me late. They finally threw him out of the game. I remember after the game, the reporters were in the locker room and I was sitting right next to Cas, and they wanted to know about the game, and they were insinuating that the Huskies were the toughest guys we played all year. 'They were really tough.' I said, 'That's the 'dirtiest team I've ever played against in my life.' I said, 'They're not tough. They're dirty players.' I said, 'It starts with their coach.'"

Bob Berry

Cas would always have problems with Washington. It started the year he was at Oregon, 1951. He lost in Portland, 63-6, and set a record for the worst lost in Pac West history.

It would go on through the years with gruesome games. Jim Owens played at Oklahoma. Somewhere along the line on

Chapter 6

Washington's road to numerous Rose Bowls, the defense was coached to outhit and "out-physical" their opponent. Owens was from Oklahoma and coached with Bear Bryant at Texas A&M, and was part of the "Junction Boys." The Huskies became very successful, especially on defense, and they had a number players go on to the pros. As time went on, Oregon had physical players also. First, Ron Snidow and Steve Barnett, then Mickey Ording and Dave Wilcox, then Linebackers like Tim Casey and Dave Toby and Lowell Dean. The other part of this was the psych-out part. When playing in Husky Stadium, the Huskies would always come out early from the locker room and at half time. They would hit their helmets against the wall, and head butt the door again like some medieval knight before the battle began. As Jack Roche was quoted as saying, "This is not just a game, this is an all out war." In 1962, Cas was walking down the runway to the field, and some of the Huskies knocked him down to the ground. The next year, 1963, in Portland, the Ducks were playing the Huskies. The Huskies kicked off to the Ducks who, minutes before, had scored on a pass play by Berry. But Berry injured his knee on the score. Cas was about to put Mel Renfro in at quarterback; a position he played in high school. But Renfro received the kick off from Washington, and advanced it 17 yards. He was tackled by Washington's Junior Coffey with a vicious blow. The collision caused cracked ribs and put Mel out for two games.

In 1964, the Ducks played the Huskies in Seattle. Nothing was easy. Because of fog in Seattle, they had to go by bus. Cas read the sports page the morning of the game, and became livid. He had it rolled up, and in his pep talk, it was all about the article that said the Huskies would win. It was because they were tougher, and were going to out-hit Oregon, and that Berry would fade because he would feel it in his knee. The bottom line was that Oregon would do the out hitting and would win, 7-0. Cas had had it through the years. Enough was enough, we were going to win.

Cas willed his determination on Oregon, and especially that day, for a victory. "We're playing Washington at their place, which is legendary. I got half my team from a year ago. These young guys are throwing up before the game, they're so nervous. 'Come on, guys. We gotta go play football. Get out of the bathroom.' I'll never forget it. They were so nervous. I just got them fired up. Let's go, 'Come on,

They called Him Cas

man. We'll kick their ass no matter who they are. We're gonna show them how we do it in Oregon."Bob Berry

The element of surprise, a tenacious defense, and great desire gave Oregon its long-awaited football victory over Washington on a Saturday afternoon. There were 55,300 in attendance. Lowell Dean, offensive right tackle, scored the only touchdown on a tackle-eligible play, not seen in the Oregon offense since 1961. Dean took a pass from Berry on the two-yard line and bowled his way into the end zone for a 14-yard play. Herm Meister made the PAT. Junior Coffey, who had 30 carries for 110 yards in Portland the year prior, and scored the first and last touchdown for Washington in their 26-19 victory, had just 12 yards on six carries. He was supposed to have been suffering a hurt hip. When asked about it, Owen said, "What can I tell you, he just didn't get his jersey this week." Washington had a deal where you had to earn your starting job each week. "Coffey didn't get his jersey." Many players, when recruited by Washington, felt Jim Owens was impersonal. Washington could bring in twice as many players as Oregon in this era because they could afford it and it was legal to do.

Len Casanova delivered his pregame pep talk, Saturday, by reading from a newspaper. It was a sports column in the University of Washington Student Daily which said:

"Oregon is riding for a fall. They have not met a really tough line yet this season, and although they are probably not admitting it to their teammates, deep in their hearts they all remember last year's bone- crushing defeat at the hands of the Huskies."

"I'm betting," the columnist continued, "that each time Bob Berry puts on his knee brace, he remembers how it feels to be really hit. The Ducks did not have what it takes to handle a real hard hitting football team last year. And I doubt if they have forgotten it."

That sports columnist had to eat his words. Oregon's Webfoots had what it took, and apprehended Washington Huskies, 7-0, before an estimated crowd of 55,300 spectators under cloudy, chilly skies.

It was Oregon's sixth straight victory without a defeat, and the 10th straight over two seasons, equaling an all-time record. It was the first victory over the Huskies since 1961. Cas was searching for a game ball. He wanted to give it to the two co-captains, Bob Berry and Lowell Dean. Finally, one of the Oregon managers found a game ball

Chapter 6

and gave it to Berry who replied, "Give it to Lowell. He came through." Lowell Dean, 235-pound offensive tackle wound up with the game ball for his part in the play. It not only surprised the Huskies, but won the ball game.

Berry took the snap from center, stood straight up without moving back, and fired downfield to Dean. He was sandwiched between two defenders a couple of yards from the goal line. Dean simply grabbed the ball and carried those offenders over the goal line with him. The Oregon coaches had the tackle eligible play ready for last week's game against Arizona, but decided to save it for the Huskies. It was the first time the Ducks had successfully worked the play since 1961. Dean said, grinning, "It is the first time I ever got close to the ball in my collegiate career." He was an All-State tight end at Medford High School. He said, "I wanted the ball. It was a perfect pass. I just had to grab it. That's all I had to do."

It was defensive back, Jim Lambright, playing up on the line, who did the number-one job catching Berry. Before he could throw, another rusher, Dick Wetterbauer, was called for a personal foul against Berry, and was taken out of the game. Husky coach, Jim Owens, gave Jim Lambright—credited with 11 tackles and six assists— "lineman of the game" honors. As for Oregon, Cas said, "We just out-toughed them."Eventually, Jim Lambright would become Head Coach of Washington from 1993-1998.

It was a fumble, with Oliver McKinney recovering on Oregon's one-yard line, that stymied Washington's best offensive thrust. Harry Cartales intercepted a Bill Douglas pass and returned it 32 yards to Washington's 36-yard line. Cartales also blitzed Husky quarterback, Jim Sartoris, and threw them for an eight-yard loss on a fourth and two.

As he talked about the young defensive team, Cas said, "I thought our defense was real good. They were nothing at the beginning of the season. Seven had never played in college games before this year and two are playing in new positions." He credited defenses of guard, Ancer Haggerty, who had seven tackles, two assists, and one pass interception. He also praised the defensive work of Harry Cartales and Tim Casey.

There was no question, either, that Washington hurt itself with what some called, euphemistically, illegal play. Others didn't mince

They called Him Cas

words, and just called it dirty. Berry was the special target of it, being hit hard numerous times long after he had gotten rid of the football.

Wetterbauer, first man assigned to rush Berry, got him five times early in the game before an official called a personal foul penalty. It gave the Ducks a 15-yard assist in the touchdown drive.

Lambright was there on the line to keep on Berry. He hustled like the Devil. Said Coach Owens, "He was in the right place at the right time."Back to penalties again: The Huskies lost 125 yards on 12 infractions. There were just too many penalties, and the two crucial fumbles didn't make the offense go, Owens said.

AsHarry Cartales said, "It was a great call by Robbie (John Robinson)." He called it with both linebackers stunting to the weak side. Cartales pulled down Sertorius from behind, grabbing the neck of his jersey.

In the fourth quarter, Casanova himself stormed on the field as Washington defensive tackle, Jim Norton, knocked Berry down long after he'd handed off to fullback Dick Winn. He had kept him down, using his elbows on Berry, but no penalty was called. Casanova literally pulled Norton off of Berry as he was trying to injure his right knee and get him out of the game. What kind of a coach is this that cares for his players that much? I want to play for a coach like that.

Altogether, three personal foul penalties were called on the Huskies to one against the Ducks.

After the game, the Ducks were able to book a flight late. The team had dinner while some of the players waited on the bus half full to go to the airport, Pat Matson was egged on by Tobey and few others to go ahead and drive the bus. So Matson got in the driver's seat, put on his bus driver's hat, and took the bus down almost a block. The bus driver came running out from a smoke break saying, "What the hell are you doing, don't you know I could lose my license over this?" Pat, being real soft and cordial, said, "It's okay. You take over, I was just playing around." The joys of victory and the antics one pulls.

Johnny McKay had gone to USC in 1959 as an assistant coach. He was head coach of USC from 1960 through 1975. In 1960 he went 4-6. In 1961, hewas4-5-1. At this point in McKay's career at USC there was pressure. The alumni wanted to fire him, but President Norman Topping resisted the pressure and gave McKay

Chapter 6

one more year to field a team and use the players he had recruited. In 1962, USC was 11 and 0 and won the Rose Bowl and the national championship.

USC was playing Washington in Seattle that year. They were in the locker room at halftime and the Huskies would go by and head butt the door with their heads to intimidate the opposing team. Accidentally, the door opened because of the head butting. It was now wide open and McKay said his last few words at the chalkboard. He quickly reacted by saying, "Well, what the hell are you waiting for? Let's go out and kick their asses. Come on." Spontaneously, everybody got up, ran out, and had a little mayhem in the tunnel, with USC ultimately winning the game. This win guaranteed USC a spot in the Rose Bowl and there was crowd of thousands of people welcoming the Trojans players home back in LA. McKay got off the plane first, to large cheers, and several players followed. Finally, the last player got off the plane carrying a door. People in the crowd were asking what was is that all about? The memento was quite meaningful to those who knew the locker room door that was head butted.

Loss to Stanford, 8-10

Despite a dismal offensive showing, seventh-ranked Oregon was ahead until the last 13 seconds when Braden Beck's 27-yard field goal gave Stanford a 10-8 win.

After watching movies of the 10-8 loss to Stanford, Casanova reiterated what he said immediately after the game: That quarterback, Bob Berry, had a bad day and so did his receivers. Neither was he pleased with defense. They were just a step slow all the time. They weren't hustling the way they did before. Somebody was falling down.

One factor of Oregon's poor offensive showing: Stanford's punting the ball. It was downed twice on Oregon's 14 yard-line, once on the 12-yard line, and the last time on the one-yard line.

Ray Handley, one of the nation's leading ground gainers, was named back of the week by the Pacific Athletic Conference. This was for his performance in the Indian's upset 10-8 win over Oregon the

They called Him Cas

previous Saturday. He made 113 yards running, and also caught three passes for 25 yards.

Bob Berry had a bruised shoulder and sore knee, but in no way was his future being impaired. The medical man told me and added that it looked like there were 10 other guys who weren't playing tough.

Everybody knew or should know that Oregon lived and died by the pass and that's Berry. He would not be playing for the Webfoots unless he was reasonably healthy, regardless of his desires. Len Casanova did not value winning to that degree. There is no question Bob Berry picked up a number of bumps and bruises and some strained ligaments. He had been a marked man since the season started, although no opponent other than Washington appeared to be out to get him. He could very well be the target of Washington State's defensive plans at Hayward Field. I asked Jim Shanley—Ex-Webfoot half back and member of the Washington State staff who scouted Oregon against Stanford—if the Cougars would play Berry like the Huskies did. Shanley said, "Definitely not, according to what I heard about the Washington game, but we are aggressive and we do hit hard."

Tie With Washington State, 21-21

Mike Brundage started and finished the game in front of a crowd of 19,000. Brundage was called on to fill the shoes of the healing Bob Berry. By the time the game was over, the Webfoot followers were considerably less worried about what Oregon would do for a quarterback after Berry graduated. Brundage passed for 239 yards and two touchdowns and executed a two-point conversion pass that gave the Ducks a come-from-behind tie. Coach Casanova said that Brundage did a fine job. Max Coley called the plays from the press box. Brundage completed 11 of 18 passes for 144 yards. Brundage drilled three passes: 12 yards to Ray Palm, 14 yards to Steve Bunker, and 31 yards to Arlen Elms. Dennis Keller had a five-yard sweep for a touchdown. Ron Martin and Harry Cartales put on the finishing touches when they tackled Washington State's Clancy Williams for a one-yard gain on a fourth and two. Ducks took over on the five-yard line.

Webfoot defensive halfback, Ron Martin, claimed, "That's exactly what happened." The safety man, Tim Temple, was covering Shaw on the play. The ball went through his hands. Martin said the ball hit the ground and he put his hands on it. The referee was on the blind side. It would show up in the movies. The official signaled the touchdown, though spectators in the end zone seats, and Martin himself, said the ball went through Shaw's hands and he trapped it on the ground. With two minutes and 40 seconds left, the Ducks had 4th and four on the WSU eight-yard line. Brundage unleashed a pass that head coach of WSU, Burt Clark, remembered with a shutter for a long time.

Intended for Ray Palm in the end zone, the ball was knocked up in the air by a Cougar defender and plopped into the open arms of Corky Sullivan on his knee about 10 yards away.

After that Brundage to Palm to Sullivan spectacular, it was up to Brundage to make good on the two-point try, and he did. As the flow of the play went to the right, Brundage threw left to his former Roseburg High School teammate, Ray Palm. He was all alone and unguarded in the end zone. Time remaining was two minutes, 45 seconds.

The Ducks decided against an onside kick attempt. Casanova explained afterwards, "We thought we had better get the kick down in there deep. They got a pretty good field-goal kicker." Toby kicked the ball deep. The Duck Defense held and forced the Cougars to punt.

Ron Martin fielded the punt on the 50-yard line at a dead run. As he was hit on the WSU 46-yard line, the ball was knocked away, and Cougar guard, Wally Dempsey, fell on the ball. The Cougars could not advance the ball and time ran out. So did chance for the Ducks pulling out a victory.

Burt Clark said afterwards, "You have to give Oregon a lot of credit for coming back the way they did."

Win Over Indiana, 29-21

Len Casanova wasn't much for pep talks at halftime, but he gave one here Saturday. It was a blistering one. As center Dave Toby recalled later, "I think it was the maddest I've ever seen Cas right there. He was really upset." And his words had the desired effect.

They called Him Cas

Oregon Webfoots, with a record breaking individual performance by quarterback Bob Berry, staged a magnificent second-half comeback for a 29-21 victory over Big Ten opponent, Indiana. It was the second defeat in two weeks for the Hoosiers at the hands of a Pacific Athletic Conference team. Oregon State had done it the week before, 24-14. Attendance at the game was 20,708.

Things turned out all right, but Cas was so upset at halftime that I might have walked back to Eugene if possible. I wouldn't have wanted to be on that plane with him.

Cas went in at half time thinking to himself, "We peaked beating Washington, we lost to Stanford in the last 13 seconds, we tied WSU without Berry last week, and now this is the third game in a row we are falling apart. We're down 21-0. I am not going to let this happen. I am going to wake these guys up and get them playing the way they should, and I am going to will a victory."Cas could will a victory maybe one game a year. There was Washington and now this one. This was, quite frankly, a very similar halftime to the University of Portland game in 1934, though he did not say, "You're not worth a bucket of shit."

Ironically, Cas had invited a dozen priests to come in at halftime. I am not sure why, and they were standing in the background watching all this go on. How does this man of God handle himself at halftime? Unforgettable. Robbie started talking and said, "OK we need to make a few changes on the defense." Cas cut him off and said, "No! we're not changing a damn thing!" Then he made a big scene by kicking the galvanized bucket full of sliced oranges across the room. Then he kicked the water cups too. He shouted, "Don't give them any oranges or anything to drink. They don't deserve it!" Toby got up because he needed to go to the bathroom. He said, "I got up to go to the bathroom. We always did that. You go to the bathroom and then you get some orange slices." Cas yelled, "Toby, sit down!" I was just quivering. This is one time he was picking his words. He was just like a drunken sailor. He didn't care who was there listening, he called out guys by name. He challenged them. He said that they had to do better. And then we get the knock on the door from the referee saying it was time to go on the field. By now I really had to go bad, so I stood up again to go to the bathroom. Cas

Chapter 6

yelled out again, "Toby sit down!" So was just quivering, then Cas said, get out on the field.

So we were kicking off to start the second half. Toby went out to kick it off. Toby was trying to kick it off down the middle down to the goal line. Instead, it went about ten yards down the field hard to the right. Les Palm, the farthest man to the right, fell on the ball as Toby kicked a perfect onside kick. The offense came in and scored. The offense continued to score, and Oregon won the game, 28-21. The real question was: Did Toby go in his pants or did he hold it? Either way, it was very uncomfortable to kick off.

There was an article in Sports Illustrated and Robbie claimed in jest that he was fired during halftime, and Cas wouldn't let the kicker go to the bathroom.

"George Pasero, Oregonian sportswriter came up to me after the game with that big smile of his and said, 'Toby that was really a brilliant onside kick. Did Cas tell you to do an onside kick?' I said, 'No, Cas wouldn't let me go to the bathroom, and I felt so bad I couldn't even kick the ball.'"

Casanova was still trying to figure out Sunday what caused Oregon's poor first half against Indiana. He said, "Maybe we sent them to bed too early. Usually, we leave on Thursday and have time to adjust to the time change." The Webfoots left for Indiana Friday. This time, Cas said they were sent to bed at 10:30 PM. That is 7:30PM Eugene time. "I went to bed at 11:30 and last time I looked at my watch, it was 5:20." Casanova said.

Cas said there were a few encouraging points about the Indiana game, notably the return to form of quarterback, Bob Berry. Also, the second-half comeback, the play of quirky Sullivan, and the offensive blocking of guards Mark Richards and Dale Wilson.

Cas said of Wilson and Richards, "They're the ones who made us go. When Bob Berry took off on a run, they really got out there and blocked." Casanova said Sullivan played well both offensively and defensively. He said that the fact Barry was healthy enough to run the ball improved Oregon's entire running game. Everybody had been defending us on the pass, figuring he couldn't run.

What about the priests? I think human emotion does take over in all of us whether we want to admit it or not.

They called Him Cas

Loss to OSU, 6-7

Strangely, the Beavers beat Oregon in the way Prothro never would have predicted. In front of 30,154 people, OSU fumbled five times and lost three of them. Prothro called it, "a lack of poise." "We didn't have it in poise today. Today we won, making mistakes." OSU had lost only seven of 12 fumbles in nine previous games. The winner of this game would go to the Rose Bowl. Oregon State won the game. After that, Prothro would become the new head coach at UCLA.

Oregon Webfoots trudged slowly by ones and twos into the dressing room of the Gill Coliseum basement. They made no move to take off their muddy jerseys on which more than a few bloodstains could be seen. Some set on a long bench as others stood. A few had tears in their eyes. And through the subdued group moved the assistant coaches with pats on the back grips and on the shoulders, and soft-spoken words. There was little sound.

Casanova walked among the players and began speaking. His voice was firm and loud: "I told you before the game that I wanted to be proud of you. I am."

Casanova brought cheers from the players, something ordinarily not heard in the dressing room of a team that had just suffered a heart-rending defeat. The celebratory cries let out as he announced that the Webfoots two co-captains, Bob Berry, and tackle, Lowell Dean, plus senior Corky Sullivan, had been invited to play in the East-West Shrine Game in San Francisco.

How did Berry feel about Oregon's chances of pulling the victory out of apparent defeat in those 53 seconds remaining?

"We did it before," he answered, as he put on a tie in front of his locker. "If you have forgotten last year's Indiana game when the Ducks stormed to a winning touchdown in the final one and a half minutes." But Berry added, "It is pretty tough, you know."

Dick Winn, the chunky fullback who piled up 85 yards rushing on off tackle slants, wouldn't take any congratulations for his repeated long gainers. He said, "The linemen did it. Those were real big holes they opened. They really were the biggest all season."

Chapter 6

At the annual football banquet, Bob Berry won the Hoffman Award. In accepting the award, he made it clear that he did not do anything on his own, and that there were ten other guys out there trying their best to make him look good. With Berry's frequent injuries to his shoulder and knee, and all the physical therapy he needed, he got the Tape Can award from Two Gun also.

The Clark Award went to tight end Corky Sullivan who performed amazingly well for a rookie. Seniors leaving the program were Lowell Dean, Doug Post, Oliver McKinney, Dennis Maloney, Jerry Anderson, Ron Martin, and Ron Stratten.

Lowell Dean and Bob Berry were invited to play in the Hula Bowl. Cas was invited to be an assistant coach at the East-West Shrine Game and Hula Bowl.

Tony Amato was the banquet speaker. He played at Oregon from 1934-39, and was also a practicing lawyer in Portland. For years had been a football referee for the Pac 8 Conference. He stated that we were human, and we try to make as few mistakes as possible. The movies show that we were, 99.9% of the time.

They called Him Cas

Chapter 7

(1965 and Beyond)

Season Record 4-5-1

Date	Home Team	Score	Visit Team	Location
Sat. 9/15/65	Pittsburgh	17-15 (W)	Oregon	Pittsburgh
Sat. 9/25/65	Utah	31-14 (W)	Oregon	Utah
Sat. 10/2/65	Oregon	27-14 (W)	Brigham Young	
Sat. 10/9/65	Stanford	14-17 (L)	Oregon	Stanford
Sat. 10/16/65	Oregon	18-18 (T)	Air Force	Portland
Sat. 10/23/65	Oregon	20-24 (L)	Washington	Portland
Sat 10/30/65	Oregon	17-14 (W)	Idaho	Eugene
Sat. 11/6/65	Washington State	7-27 (L)	Oregon	Pullman
Sat. 11/13/65	Oregon	0-24 (L)	California	Portland
Sat 11/20/65	Oregon	14-19 (L)	Oregon St.	Eugene

1965

4-5-1

The season started off with three straight wins, a close loss, and a tie. The team looked impressive, similar to 1964. This year may have been even better, especially on the defensive and offensive line. The obvious fact: Bob Berry had graduated. Max Coley had the creative idea of replacing him with two players: Mike Brundage to pass, and Tom Travato to rollout, run or pass. It worked well, especially for the first three games. Max Coley was excited about another offense addition he had created that year; A four-wide receiver look with no tight end. It seemed to be working until the Stanford game. As Tom Trovato said, "I don't know what the deal was, but every play the outside backer would blitz me, and I could not rollout." There was no tight end to block for him. Steve Bunker, the flanker, came back. He had gained 30 pounds, so that didn't help either.

They called Him Cas

In looking at Max's four-wide outs, it did look like a run and shoot offense in many ways. It worked, and then it did not work.

Win Over Pittsburgh, 17-15

The team flew back to play Pittsburgh and had a great game. A veteran line, offensive backs, and receivers all performed well. Scott Cress, sophomore halfback, even played a role as a runner and receiver, like Larry Hill of the Firehouse Four.

Win Over Utah, 31-14

The Ducks traveled to Salt Lake City again, this time with dual quarterbacks who could do no wrong.

Win Over Brigham Young, 27-14

Len Casanova finally got his hundredth win. The silver-haired Oregon football coach reached the century mark in victories that Saturday as the Webfeet defeated Brigham Young, 27-14, at Hayward Field. After being carried off the field, Cas said, "I thought I was going to be 100 years old out there this afternoon the way we kicked the ball around." The victory, Oregon's third in a row, came in the home season opener. A full-house crowd of 20,500 saw an awesome Duck defense virtually skin the visiting Cougars. The explosive Oregon offense scored in every quarter behind the two platoon quarterbacking of Tom Trovato and Mike Brundage.

Head coach, Tommy Hudspeth, said, "That was a fine football team, they just beat the tar out of us. Trovato and the other Brundage will make them forget Bob Berry, and he's the best quarterback I've ever seen. I hope to goodness we don't play anybody like that anymore." He was talking about the current edition of the Webfeet, not last year's Berry-guided team. Casanova shuttled his players, including quarterbacks Trovato and Brundage, back and forth onto the field to give them rest.

Chapter 7

Loss to Stanford, 14-17

Oregon recovered two Stanford fumbles at midfield, but could not move the ball. Ancer Haggerty recovered a third Indian fumble on the Stanford 29-yard line, leading to a field goal attempt by Mark Scholl from the 20-yard line. The ball sailed wide. Pat Matson fell on a ball at the Stanford 28-yard line. Tom Trovato completed a 20-yard pass to Scott Cress. Trovato passed again to Cress at the 5-yard line. Casanova called for a field goal; a 39-yard attempt. If they made it, the game would be tied. Cas praised linebackers Tim Casey and Dave Toby for their excellent plays, with 13 tackles, and Mattson's offense and defense with 11 tackles.

Tie With Air Force, 18-18

A tie is neither a win nor a loss, but that is not the way coach Len Casanova felt on this Saturday. The upset-minded Air Force Falcons fought to an 18-18 standoff with Oregon's favored Webfoots at Multnomah Stadium. The grim-faced Casanova snapped: "Hell, I consider it a besting."

Ex-Oregon linebacker, Spike Hilstrom, who left a head coaching job at North Salem High to become an assistant coach at the Air Force Academy, had scouted his alma mater the last three Saturdays. He did a tremendous job putting together the format. Martin head coach said it was Hilstrom's suggestion they carried out.

Cas explained Oregon's second half comeback by saying, "Well, we had the ball a little bit; we never had the ball in the first half. I'm sure no one on the Air Force team got hurt, we didn't hit them hard enough."

Loss to Washington, 20-24

Somehow, it was the same old script for an Oregon-Washington football game: Tense, exciting, close, and undecided until the final minute. Washington's Huskies, reputedly a team that got airsick at the thought of putting the ball in the air, outplayed Oregon's Webfoots at their own favorite game of passing. They emerged with a 24-20

They called Him Cas

victory before 33,437 spectators at Multnomah Stadium. The unexpected switch saw Jim Owens' Huskies bomb Oregon, scoring all three touchdowns on passes.

Owens smiled, "It was another close one, but this went our way." He was glad he could smile. He said, "That Oregon ball club is dangerous and explosive. They had us fighting right down to the wire." Cas said, "We killed ourselves with mistakes. We had a lot of them, punts should've been fielded, kickoffs should've been run up the middle, our pass coverage was poor." Tom Sparlin, Husky quarterback from Grants Pass, completed 11 of 20 passes for 230 yards. His favorite target was Dave Williams who got five passes for 177 yards and was named lineman of the game.

Once again for the Webfoots, the Trovata and Brundage quarterback combination guided the offense. Tom & Mike, interchanging frequently, both combined on the first touchdown drive by Trovato. He threw an eight-yard pass to Steve Bunker. In the third quarter, Trovato, running the show, charged over for a touchdown after the Ducks recovered Holland's fumble on Washington's 28-yard line

Win Over Idaho, 17-14

It was Homecoming game at the University of Oregon. Oregon would win, 17-14, using a balanced attack with Dick Winn effectively carrying the ball with Pat Mattson blocking. Both Trovato and Brundage at quarterback were a dangerous dual that would be effective. It was a close game. Idaho had their junior fullback Ray McDonald, a 6'4, 248-pound phenomenon.

Loss to WSU, 7-27

Washington State Cougars were for real. It was no fairytale game on this sunny Saturday at Rogers field. The sophomore-loaded Cougars out blocked, out tackled, hit, passed and outran the Webfoots for a 27-7 homecoming victory. The game wasn't as close as the score indicated.

The 20-point margin was the worst beating taken by an Oregon club since losing against Penn State, 41-13, in the Liberty Bowl in

Chapter 7

1960. A disappointed Casanova told Jim Shanley, former Webfoot backfield star who was coaching the Washington State defensive secondary, which incidentally intercepted three Webfoot passes, "You kicked the hell out of us, Jim. We were just awful. This is the worst we have played in I don't know how many years. We just couldn't move. WSU outplayed us, out fought us and we were stupid. We were always a step behind."

Loss to Cal, 0-24

It was perfect weather for Duck hunting, and California's Golden Bears took full advantage of it. The Bears used a 12-gauge ground attack on Saturday to shoot down Oregon's Webfoots, 24-0. Cal, which used a muddy field offense even on dry turf, found the Multnomah field made to order for its power running. The turf was muddy after the weeklong rains. It grew slicker and more slippery as it rained throughout the game. This forced the less brave among the 16,890 spectators to seek shelter underneath the stadium roof.

They ended up with the first shutout of an Oregon football team since losing to Michigan, 21-0, in the second game of the 1960 season.

The Webfoots had lived by the pass and they died by the pass as Cal defenders intercepted four of the quarterback's aerials. Three of the interceptions set up scoring opportunities. Oregon quarterback Mike Brundage said, "It's pretty hard to throw when it's that muddy. But that's no excuse for four interceptions." Brundage had just experienced his worst day as an Oregon passer, completing only 14 of 36 passes.

Loss to OSU, 14-19

Dee Andros tried hard to live up to his own words, but it was difficult. The Oregon State head football coach said, "There's a lot of Saturdays left. I'll take this win and be very humble." Andros tried hard to be humble after watching the Beavers win over Oregon, 19-14, on a soggy Hayward field turf.

It was a free for all after the final gun took some of the enthusiasm away from Andros, but he was still obviously jubilant. He

They called Him Cas

told reporters after the game, "They're all good kids. They just wanted to win and tempers flared." The game was the first Civil War contest for Andros and he savored the win saying, "I've been around for the big ones, seeing Cal, UCLA, Michigan, Illinois, like that. This being just my first of the Civil War, it was the greatest win."

In the first 30 minutes, Tom Trovato and Mike Brundage, Oregon's quarterbacks, threw 13 passes between them, completing two with three interceptions. Brundage was caught trying to pass five times and was thrown for losses totaling 24 yards with about one quarter left in the game. Oregon State reverted to its prevent defense or victory defense as Andros called it. Said Andros after the victory defense almost lost the game, "I probably wouldn't call the victory defense again if I had it to do over." On a Brundage to Bunker touchdown pass which covered 50 yards, Oregon State had three men-covering Bunker. Brundage had time to throw a perfect pass. Thurman Bell, defensive back and one of the three men covering the Oregon flanker back, "Actually that was a play we hadn't seen before." Brundage threw to Ray Palm in the end zone for a second touchdown for another six points. Then came the long throw to Oldham who was somehow in the clear on the OSU 10 yard-line. Smith, however, recovered in time to race over and make his game-saving deflection.

The Webfoots ended the season with a 4-5-1 record; the first losing season for a Len Casanova-coached team since the 1961 squad went 4-6. The Beavers, meanwhile, averted a losing season by finishing 5-5.

Peter Pifer finished the afternoon with 136 yards; giving him 1,005 yards for the season, and making him fifth back in conference history to top the thousand mark in a single season.

Quarterback, Mike Brundage, passed on 13 completions in 32 attempts. He finished the afternoon with 212 yards and said he thought the interception he threw in the second quarter to Thurman Bell—who returned six yards for a touchdown—was the thing that killed us.

Chapter 7

1965 Football Banquet

At the 1965 Football Banquet, Hoffman Award went to Dave Tobey. Clark Most Improved Player went to Jerry Inman, and Tape Can Award went to Ancer Haggerty. It was a losing season; the first one since 1961. Cas said, "May you carry on as you did in last part of the last game,19-14 (L)."

The guest speaker that night was Dick Daugherty who played on the 1949 Cotton Bowl team, and then played 8 years as a linebacker with the Los Angeles Rams. He was funny, and tried make light of the season, saying, "You were 4-5-1. How would you like to be on the Rams and go 1-12. I put in a collect call to my wife and she wouldn't accept it."

"One of our Ram teammates was injured and in the hospital and was being fed intravenously through his rectum. He loved hot chocolate, and so we thought that we would surprise him with a nice hot thermos of hot chocolate. We talked the nurse into putting some

They called Him Cas

hot chocolate in his tube so he could enjoy it. So she put it in and all of a sudden the patient goes, 'Ooh, ooh!' The nurse asked, 'What's the matter? Is it too hot?' He said, 'No, no, too sweet.'"

The coaches thought it would be good to have each senior get up and say something short about their experience at Oregon. A funny thing happened. They thought everyone had spoken, and then someone asked, "What about P. K.? He hasn't spoken yet." This was, of course, P. K. Hoffman, a 5th year walk on who majored in pottery in the school of Art which was known as Potsalvania. He was funny, different, and the in-house hippy or as close as it got. His favorite line was, "Hey Bipster, how's it going?" So P. K. got up to the microphone and said something very serious: "I have been here for five years as a part of this group. It has really molded me into who I am today. As I walk out of here tonight, that will end. I will really, really miss all you guys." It was very touching. The evening ended shortly after that. For the seniors, it did end as P. K. said.

Pat Matson went on to play 10 years of pro ball with Green Bay.

Dan Archer would play in the next Super Bowl with Oakland, and for the Cincinnati Bengals. Then he went into architecture.

Tim Casey played for the Bears a few years, then went into various businesses in Portland.

Ancer Haggerty

Ancer wanted to go into pro football. Cas advised him to go into law. He was one of the most highly decorated black Marines in the Vietnam war. He received the Silver Star.

Haggerty graduated from the University of Oregon in 1967 with a BS. After service in the United States Marine Corps from 1967 to 1970, he entered Hastings College of Law of the University of California, earning a JD in 1973.

After four years in the Metropolitan Public defender's office in Portland, Oregon, Haggerty entered private practice. He served as Chief Judge of the Court from 2002 until 2009. He served as judge in Oregon Circuit Court and as Chief Justice for the United States District Court for the District of Oregon from 2002 to January 31, 2009. He was nominated by Bill Clinton. He was the first black to serve in these two capacities.

Chapter 7

Jack Clark went into the business world and wound up in Eugene running a company for several years.

Dave Tobey played eight years of Pro ball with Pittsburgh, the B.C. Lions, and Minnesota, before going into the medical parts business.

Bill Smith played with the Pittsburgh Steelers and then coached at various colleges.

Jim Kolman played with the Chicago Bears, then ran various businesses.

P. K. Hoffman became a professor of Art and Pottery at Columbia Gorge Junior College in The Dalles, Oregon.

Les Palm went on to a 30-year career in the US Marines, rose to being the Head of the Marines with a rank of General, and Director of US Marines. Les's dad, Les Sr., also played for Cas at Santa Clara College.

1966

Overall Record 3-7

Date	Home Team	Score	Visiting Team	Locations
Sat. 9/17/66	Oklahoma	0-17 (L)	Oregon	Oklahoma
Sat. 9/24/66	Oregon	14-17 (L)	Utah	Eugene
Sat. 10/1/66	Oregon	7-21 (L)	San Jose	Eugene
Sat. 10/8/66	Stanford	7-3 (W)	Portland	
Sat. 10/15/66	Air Force	17-6 (W)	Oregon	
Sat. 10/22/66	Washington	7-10 (L)	Oregon	Seattle
Sat. 10/29/66	Idaho	28-7 (W)	Oregon	Boise
Sat. 11/5/66	Oregon	13-14 (L)	Washington State	Eugene
Sat. 11/12/66	Arizona State	10-14 (L)	Oregon	Phoenix
Sat. 11/19/66	Oregon State	15-20 (L)	Oregon	Corvallis

This would be Cas' last season of coaching. He would not coach a game at Autzen Stadium. Ironically, it would open in 1967, the year after he retired. Autzen Stadium held 42,000 at the time. Cas would become athletic director.

Oregon used four different quarterbacks during the season. Unfortunately, they couldn't get it right. The quarterback had to run, pass, and handoff. Brundage and Olson could pass and Trovato and

They called Him Cas

Barnes could run but not pass. It would be a long time before that would become a reality.

Norm Chapman

1966 would see Norm Chapman return to Oregon as a coach. He would take Eddie Johns place as freshman coach. Eddie would go on to Utah and coach with Mike Giddings, his old marine buddy. Norm was excited to be back at Oregon. He was running around giving emotional put ups to guys on the defensive side of the ball. Sometimes you would almost think he made the tackle in that he was in there in the pile encouraging guys just after the play was over. At the end of two days we had a barbeque dinner out on the Freshman field. This would be produced by the freshmen and directed by Norm Chapman, their coach.

At dinner, Norm was yelling at the freshmen to go over and get ready for the show, just like a drill sergeant. Norm was really having fun and enjoying his new position.

The first sign of the show running late was when Nino Pedrini—a freshman who on one hand only had one finger from a farm accident—Nino sticks his hand out in front of the curtain and said loudly, "Hey, guys it will be just one minute!" He held his hand up with the one finger. Everyone just howled.

A few more minutes go by and Cas was sitting in the middle of several players on the floor. Cas stood up, and with anger on his face, yells at Norm Chapman: "Norm, get over here!" Norm jumped up and immediately ran over to Cas standing at attention in front of him like they were in the marines. Cas grabbed him by the shoulders and started shaking him back and forth and yelling: "I thought you were going to get this thing started on time, what's going on anyway!" Everyone was shocked. What happened? Norm was like putty in Cas's arms. You now can hear a pin drop. Everyone was shocked and confused. Then all of sudden, Cas starts laughing, with a big smile on his face, as if to say, "I sure fooled you guys." Now everyone else was laughing and talking about how shocking the whole thing was. What a fake out by Cas! Eventually the "Rookie Show" began and it was a nice way to bring in the 1966 "two a days" to a close.

Chapter 7

Loss to Oklahoma, 0-17

On September 17th, 1966, Oregon played Oklahoma in Norman. Attendance at the game was 51,100. Mike Brundage completed only five passes in 18 attempts, for 31 yards. Len Casanova said afterwards, "It was a combination of good defense and the fact that they were double covering us out there. We got beat by some bad mistakes, but the Duck defense looked better than I expected. I think we have pretty damn tough kids. They lost their poise a little bit in the third quarter, but they recovered from that. They pride themselves on how tough they are, but I don't think they out toughed us one bit."

Loss to Utah, 14-17

On September 24th, 1966, Oregon lost to Utah before a crowd of 16,500. Paramount in the minds of many Webfoot partisans on hand in Eugene, was the post-game question: If the Ducks can't beat Utah, whom can they beat?

Brundage started the second half, but after two series in which the Ducks couldn't make a first down, Trovato got the call again. Then Brundage returned late in the final quarter, and Eric Olson also made a brief appearance.

Mike Giddings, was the enthusiastic former head assistant to John McKay at USC, whose Utah team had just made his head-coaching debut successful. He thought highly of what his Utes had done because he thought a lot of Oregon, and believed they had a good team. Mike Giddings would eventually get fired a few years later, and become the linebacker coach of the San Francisco 49ers. He would coach Dave Wilcox for several years and would be the speaker Dave chose to induct him into the NFL Hall of Fame.

Mike Giddings was always a great analyzer and tendency guy. He had cards for the upcoming team's favorite plays in practice. At half time he would literally put on the chalk board all the plays run by the opponent the first half. He was a very efficient and good assistant coach. While at USC, there was a game where the defense was not doing well, and at halftime Mike just ranted and raved, and was livid at how poorly the defense was performing. Because of Giddings' outcry, his assistant couldn't put the plays on the chalk

They called Him Cas

board. Giddings asked the assistant for the card with all the plays on it. Giddings looked at it and then says to his assistant, "Yeah, they're just beating the hell out of us."Dave Levy Assistant coach USC

Loss to San Jose State, 7-21

On October 1st, 1966, Oregon played San Jose State, in Eugene, in front of 16,000 fans. Some of the San Jose players said after defeating the Ducks, 21-7: "They are the toughest team we've played this year." Tom Keele, assistant coach for San Jose State, was a member of the 1958 Rose Bowl team, and co-captain of the 1959 Ducks. Danny Holman connected on 18 of the 22 passes for 252 yards in the second half.

With sophomore quarterback Mike Barnes at the helm, they were moving the football over the field. They ended up with 353 yards in total offense, identical to San Jose State. Eric Olson completed three out of five passes on a drive to San Jose State for two rushing plays.

It was San Jose State with the upset at 24-0. Danny was invited to participate in the East-West Shrine Game. The 6', 200-pounder was known as the splendid splinter and was the national passing leader

Win Over Stanford, 7-3

Oregon bussed up to Portland the night before the game. The normal routine was to have dinner, have meetings, and watch a movie. For some reason, the projector didn't work, so no movie. The coaches adlibbed. Max Coley got up and asked, "How many of you have been in a street fight?" I looked around and saw a fair amount of hands go up. He then said, "The key to street fighting, as you know, is you've got to keep moving forward. That will be the key to the game tomorrow. It's going to be just like a street fight. You've got to keep moving forward and attack." Everyone became quite serious, and I was shocked because I'd never been close to anything like that. Cas said a few things. It was serious, quiet, and we knew we had a war to fight the next day. Just before we went out to the field, Cas said he would like to say a prayer in his mother's native Swiss language; a prayer she said every day before he went to school. Something like, "May God protect you and guide you in all ways."

Sophomore, Gene Washington, was quarterback. He eventually played wide receiver for the 49ers, and became John Brodie's favorite target for years. The Ducks came out as winners that day. After losing three in a row, learning about street fighting, and saying a prayer, we won a big game, 7-3.

Win Over Air Force, 17-6

At 6,200 feet in elevation, you can lose your breath easily in Colorado Springs. We matched up equally with Air Force, and things went well. To put icing on the cake, Kenny Klein intercepted a pass and ran it back for a touchdown. Everyone wanted to hug him and grab him. He pushed us away because he needed to get air after a long run and the high elevation.

Loss to Washington, 7-10

We held Washington to 10 points, but our offense couldn't score again. I remember having a nice block on a punt return, knocking the guy down, and being underneath him. He got up to run off the field, and his first two steps were on my legs. Welcome to Seattle, and button your chin strap. This game could have easily been a win.

Win Over Idaho, 28-7

We played Idaho in Boise. Ray McDonald was still their fullback and he was good. Somehow, our offense went well. Claxton Welch, a sophomore back who went on to pro ball and two Super Bowls with Dallas, was getting more time, and had a good game. Claxton came from David Douglas in Portland. He had three good years with Oregon.

They called Him Cas

Loss to Washington State, 13-14

This was our Homecoming game, and it was rainy, wet, and soggy on the field. I remember the first time on defense when the WSU offensive line was coached to grab each lineman and throw him down on the field to shock him. The center did that to me, and it was never called. Burt Clark, another guy from Oklahoma, was head coach. At the end of the game, Mike Barnes, quarterback, lost count of downs. We were on the three-yard line ready to score and go ahead. He looked over and thought it was third down. The referee then changed it to fourth down as Mike turned away. He took the ball and spiked it to stop the clock. We lost the ball on downs and the game was over. With one less mistake we could have won.

Loss to Arizona State, 10-14

A night game in Tempe. Again, a close loss with little offense. Defense did well, but offense was inept again.

Loss to Oregon State, 15-20

Dee Andros inherited many good players from Tommy Prothro two years earlier. Most were still on the team; big linemen and fastbacks. Rockne Freitas, 6'7, 270-pound center, went on to play several years for the Detroit Lions. Paul Brothers, Pete Pifer, and Bobby Grim all went on to play pro ball. Bobby Grim became a Minnesota Viking and receiver for Bob Berry. OSU had the unstoppable fullback option offense with some passes here and there; a similar offense to Ohio State. With the score at 20-8, Harry Cartales intercepted a pass with only seconds left in the game. He ran with it and then he had the wherewithal to pitch it out to Jimmy Smith next to him on the outside. Jimmy ran about 60 yards for the touchdown. That made the score seem closer than it really was.

The Ducks' offense was only able to make a touchdown. Pete Pifer told me later that he watched Andros on the interception. Dee wouldn't be caught dead without a big full package of Beechnut chew in his mouth on the sideline. As Jimmy was at midfield, Dee was

Chapter 7

pretty unemotional. As Jimmy was breaking away from everyone, Dee turned toward him and was walking down the sideline. He was yelling because he saw Jimmy was going all the way for a touchdown, and untouched. Dee went crazy yelling and was very upset. He turned around to come back to midfield with his head down. Pete said that the outside of his pudgy face was filled with strands of Beechnut tobacco and spit. Lesson: Don't yell uncontrollably with Beechnut in your mouth.

    Denny Schuler would go on and coach over 30 years of college ball throughout the west coast, and have a long, successful job as defensive coordinator at Oregon under Rich Brooks. He also coached for the Rams.

    Gunther Cunningham has coached over 30 years in the NFL. Mostly as a fine defensive coordinator.

    Terry Shea became Head Coach at San Jose and Rutgers and held several offensive coordinator jobs in the NFL.

    Scott Cress, Nino Pedrini and Jim Nicolaisen all went on to become successful businessmen.

    Roger Stahlhut became a successful coach and pastor in Southern California.

    Here are four coaches who played at Oklahoma at the same time, and, ironically, three of them wound up in the Pac-8 Conference for several years:

Position   W-L Record as Coach

Darrell Royal, Oklahoma, played 1946-1949 at quarterback: 184-60-5
Jim Owens, Oklahoma, played 1946-1949 at end: 99-82-6
Dee Andros, Oklahoma, played 1946-1949 at guard: 62-80-2
Bert Clark, Oklahoma, played 1949-1951 at center: 15-24-1
Bear Bryant, Kentucky, Texas A&M, and Alabama: 323-85-17
Woody Hayes, Denison, Miami of Ohio, and Ohio State: 238-72-10
Len Casanova: 104-94-11

    Reaching the milestone of winning 100 games in Cas's era was quite an elite list: The top two percent of coaches. There were some super coaches that far exceeded 100. They were few and far between and had elite programs which were few and far between. That Cas was able to surpass the 100 mark while at Santa Clara and

They called Him Cas

Oregon says a lot; both for enduring in the program, and being able to recruit talent successfully over the years.

In 1967, a new priest, Father Labelle, showed up at the Newman Center. By now, the Newman Center had a new location and church building. It was in great part because of Cas and Margaret's efforts and financial support that this became a reality. Father Labelle was a large man. I would say, 6'0," 275-pounds. After his first Mass in the Newman Center, it came time for the collection plate to be passed. Cas came to the front with the plate. He was chastising the parishioners about how small the offering was and said, "We are going to pass the plate once more. Now let's give." He dropped the plate off to the front row again, then walked by father Labelle. He looked at him up and down and said, "Besides, we've got to feed this guy." Over the next several years Father Labelle endeared himself to many people—Catholics and non-Catholics—at the University of Oregon. He had a wonderful way about him. It was just hard not to love the guy. Margaret and Cas loved him and became very close to him. I eventually became the cook for a time for the three priests at the Newman center. What a wonderful experience and learning time that was. It was all because of Father Labelle. Many students had Father Labelle do their marriage ceramonies.

"It is a testament to Cas, he made something great with limited resources. In those years, the state population was less than two million. With a small budget and poor facilities, very little money was available to do recruiting. In terms of resources, it was the exact opposite of the financial largesse and support of top programs today. But we still gained a great deal of acclaim and won games because of who Cas was; because of the assistants he hired, and players we were able to recruit and coach. It was a real tribute to how he managed the job." Norm Chapman

"On Ash Wednesday, if Cas saw a Catholic player without ashes on his forehead, he would tell them to go to the Newman Center. I can remember, he grabbed two players. He parked right outside the athletic department. He told the players, 'Get in my car,' and he took them over. He was very devout in his beliefs," said John Marshall.

"More than that I think Cas lived integrity. He did that because he felt it was the right thing. He had a football coach's mentality, but what he did, he had an integrity mentality. What is the right thing to

Chapter 7

do? That's what we're going to do. My wife and I happened to be neighbors of Cas and Margaret. And so I think that's where Cas' and my relationship got a lot closer. Cas wanted to build a garden. He said, 'I need help,' and I helped him with rototilling, etc. He asked, 'What do you want in the garden?' So we planted tomatoes, corn, beans, and bell peppers. Cas said, 'I don't like bell peppers.' Again he said, 'I don't like bell peppers.' I told him that I would plant them outside of the garden. Then when he would water, he wouldn't water the bell peppers. I would go by to check the growth and the watering that Cas was responsible for, and everything was OK except the bell peppers weren't being watered by him; and they were wilted and dried out. I mentioned that to him and all he said was, 'I don't like bell peppers.' That was going to be Cas's way. I watered my bell peppers.

But the most impressive thing about Cas was how he stuck to what was right and what was wrong. You know, his integrity is what I took from Cas."John Marshall

In the winter of 1967, George Siefert came in as freshman coach and defensive line coach. Just after Cas had resigned, he came from Utah. There is a story that the assistant coaches got together and thought it would be nice to all go out on a boat, on the McKenzie, and go fishing on a Saturday, put the boat in. It was just raining cats and dogs, and they all got into one car to talk about their next move and possibly call a rain check. George gets in the back seat of the car last, rubs his hands together with excitement and says, "Guys, isn't this just great!" This shows how much George loves fishing. Every morning, I wouldn't doubt that he says that every time that he goes out fishing rain or shine. George is a real lover of fishing, has been for years.

Cas was athletic director until 1970, when he retired at age 65. Then he became the greatest fundraiser the Oregon Athletic Department had ever seen. He continued to be Ambassador for the University until his death in 2000. He and Margaret went on every road trip with the team until he was 94. He continued to reconnect with old players and friends on these occasions.

They called Him Cas

John Robinson, Ron Stratton, Jerry Frei, George Seifert
Jack Roche, Ed Johns, Norm Chapman John Marshall, Bruce Snyder
Jerry Frei, Head Coach at Oregon, 1967-1972

Record at Oregon
1967, 2-8
1968, 4-6
1969, 5-5-1
1970, 6-4-1
1971, 5-6

After the 1971 season, Jerry Frei was asked to let his assistant coaches go. Jerry refused and instead, resigned. Jerry and most of the assistants stayed in football and found other jobs. It is absolutely awe-inspiring to see the list of names; where they went and what they did in the coaching ranks.

"Jerry Frei came in after Cas. It was the toughest time for all of us, social unrest, etc. If you are radical, then you wanted to go to Cal. But there were a few less radical and they sent you to Oregon. We had a lot of tough, radical people out there. Jerry had to coach in that environment, fighting through almost every social unrest situation. Jerry Frei was a great, great man." John Robinson

It would be eight years before Oregon would have a winning season, and 18 years before they would go to another bowl game.

Chapter 7

Where They Went

- Jerry Frei: Assistant Coach, NFL, 1982-1982, Scout, 1983-2001
- John Robinson: Head Coach, USC, LA Rams (NFL)
- George Seifert: Head Coach, San Francisco 49ers, Assistant Coach & Head Coach. Won 5 Super Bowl Championships
- Gunther Cunningham: Head Coach, KC Chiefs (NFL). Has Coached in NFL since 1981. Many assistant coaching jobs for 33 years
- Bruce Snyder: Head Coach Cal and ASU
- John Marshall: Assistant Coach for 32 years (NFL)
- Terry Shea: Head Coach, college: San Jose State, and Rutgers Assistant Coach, NFL - Several teams
- Ron Stratten: Head Coach at Portland State. First black as head coach of a major college, worked several years for NCAA
- Eddie Johns: Assistant, high school team, and private business
- Norm Chapman: Private business
- Phil McHugh: Went on to become a successful building contractor in Portland
- Jack Roche: Retired after 1971 season, and 30 years of coaching
- Denny Schuler: 1969-70, graduate assistant

Thirty years of college coaching, including Defensive Coordinator for U of O, eight years at other colleges including Stanford, Cal, OSU, Utah and, in 1985, the Rams

Bruce Snyder: Head Coach: ASU, Cal, Utah State. Assistant Coach:USC, LA Rams

Other College & Pro Coaches

Tom Keele: Cal, several other pro and college jobs
Dick Arbuckle: ASU, Cal, Oregon, OIT and various high schools

They called Him Cas

Bill Smith: Northern Arizona University, Utah, University of Montana, Weber State, Portland State

Players that went on to business careers

Jimmy Jones, Don Sloan, Dick Stoutt, Fitz Brewer, Phil McHugh, Bruce Brenn, Larry Hill, Duane Cargill, Rich Schwab, Les Palm, Dr. Ron Jones, Dave Tobey, Dick Winn, Mark Richards, Jack Clark, Ancer Haggarty, Tim Casey, Dr. Eric Olson, Jim Smith, Claxton Welch, Roger Smith

Cas had many players go on to pro football, but had two players receive pro football's highest honor of being inducted into the NFL Hall of Fame. Ironically, both players played the very same years at Oregon together; highly unusual.

It was 1959, and Seaside High was playing Vale High for the A-2 State Football Championship. P. K. Hoffman was star halfback for Seaside. P.K. said, "I saw the Vale team trotting out onto the field in a straight line from behind the stadium, and all of a sudden, here's the last guy. He looked like a frigging giant. He looked seven-feet tall compared to the rest. I thought to myself, 'Oh no!' During the game, he played on the line and just annihilated guys. He also would line up in the backfield and run with the ball. What a scary guy to tackle. Somehow we eked out a win that day in the closing seconds, 28-21. That was my first exposure to Dave Wilcox, a true giant." Dave and P.K. would both find their way to Oregon.

Dave was born in Ontario, Oregon and graduated from Vail high School in 1960. He played two years of college football at Boise Junior College, now Boise State University. He transferred to the University of Oregon, in Eugene, in 1962, for his final two seasons.

Both the Houston Oilers of the AFL and the San Francisco 49ers of the NFL sought to sign Dave. Wilcox opted to sign with the more established 49ers where he went on to play for 11 seasons. Converted to outside linebacker, Wilcox, nicknamed The Intimidator, quickly established himself as the league's finest linebacker. He was ideally suited for the position both mentally and physically. Known for his ability to disrupt plays, he was particularly tough on tight ends. He did not let anybody easily off the line of scrimmage, and was there to block or get into a pass route. He was always prepared, and was a true student of the game. He worked to be fundamentally correct and made almost no errors in his play.

Following each season, San Francisco would rate their players based on their performance. The typical score for linebacker was 750. Wilcox's score in 1973 was 1,000. That season, the veteran linebacker recorded 104 solo tackles for forced fumbles, and tackled opposing ball carriers for a loss 13 times. Durable Wilcox missed only one game due to injury during his career. Four times he was named All-NFL (67, 71, 72, and 73) by VAP, and two times, All-NFC (71, and 72). He was also selected to play in seven Pro Bowls. Dave was inducted into the NFL Hall of Fame in 2000.

They called Him Cas

Mel Renfro

    Mel was born on December 30, 1941 in Houston, Texas. Mel went to Jefferson High School in Portland. Jefferson won the state championship in football Mel's junior year. Mel was quarterback his senior year, and lost in the finals to Medford High, 7-0. Lowell Dean of Medford made a block on a punt return that took out three players and Ken Durkee of Medford was able to run 70 yards for a touchdown. It was the only score of the game. Both Mel and Lowell would go on to Oregon. Mel excelled as a track star and a two-way football player; an All-American halfback and defensive back. In his three seasons with the Ducks, Renfro rushed for 1,532 yards, and scored 141 points.

    In 1986, Renfro was enshrined in the College Football Hall of Fame. He is a member of The Pigskin Club of Washington, D.C., a National Intercollegiate All-American Football Players Honor Roll. As a track star at Oregon, Renfro was part of a world record-setting 440-yard relay team in 1962, with a time of 40 seconds.

    Renfro was drafted by the Cowboys in the second round of the 1964 NFL Draft. He was initially placed as a safety, but was switched to cornerback in his fifth season. The speedy Renfro became an exceptional threat to wide receivers. Mel led the NFL with 10 interceptions in 1969. Renfro was selected to the Pro Bowl in each of his first ten seasons in the League, including five All-Pro selections in 1964, 1965, 1969, 1971, and 1973. Mel also was a significant threat on special teams, performing punt and kickoff return duties, in addition to playing on defense, leading the league in punt and kickoff return yardage in 1964.

In his fourteen seasons, Renfro intercepted 52 passes, returning them for 626 yards and three touchdowns. He also returned 109 punts for 842 yards and one touchdown, 85 kickoffs for 2,246 yards, and two touchdowns, along with recording 13 fumble recoveries, which he returned for 44 yards. In the 1970 NFC title game, Renfro had a key interception. It led to the Cowboys' game-winning touchdown over the San Francisco 49ers and helped them get to Super Bowl V, where they lost to the Baltimore Colts. He played in Super Bowls VI, X and XII, retiring after the final one, a Cowboys victory over the Denver Broncos.

Renfro was added to the Texas Stadium Ring of Honor in 1981, and was elected to the Pro Football Hall of Fame in 1996.

Source: Wikipedia

College Football Hall of Fame coaches from Oregon

Len Cassanova inducted in 1977   104-94-11
John McKay inducted in 1988   171-128-9
John Robinson inducted in 2009   211-151-4

Herb Yamanaka

"I worked with Cas when he was a coach first, and he became athletic director when Leo Harris retired. And then, five years later, he was in major gift fundraising. I worked with him under all three different jobs. Throughout his career, he taught us the fundamentals of life and that was where he said the four primary things in life are your health, family, friends, and a love for the Lord. Everything else is secondary, and how true it is.

When I first started working for Cas, he said your primary job is to take care of the student athletes, the coaches, and the donors. Sixty years later, I'm taking care of the student athletes, the coaches, and the donors. I'm loving it and they loved me. So these are gospel truths. He always said life is not a bowl of cherries, each meal is not a banquet, and the body can stand a lot of punishment. That was really true. He taught you the fundamentals of life and how to respect your elders and bring honor to the University and to your family. Everybody looked up to Cas. He was a wonderful, wonderful, person and a great, great, teacher. Even after players got through school, he remembered them when they had kids. Kids graduate, he always wrote letters to them. He wrote it in long hand. He didn't type it, he wrote it. He had great penmanship."Herbie Yamanaka

We went to see John Jaqua one day. John was one of the most prominent attorneys in Eugene, and helped Nike in legal matters. He became a prominent stockholder in Nike as a result. We got to the front desk of his law office, and the secretary asked, 'What can I do for you?' and he said, 'Tell John that Len Casanova and Herbie Yamanaka are here to see him.' So she called him and he said, 'Okay, I'll be out in a minute.' He came out with a check for $5,000. He said, 'Okay, Cas, I know why you're here. Here's a check for $5,000.' Cas looks at the check, he tears it in half and says, John we came for $10,000. So John walked back and wrote a check for $10,000 and gave it to Cas. If I would have tried that on my own, I would have gotten thrown out of the office, but not Cas.

Cas wanted to smoke a cigarette. We were at the Eugene Country Club. Cas said, 'Let's sit over here,' and I said, 'Cas, I don't know these people.' He goes over there and says, 'Hi Bob. What are you smoking today?' Bob says, 'Lucky Strikes,' and he said, 'Give me two or three.' He just walked up and bumbed some cigarettes off these guys.

Cas was having lunch at the Country Club with other friends and they were talking about some athlete signing for a multimillion dollar contract in the NFL. Cas said that it was outrageous. 'As head football coach at the University of Oregon, the most I earned in one year was $25,000.' Meredith Wilson, the retired University of Oregon President, said, 'Cas, I don't feel sorry for you, because at the University, the highest salary I made was $23,000.' Herbie Yamanaka

Paying Off the Mortgage to Cas's Home

Dave Wilcox, Norm Chapman, Dick Winn and all the rest, gathered the athletes who played for Cas, and had them make contributions. They presented that amount of money to Cas to pay off his mortgage, and there was enough left over so that he and Margaret could take a trip to Switzerland and Austria to visit the homeland of his parents and grandparents. Cas wrote a note to Tom Keele when he was having a beer at Hitler's Eagle's Nest in the Alps. He said, "Tom, I think that beer that you had at Maxi's tasted better than the one I had at Eagle's Nest."

Cas had a life insurance policy on the mortgage that when he died, the house would get paid off by the insurance. So they put the cash in a trust fund to draw interest, and they used the interest to pay off the mortgage insurance policy each month. When Cas died, the house was paid off and Margaret still had the corpus of the endowment. The good part is Margaret Casanova was able to live in a retirement home for the rest of her life, and all these guys helped her by paying for her living expenses also.

"I was head coach at USC, and we were going to play Notre Dame back in Notre Dame. I invited Cas and his wife, Margaret, down to LA and they went on the team plane with us. We went back to South Bend and it was a big time game. We were both in the top five, we played great and won. We got on the plane to come home and everybody's sitting there happy and talking, and Cas came up to me, sat alongside me. I thought he was going to say something great. But he said, now Robbie you know you have a tendency to get really cocky when things go good for you. Now I don't want you to get all puffed up. So here he is giving me a lecture on the plane after a big win. John Robinson

"Different guys would call Cas unexpectedly all the time. For instance, Bear Bryant would call Cas. He wanted talk about the timber, because we had timber out here. How's the lumber market? They were back and forth, and Bear Bryant was that kind of guy. But anyhow, he had that friendship with all the well-known coaches of his era." Norv Ritchey

They called Him Cas

Gofub-A Golf Outing at Black Butte

Rich Schwab, Dave Wilcox, Doug Post, Daryl Aschbacher, Norm Chapman, Jack Crabtree, and Mike Corno started Gofub:"Golf, Have Fun at Black Butte." It started with these guys bidding and winning a fishing trip to Central Oregon at a Duck fundraiser in 1987, in Eugene. They had such a good time they decided to do something similar. Over time, it evolved to the location of Black Butte. A few guys owned cabins there and you could play golf. Mike Corno, ex-restaurateur, made delicious meals. It seemed to grow each year as other ex-teammates were added in.

About the second or third year of the gathering, Cas was invited. It was inspired by guys loving each other, loving the memories of playing together, and loving to be coached by Cas. Cas enjoyed it and became an integral part of it. He went to almost every one from then on. We all wanted to be on Cas's golf team because he would always hit it right down the middle. It would go about 125 or 130 yards, but always down the middle. When we played a scramble, we usually ended up using Cas's shot. We all wanted to play with Cas. Dave Tobey

It was just really fun to be able to be in his foursome. Schwab and Wilcox improvised and moved Cas around so he would get to play with everyone at some point over the two-day period. Over the course of three or four years, almost everybody got to golf with him.

Chapter 7

You always remember that time you golfed with Cas. I have a picture of Cas on my desk. I think the year was 1998.

Not too long after that, the old assistant coaches were invited to come also: Jack Roche, Phil Mc Hugh, Bruce Snyder, John Robinson, and Eddie Johns. This was a very important time for all these guys. They got to see other former teammates and other players they coached. A funny memory: Phil still smoked and Cas would see Phil and Cas from his golf cart would say, "Phil, give me a cigarette."Cas was in pig heaven and he knew who to bum cigarettes from. At every turn were some of his greatest students of the game of football, and wonderful people in life. He could smoke whenever he wanted, not like at home.

At different times, sitting around talking about different ex-players after dinner, Cas would tear up. He would talk about things that meant a lot to him; some things he never shared before because perhaps it wasn't appropriate in a player-coach situation. It was a special time.

The players who were invited were from the three bowl teams that Cas coached. Eventually, the group invited other ex-players from various years Cas coached. As the years went by, the food was great, the golf was good, and the fellowship was special.

There were a lot of funny things that happened at Gofub. Craziness, like going to bars in Sisters, and confessing to Cas in the morning. Cas always brought his Bible and would never miss his daily study. He gave funny talks and would always be reminiscing about old memories.

The Rose Bowl group stayed together and, inevitably, opened up old year books and looked at different pictures, reminiscing about a game. We would always go to dinner at the big house. The dinners were top notch. Every year they were cooked by the Corno brothers.

All came to Oregon from different cities, different walks of life. Some were rich, some poor, some refined, some rough around the edges. All were expected to be molded into a great team in Eugene at the U of O; to live in the rain, to call it home. Cas was an expert at bringing guys in from all over the west coast and having them stay around. These men had pressure on them and so they came back to Gofub to reconnect and relive some important memories in their lives. They wanted to see old friends they normally did not get to see.

They called Him Cas

Long ago it was a pressure cooker, today it was releasing some of that pressure, and it was emotionally healthy and fun. They all wanted to see Cas.

It started in 1988 and went 28 years. It grew from eight to 35 guys. There were many fond memories. One of the Gofubbers told me, "Every year I come here, I am reminded of what I did. I cherish the fond memories, I interact with some great old friends, and this just helps me define who I really am and where am I going in life, as time marches on."

"He was obviously an outstanding football coach. And in my three years as a varsity player at Oregon State—my first game was a 14-14 tie—and then we were able to win the second one and the third one, and the third one being whichever team won went to the Liberty Bowl in 1962. And Oregon was favored, but we were able to eek out a win when we came back in the second half. That's the Mel Renfro team. And Cas was obviously an outstanding coach and had great success at Oregon before the onslaught of basically unlimited scholarships and players going one way instead of both ways. And then the facilities boom when Oregon and Oregon State both got left in the wake, because they didn't invest enough money in their football program.

Well, Cas was Athletic Director Emeritus, but he was in the office basically every day, he went on every football trip for my 18 years.

So he was just a tremendous sounding board for me and was the first one when things weren't going well, to come in and tell me to keep my head up, and keep plowing forward. He'd been down the road many times, and certainly was a good person to discuss problems with, and things like that, where he could help give you some advice.

Cas always reminded me that they hung him in effigy, and later the next year they went to the Rose Bowl. And, basically, the same thing happened to me, almost, when they were selling Ditch Rich bumper stickers in the parking lot before we beat Iowa at home in 1994, and ended up going to the Rose Bowl that year, and winning the conference championship. So Cas has a perspective on the good and on the bad, and was probably one of the best coaches that I have ever been around. About staying in touch with former players, and the admiration that former players that played for him, and

Chapter 7

coaches that coached with him, just was unbelievable how much they respected him.

Oh, he never quit smoking. he'd always hide when Margaret was around. He'd sneak out and we'd be at different booster functions, and if Margaret was there, he would sneak out and take a quick smoke and get back in like she could never smell it on him, you know what I mean? He wasn't really fooling her very much, but he didn't want to do it right in front of her anyway, and he would do that all the time. And he was really active in fundraising. And I can remember going up and visiting several big donors in Portland with him in tow and asking for money and having them tell me as we kind of finished up, and Cas was walking out and pulling me aside, and said, nobody can ever say no to Cas.

I mean, I just had a lot of great times with him, and different fundraisers and different events, and associating with him for 18 years was just an honor and a pleasure to have been around a person of that magnitude and quality. He was always so humble, and when it was getting near the end, it was always pretty sad because he kept saying to all of his friends and his associates and people that he'd grown up with, basically were all gone. And, of course, he lived to be 97, and it was just a remarkable life." Rich Brooks Head Coach (1977-1994)

Naming the Casanova Center

Apparently, the Center had to have the Oregon State government pass a bill to be named, "Casanova Center." Cas made the comment frustratingly to his daughter Margot, "I don't know why they have to go through so much to name a building after someone who they won't know who the hell he was in a few years."

"On a birthday, 90 something, I picked him up at home and I drove him down to the barbershop. And he was getting elderly. There was a lady barber and I paid her beforehand. So he gets out of his chair for his haircut. She says, 'Mr. Casanova are you over 90?' He says, 'Yes I am.' And she said, 'Well, the haircut is free.' He said, 'Boy, I like that lady. I'm going to come back the next time to her.'"Herbie Yamanaka

Free Chowder

"I took him over to the country club one Friday afternoon and he said, 'I will have a cup of clam chowder.' I had already tipped the waitress when he asked, 'Ma'am, how much do I owe you for the cup of clam chowder?' She asked, "Are you over 90?" He said, "Yes, I am." She said, "Well then, the cup of chowder is free. He said, 'Then I'll have another one.'"Herbie Yamanaka

"Because he was well liked by coaches all over the United States, I'd go to the coach's conventions with him, and they all loved him. He knew them all. You'd think that he was right in there with them, coaches like Bear Bryant and Woody Hayes. They were all good friends of his. But everybody liked him and were always interested in him. He was always a good speaker and was President of the National Football Coaches Association and had all those honors. And it wasn't all his winning seasons, he was just the person that he was. We just had a wonderful life together. I just loved it. Loved everything about it.

He was so good at wanting to look up people when he went through a town. That was one of the reasons people liked him so much. He didn't forget them. He would say, 'Well I'm going to look up so and so.' Someone he had known years before. He was so interested in people from the past, and wanted to keep up with them. Most people don't take the time to do those little extra things that he did. That meant a lot to people.

I grew up in Idaho, just across the Snake River from Ontario. Every time we'd go visit my relatives in Idaho, we would have to stop in Vale, Oregon and see the Wilcoxes and the Schaffelds, the parents of Dave and John Wilcox, and Joe Schaffeld.

Cas was always a part of the 24-hour prayer chain and it was during the night, sometimes. But he would be there. Those kinds of things meant so much to him. He was just a very devout person. But you wouldn't really know it just to know him.

His religion was the most important thing in his life. Whether people knew that or not. I guess maybe his girls and his wife did. And I had, of course, never been around anybody so devout, and it was a good thing for me too. I was raised a Protestant and I had to become a Catholic to marry him, which I was happy to do. It didn't

Chapter 7

make any difference to me. And so I was just amazed that anybody was that devout, and to see how much it did mean to him.

He visited sick people in the hospital, whether he knew them or not. He just took it upon himself. He was a great one to go to the hospital. He might have been up there to see somebody he knew and just dropped in on some he didn't know.

Darrel Aschbacher told me that early in the football season he would ask how many players went to church? He would say, 'I want you to go to church. I don't care what church you go to, but I want you to go to church. And if you're a Catholic I will see you in church.' He said that, after a while, people wouldn't tell him if they were Catholic because they didn't want him telling them that they missed church." Margaret Casanova

Len and Margaret went to every football game, whether home or away, until Cas was 94. He went to his office until he was 96. Bill Moos jokingly said, "Cas, I haven't seen you around the office, I'll have to give you a pink slip." Cas flashed a smile and said, "I've got tenure." At his 96th birthday party, held appropriately at the Casanova Center, Herb Yamanaka handed him a beverage. The response was classic Cas: "We usually give him apple juice," Yamanaka had said. "For his birthday, we filled his cup with Jack Daniels." He tasted the drink and blinks his eyes and said, "What was that? Jack Daniels?" Then he handed the cup to Herb and said, "I'll have another."

Cas had spent a half-century of his life at Oregon. When he started there, the Korean War was going on, and the President was Harry Truman. He put U of O football on the map, and went to three bowl games. His record at Oregon was 82-73-8 in 16 seasons, from 1951-1966.

One of my last encounters with Cas happened on a golf course, approaching the 18th hole. It was a special day, because Bucky Wilcox had driven 97-year-old Cas up to Black Butte that morning. Dave Wilcox was driving a golf cart with Cas as his passenger. I will never forget this ironical sight: Dave, the greatest lineman Cas had ever coached, an NFL Hall of famer, with a big smile and cigar in his mouth. Next to him, Cas just barely hanging onto a cigarette stub with two weak fingers. A picture of health for two great athletes.

Later that day, Bruce Snyder, who had played and coached for Cas then became head coach at Cal and Arizona State University,

They called Him Cas

would drive Cas home in the early afternoon. It was like any other Gofub where everyone wanted to see Cas and be around him. It was amazing how he remembered everyone's name. Bruce drove Cas home and the trip was smooth and uneventful. Cas even took a nap. They arrived in Springfield and as they went over some train tracks, Cas woke up. He made what Bruce thought was a garbled comment about "Third Street." Bruce said, "Oh yes, we just crossed Third Street, that's right." Then Cas said, "No, I said Turd Street! You see my mother grew up in Switzerland and she could never pronounce the 'TH' properly. There was another silence and then Cas said, "I was sure glad when I got out of the Turd grade."

"One day I went over and I said, 'Cas, I won't be over at dinner time because I'm going to be at my retirement dinner.' He said, 'Herb, you made me a promise that you would be here when I died.' I said, 'Cas I'm going to come right back. I will be here tomorrow morning.' He said, 'You can't quit. You made me a promise.' I said, 'tomorrow morning.' So I had my retirement dinner, I came back, and he died that night. At the funeral service, Cas's family presented me with the 1958 Rose Bowl ring, the coach's ring. It was a ring for seven years. And seven years later, an astronaut from Sheldon High School, who was a colonel in United States Air Force, was going into space, and he wanted to take something to commemorate the University of Oregon. His grandfather was Chuck Harvey, who knew Cas, so I gave him the Rose Bowl ring. He took it into outer space and brought it back and presented it to Margaret and me at a football game the next year. That ring will be put as memorabilia here in Cas's showcase. They're making a duplicate to put in the new football building." Herbie Yamanaka

Much of what the University of Oregon football program is today, it owes to Len Casanova. From 1951-2002, he was a pillar of strength. He modeled respect, dignity, and integrity for more than 50 years, and his influence continues to this day. Bill Moos

"Cas was the glue that held things together." Ron Stratten.

"He was a mentor to all of us. A man who set an example, and he loved us. He genuinely cared about us as players. He would get on our butt if we didn't go to church, and if you didn't go to school he would darn near punch you out." John Robinson

My Life Timeline

1958

I was in the 4th grade and I attended the high school football banquet in Medford, Oregon

1963

I watched the Idaho-Oregon game in person as a senior at Medford High School. It was the first in-person college game I had ever seen. I was a 165-pound linebacker and had only started the second half of the season. I was taken by Tim Casey as a linebacker. He weighed 195 pounds. My goal from there on was to weigh 195 pounds by next fall as a freshman at Oregon. I felt then I could at least turn out for the freshman team at Oregon at that size.

1964

I came to Eugene in the fall and registered for my classes at Oregon. Then I went out for freshman football with everyone else. There were about 30 guys on scholarship and 30 "walk-ons." The head coach was Eddie Johns. His assistants or graduate assistants were Rich Schwab, Larry Horyna, Larry Hill, Ron Stratten, and Paul Burlsen. Suddenly, I learned unless I really stuck out, I was not going to make it as a "walk on." I did weigh 195 pounds.

We would continually have physical blocking and tackling drills much more than high school. Unknowingly, I gained a lot of experience in hardcore hitting on both offense and defense, thanks to Eddie Johns, Larry Horyna, and Ron Stratten. At first, I absolutely hated it, but it paid off later. One time, I had a good week and outhit everyone. I assumed I would be rewarded by making the game road trip to Seattle, but did not. Ron Stratten went out of his way to talk to me. He said if I waited until spring ball I would get my chance. That moment with Ron was the highlight of my freshman season.

I went on academic probation with a GPA of 1.78. We were not wealthy people. My dad was taking a loan out to finance my education. In winter quarter I was determined to get my grades up and got a 3.00. On spring break I went to a Christian conference in Southern California. I gained a deeper appreciation of the love God has for me, personally, and how He died for me. I made a personal commitment to follow Jesus. It was out of His love for me that he gave His life. Incredible.

1965

Spring term, I went back to Oregon and faced going out for spring ball. I prayed to God, and said if He wanted me to play football, I would know by making the team, though it seemed like a long shot with little hope. I said, "I give this to you, God." At that point it was the last stop.

I went out for spring ball. All I knew how to do was hustle, so that's what I did. I was about 200 pounds from lifting weights and running. I had learned great fundamentals in freshmen ball from some great Oregon linemen. There were a ton of guys out there. I handled the drills pretty well and continued to hustle. I got into a few scrimmages. Coach Casanova said something at the end of the last practice about, "these guys go to the right" and "those guys go to the left." Then I will never forget that Jack Roche singled me out and said, "You know you are going left. Do not go to the right. Again, do not go right." So I went left, and it was the greatest left I ever took.

A few coaches were huddled around me, and Roger Smith saying they wanted us to come back for fall ball. I couldn't believe it. I was being invited to be on the Oregon varsity team for next fall. Roger Smith from Yankton, South Dakota, and I, were the two walk-on freshmen invited back. Roger went on to be a starting halfback on offense. He had a good career at Oregon.

1965

The next fall came, and I continued to work out, getting up to 210 pounds. I lifted more weights and ran, and worked in a lumber mill during the summer. Early on, Cas met with most of the sophomores, except one or two, and told us we were going to be red shirted. This meant we would practice with the team, but not play in games, and not lose a year of eligibility. A lot of guys took this as a big insult. Some quit. For some reason, I took it as a time to amp up and improve myself. I would play on the defensive line, and mimic the

My Life Timeline

opponent's defense for that particular week. We were helping prepare the offensive line for their next opponent.

Bruce Snyder was my coach. From that very first week of red shirting I would give my all on every play to prepare the players for their next opponent. They got mad at me, but they couldn't stop me. Each week my game was the four days of playing the opposing team's defense. During the season, at different points, each coach personally came up to me and complimented me on my hustle. That meant the world to me. I really didn't need a ride with those compliments.

1966

In spring ball, Phil McHugh, defensive line coach, visited the Alabama's spring practice for a week. Alabama had won the national championship, and at that time, they were small, quick guys. During an early spring practice, Phil said, "George, get in there at nose guard." Phil needed a new nose guard due to graduation. It was a familiar position from the fall, but I had had no coaching at it. Plus, I was playing linebacker. At least that's what I wanted to do.

I came up against Bill Smith, one of the best centers to ever play at Oregon. Lyle Smith, Boise State's head coach, is Bill's son. Bill Smith was 6' 3," 250 pounds. He snapped the ball, and I saw his head go left and I moved left. I beat his block and there was the ball carrier, and I made the tackle. Phil came running up and said, "That's the way to do it George. It's that quickness, just like at Alabama!" From that day on, I became a nose guard, and Phil would drill me daily on reading the head of the center.

Usually, any defensive position comes down to reading something. Then, you instantly react to it as quickly as you can. The quicker you are, the more successful you will be. It eventually becomes instinct. Thanks to Phil demanding that drill with him multiple times in each practice, it became instinct to me. It was foundational for me playing nose guard.

1966

Summer in Medford, I read in the newspaper that Cas was going to be one of the coaches attending the Fellowship of Christian Athletes camp at Southern Oregon University in Ashland. I drove over for an

They called Him Cas

evening meeting. I saw Cas afterwards. He said to me, "I was thinking about you. I am speaking tomorrow. What if you came and spoke with me?" That encounter changed my life forever. That is just how Cas was. Cas and I spoke to the group the next day—500 high school athletes from all over the West Coast—for a few minutes. I told my story. I went from 165 pound-high school linebacker to 210-pound college nose guard. I talked about how I walked on, how I went from last string my freshman year to a starter; how I became a Christian and gave the Lord my future football career when it seemed hopeless. It was my rags to riches story. Cas spoke and did a great job. He told jokes, talked about the Rose Bowl, about other players, and his thoughts on life. We were done and I was headed over to get off the stage, and I saw about 20 guys who wanted to talk to me.

This was the greatest thing that had ever happened to me. I was playing the sport I loved and was telling my story on how I became a Christian to other athletes. Playing football and telling my story was like a hand and glove to me for years. Cas got the whole thing started. That's just how he was. He would magically show up at the turning point in players' lives. It was a spiritual thing.

1966

By fall I was nervous because I had not really played football in a real game since my senior year of high school against Roseburg High. Here I was in Norman, Oklahoma, in front of 50,000 people. All I had done was practice, practice, practice for going on the third year. What I didn't realize was that I had been practicing against probably the best center in the nation, bar none. I was scared. I had doubts. The Oklahoma center ran up to the ball and I thought the guy was really skinny compared to Bill Smith. Not only was he light, he was not as quick as I was ,nor as strong. Oklahoma had the same belief as Alabama in recruiting quick guys. I have to say, I had the most fun that afternoon that I had had in three years. I made around 15 unassisted tackles. I could not believe that football could be so fun.

For the next three years, I enjoyed beating centers by reading their head or stunting, depending on what the call was. I created my own techniques on stunts that made my rush more effective in my junior and senior year.

I received the Clark Trophy for most improved played at the annual banquet.

1967

Injured O.J. Simpson in the Coliseum in Los Angeles; his only college injury.

Was All-Coast

1968

Was All-Coast and Pre-Season All-American, and received the Hoffman Award.

I frequently had the opportunity to speak to various high school groups and share my life's story. What a privilege that was.

I played in the Hula Bowl. In the off season, I became the first State of Oregon Fellowship of Christian Athletes representative to promote and help start local high school FCA groups throughout Oregon. What a fun job.

1970

I signed as a free agent with the San Francisco 49ersand stuck with them as a linebacker in 1970 and 1971, until the last cut.

I coached a year at USC as a graduate assistant for Johnny McKay, along with two other graduate assistants, Hudson Houck and Al Saunders. Both went on to have successful and long coaching careers in pro ball.

1972-1995

Coached high school football at several high schools, including a state Championship at Medford High in 1985, as defensive coordinator. Also coached at Mountain View High School in Bend, Oregon.